THE MISANTHROPE, TARTUFFE, AND OTHER PLAYS

By MOLIÈRE

Translated by
KATHARINE PRESCOTT WORMELEY,
HENRI VAN LAUN, CURTIS HIDDEN PAGE
and CHARLES HERON WALL

Introduction by
HENRY CARRINGTON LANCASTER

The Misanthrope, Tartuffe, and Other Plays
By Molière (Jean-Baptiste Poquelin)
Translated by Katharine Prescott Wormeley, Henri Van Laun, Curtis Hidden Page, and Charles Heron Wall
Introduction by Henry Carrington Lancaster

Print ISBN 13: 978-1-4209-5533-0
eBook ISBN 13: 978-1-4209-5534-7

Cover Image: a detail of an illustration for *The Misanthrope*, Act IV, Scene III, by Moliere, pseudonym of Jean-Baptiste Poquelin (1622-1673), watercolor by Henri Favre / De Agostini Picture Library / G. Dagli Orti / Bridgeman Images.

Please visit *www.digireads.com*

CONTENTS

INTRODUCTION ... 5

THE SCHOOL FOR WIVES

DRAMATIS PERSONAE ... 22
ACT I. ... 22
ACT II. ... 31
ACT III. ... 37
ACT IV. ... 46
ACT V. ... 53

THE SCHOOL FOR WIVES CRITICIZED

DRAMATIS PERSONAE ... 64
ACT I. ... 64

THE IMPROMPTU AT VERSAILLES

DRAMATIS PERSONAE ... 84
ACT I. ... 84

TARTUFFE

DRAMATIS PERSONAE ... 106
ACT I. ... 106
ACT II. ... 118
ACT III. ... 132
ACT IV. ... 143
ACT V. ... 153

THE MISANTHROPE

DRAMATIS PERSONAE ... 165
ACT I. ... 165
ACT II. ... 175
ACT III. ... 184
ACT IV. ... 192
ACT V. ... 199

THE LEARNED LADIES

Dramatis Personae 208
Act I. 208
Act II. 215
Act III. 225
Act IV. 238
Act V. 246

Introduction

THE COMEDIES OF MOLIÈRE

The great pulpit orator, Bishop Bossuet, wrote about Molière: "His comedies are full of impious and infamous expressions. He encourages disgraceful tolerance in husbands and invites the wives of jealous men to avenge themselves in shameful fashion."

Bossuet, of course, lacked a sense of humor. Most orators, except Winston Churchill, do. Otherwise, they would not be orators.

Other writers find in Molière a moralist, one who preaches the doctrine of the golden mean, of nothing too much, of follow nature. On this account he has been given to children to read and has been recommended for those who are in mental trouble, so much does he represent a sane outlook upon life.

Who is right, Bossuet or the others? I think that both are wrong if they look upon Molière as primarily either a moralist or an immoralist. I do not doubt, of course, that one can find moral—occasionally immoral—instruction in Molière's characters, that one can see in his plays the unhappiness that certain affections, certain vices bring, but I deny that this was his principal concern, that he wrote plays, like Bernard Shaw or Brieux, in order to preach, or that there is no conflict in the ideas that he sets forth.

If you read the *Précieuses ridicules*, you will conclude that, a father or guardian can choose a better husband for his daughter or ward than she can herself, but if you read the *School for Husbands*, or the *School for Wives*, yon come to the opposite conclusion. In the *Learned Ladies* Molière makes a servant, say: "When one makes oneself understood, one always speaks well," a doctrine that no poet, no professional writer can accept, though it is quite in its place in the play. Molière can preach if his characters are addicted to preaching, but this is not his main concern. If you look upon him as primarily the man of the stage, the actor-manager-dramatist, you will find remarkable unity in his life and in his work and at the same time you can explain why he has been considered a moralist or, if you agree with Bossuet, an immoralist.

Molière was not born to the stage, as were some of his colleagues. He early became an actor for love of the profession, not because he could find no other way of making a living. And he adopted the profession so completely that he is known to us, not by his real name, but by the name, Molière, that he assumed when he began to play. He was the oldest son of a successful Parisian upholsterer named Poquelin, one who was so successful that he was upholsterer to His Majesty, Louis XIII, when his son was born in January, 1622. The youngster came into the world in the heart of Paris, not far from the one official Parisian theater of the time and not far from the Louvre, to which his father was admitted in order that he might patch up the royal tapestries. Nor was he far from the great French marketplace or from the quarters of plain people that surrounded it. Born into a prosperous middle-class family, he had ample opportunity to observe Parisians of higher or lower degree than his father and himself.

He also came into contact with actors. He knew a family named Béjart. The father, who was a sergeant-at-arms, must have had difficulty in supporting his large family. The children relieved him by going on the stage. Madeleine, Joseph, Genevieve, and Louis all became actors, as did many years later the last child, Armande, who was to marry Molière. Madeleine was probably the first to play. We have a poem that she addressed to a leading dramatist. She, her brother Joseph, and her sister Genevieve joined forces with Molière as soon as he came of age and was able to make use of the money left him by his mother. He had already received a good education in the humanities and probably in law. As soon as he obtained his inheritance, he invested it in creating a troupe, composed of himself, three Béjarts, and several other young people. They called themselves the Illustrious Theater, illustrious in name alone.

This was in 1643, when there were in Paris two well-established theatrical companies, those of the Hôtel de Bourgogne and the Marais, though Paris was then about the size of Newark or Indianapolis. Molière and his friends rented a hand-ball court, had a carpenter set up a stage and some boxes for spectators, and gave plays there till they were obliged to move to another court. Their affairs were in such bad shape that Molière was arrested for the debts of the troupe and was liberated only when his father paid them. After two or three years the situation became so hopeless that the troupe broke up and left Paris. Molière and the Béjarts stuck together, while their comrades went elsewhere. Molière's departure from Paris may be compared to the flight of Muhammad from Mecca. In both cases the exile led to a period of preparation outside the capital and to a victorious return.

Molière and the Béjarts attached themselves to a provincial troupe headed by a certain Dufresne and protected by a duke who lived in southern France. They wandered all over the country, playing where they could, having difficulties with small-town authorities, in danger from those who took part in the civil war of 1649-53. Molière became more and more important in the troupe until about 1650 he was made its leader. He studied his comrades, learned how to advise them, how to make them work together. He also began to write plays for the troupe to perform. During these years he learned to know more of France than Paris; he was able to study life in villages and small towns, the ways of peasants, of petty office-holders, and of rustic nobles, all of whom were to reappear in his comedies.

Under his management the troupe became the most distinguished French company outside of Paris. In 1658 he returned to the capital and was allowed to act in theaters that belonged to the government. The year following his return he delighted Paris with the *Précieuses ridicules* and after that new plays came thick and fast from his pen. He had learned that one road to success was a provision of new plays, as these could not be acted by other troupes until they were printed. And his comedies were so many and so popular that he made his theater the chief place in France for comedy. He won the patronage of the king, who gave his troupe an annual subsidy and had it play frequently at court.

But Molière had to fight his way—first against the troupe of the Hôtel de Bourgogne, next against opposition from the church, lastly against his own poor health. Not only did he fight, but he found in his opponents material for comedy. He burlesqued the acting of his rivals. He dramatized the doings of hypocrites and their dupes. He gave his cough to one of his characters and made fun of the doctors who failed to cure him. Let's look at these three classes of opponents in greater detail.

First the rival actors. In the *Précieuses ridicules* a mock-nobleman declares that he will give a play he has written to the Great Actors, that is, to those of the Hôtel de Bourgogne, for they alone know how to roll out a verse and to wait for applause. This seems to have been the first shot in the battle. The rival actors replied by having authors parody Molière's plays and printers seek to pirate them. The more successful Molière became, the more hostile were his rivals, who felt that he menaced their preeminence. When Molière wrote the *School for Wives*, friends of the older troupe attacked it savagely. Molière replied by his *Critique*, a playlet in which the *School for Wives* is discussed, the sensible characters approve of it, and it is condemned by a jealous poet, a prude, and an empty-headed young nobleman. Then followed a number of short comedies in which Molière is criticized in turn, and a second reply of his, the *Impromptu de Versailles*, in which Molière puts himself and his comrades on the stage and he burlesques for their benefit the acting of his rivals.

This celebrated literary quarrel, distinguished from others by the fact that the majority of the documents concerned are in dramatic form, resulted in making the *School for Wives* an extremely popular play and in advertising Molière and his troupe, he remained on unfriendly terms with the actors of the Hôtel. After his death some of his actors went over to the rival troupe, but enough of them remained to keep the company going. Soon most of the actors of the Marais were joined to those of Molière's troupe, and finally in 1680 the troupe of the Hôtel and the company that had been Molière's were permanently united.

This troupe became known as the French Comedy or the French Theater, to distinguish it from the Italian troupe that was acting at Paris. It was in this way that the Comedie Française came into being, born of Molière's troupe and that of the Hôtel de Bourgogne. Molière's share in its creation is recognized by the fact that the theater in which the company performs is often called Molière's House and by the fact that his plays have been acted there more frequently than those of any other author. And this troupe, active in Paris today, has the longest history of any company of actors that has ever existed. Obviously Molière as a manager met with no small success.

And now as to clerical opposition. A number of people were disturbed by the *School for Wives*, finding in it passages they considered indecent and accusing Molière of attempting to parody the Ten Commandments. They joined the jealous dramatists and the rival actors in attacking Molière. A group known as the Company of the Holy Sacrament got wind of the fact that Molière was writing *Tartuffe* and decided at a meeting in April, 1664, to seek to have the play suppressed. They appealed to the Queen Mother, who was a devout Spaniard, and to the Archbishop of Paris. Molière managed, however, to give three acts of his five-act comedy as part of an elaborate festival at Versailles, but further performances were forbidden for five years, though he was allowed to read his play in private homes and he once gave it in his theater with altered names. By 1669 the Queen Mother had died and her son allowed the comedy to be acted. After such a build-up, *Tartuffe* became, of course, the leading attraction of the century.

During the period in which he could not play *Tartuffe*, Molière brought out *Don Juan* and introduced into it scenes in which hypocrisy is laughed at. The play was immediately criticized by a priest and was withdrawn after four well attended productions. Subsequently Molière thought it wise to abstain from controversy of this nature, Tartuffe, it is true, became his most successful play, but after *Don Juan* he wrote no play that could bring down upon him the wrath of the clergy. Instead he turned to the medical profession, substituting those who care for the body for those who concern themselves with the soul. *Don Juan* marks the transition. It is the last play to be criticized by churchmen and the first to introduce criticism of the practice of medicine.

By wearing a physician's robe Don Juan's valet has been able to prescribe for several peasants. His master thinks his prescriptions will do as well as those of the licensed practitioners, for cures wrought by the latter are usually accidental. His valet accuses him of being an unbeliever even in medicine, as he doesn't have faith in senna, or cassia, or emetics.

This was only a beginning. Soon Molière had written a farce called *Love as a Doctor*, or *The Four Doctors*, in which we see four physicians of whom one insists upon bleeding, another on the use of antimony, while the others, though willing to take milder measures, are great sticklers for form. They visit the girl who is supposed to be ill. One of the physicians, upon recognizing a servant girl he had seen at a house where the coachman was ill, gives this proof of his reverence for authority: He asks about the health of the coachman for whom he has prescribed. Lysette, the maid, answers: "He is dead."

Dr. Tomès: Dead!

Lysette: Yes.

Dr. Tomès: That can't be.

Lysette: I don't know whether it can be, but I know that it is.

Dr. Tomès: He can't be dead I tell you.

Lysette: And I tell you that he is dead . . . and buried.

Dr. T.: You are mistaken. Hippocrates says that these sorts of illnesses end only on the fourteenth or the twenty-first day, and it is only six days since he fell ill.

Lysette: Hippocrates may say what he pleases, but the coachmen is dead.

Then comes the consultation held by the four doctors, who seat themselves and cough;

Dr. Dès Fonandrès: Paris is very large; you have to take long trips when business is active.

Dr. Tomès: My mule is excellent for such trips. You wouldn't believe how far she can go in a day.

Dr. Dès Fonandrès: I have a horse that can't be tired out.

Dr. Tomès: Do you know where I've been today? I went to the Arsenal, then to the Faubourg Saint-Germain, then to the Marais, then to the Saint-Honoré Gate, then to the Faubourg Saint-Jacques, the to the Richelieu Gate, then to the Place Royale.

Dr. Dès Fonandrès: My horse did all that today and more, and besides visited a patient outside of town.

Dr. Tomès: By the way, which side are you taking in the quarrel between Dr. Theophrastus and Dr. Artemius?

Dr. Dès Fonandrès: I'm for Artemius.

Dr. Tomès: So am I. It is true that his opinion killed the patient, but, Theophrastus ought not to have had a different opinion from that of a colleague, older than himself. Don't you agree with me?

Dr. Dès Fonandrès: Certainly. We must always respect formalities, whatever may happen.

Dr. Tomès: A dead man is only a dead man. No conclusion is to be drawn from his death. But the neglect of a formality injures the whole medical profession.

The next play in which Molière ridiculed the profession was *The Doctor in Sprite of Himself.* Here we see no physician, but a wood-chopper named Sganarelle who had once been the valet of a physician and had picked up scraps of Latin and of medical talk. He is forced to put on a doctor's robe, but he soon enjoys it, for he finds that, thanks to the robe, to his bad Latin, and to his nerve, he gets along quite nicely in the profession. He is called in to diagnose the case of Lucinde, a girl who has suddenly become dumb. Here is the scene of diagnosis:

Sganarelle: Well, what's the matter? What pains do you feel?

Lucinde: Ha, hi, hom, han.

Sganarelle: What's that?

Lucinde; Han, hi, horn, han, hai, hi, hin.

Sganarelle: What?

Lucinde: Han, hi, hom.

Sganarelle: Han, hi, hon, han, ha. I don't understand. What the devil of a language is this?

Géronte (the girl's father): That's her illness, sir. She has become mute without our ever discovering the cause. That's why her marriage has been delayed.

Sganarelle: Why?

Géronte: The man she is to marry wants to wait for her to be cured.

Sganarelle: And who is this fool who doesn't want his wife to be dumb? Would to God that mine were. I'd take good care not to cure her.

Géronte: We beg you to do what you can for my daughter.

Sganarelle: Don't worry. Tell me, does this illness oppress her much?

Géronte: Yes, sir.

Sganarelle: So much the better. Does she feel great pains?

Géronte: Very great.

Sganarelle (to Lucinde): Give me your arm. (He feels her pulse.) There's a pulse that indicates that your daughter is mute.

Géronte: Yes, sir, that's her trouble. You found it out right away. . . . But what is the cause of the trouble?

Sganarelle: It is that she has lost the power of speech.

Géronte: Very good, but what made her lose her power of speech?

Sganarelle: All our best authorities will say that it is caused by an impediment in the action of her tongue.

Géronte: But what is your opinion about this impediment in the action of her tongue?

Sganarelle: Aristotle says about that . . . some very fine things.

Géronte: I believe it.

Sganarelle: He was a great man.

Géronte: Yes, indeed.

Sganarelle: To return to our argument, I think that this impediment in the action of her tongue is caused by certain humors that we learned men call peccant humors, peccant, that is, peccant humors, inasmuch as the vapors formed by the outpouring of the influences that arise in the region of illnesses, coming, so to speak, to . . . . Do you understand Latin?

Géronte: Not at all.

Sganarelle: You don't understand Latin?

Géronte: No.

Sganarelle: Cabricias arci thuram, catalamus, singulariter, nominativo, haec Musa, la Muse, Bonus, Bona, Bonum, Deus Sanctus, Est ne oratio latinas? Etiam, oui, quare, pourquoi, quia substantivo, et adjectivum, concordat in generi, numerum, et casus.

Géronte: Oh, why haven't I studied?

And the diagnosis continues, including the remark that the heart is on the right, the liver on the left, which brings a protest from Géronte, who had always supposed the heart to be on the left, the liver on the right, but Sganarelle gets out of the difficulty by answering:

Yes, it used to be that way, but we doctors have changed all that and we now practice medicine by new methods.

Géronte: That's what I did not know and I beg your pardon for my ignorance.

After emphasizing the real physician and the fake physician, Molière decided to concentrate upon the patient, upon the man who is hipped about himself, who thinks he is ill, but isn't.

Molière, of course, had never studied modern psychiatry. He did not know that, if a man thinks he is ill, he is ill, that a so-called imaginary invalid is a person mentally ill. However, in drawing his *Malade imaginaire*, he depicted a person who talks about his ailments and worships his physicians in a way that may be familiar to many of us. He is so much convinced of his doctor's infallibility, that, when he is told to walk up and down, he asks if he should walk up and then down, or down and then up. He also asks him how many grains of salt he must put on his egg.

He plans to marry his daughter to a young physician in order to have one always at hand, but his plan fails, his daughter marries another man, and, on the advice of his family, the imaginary invalid decides to become a doctor himself. This decision prepares the way for a grand ballet, in which druggists, surgeons, and physicians march in and take their places around the hall. The presiding physician than calls upon his colleagues to put questions in Gallic Latin which, if properly answered, will permit the admission of the Imaginary Invalid into their profession. The first doctor asks why opium puts one to sleep: "*Domandabo causam et rationem quare Opium facit dormire*?" The Invalid replies that there is in opium a dormitive virtue that dulls one's senses. Whereupon the chorus applauds.

Similar questions and answers follow. The Invalid swears to obey all the laws of the faculty, and the president confers upon him the right to prescribe, to purge, to bleed, to pierce, to slash, to cut, and to kill with impunity throughout all the earth.

Thereupon the surgeons and druggists dance around the Invalid, wishing long life to the new doctor who has spoken so well, a thousand years in which he may eat and drink and bleed and kill:

> *Vivat, vivat, vivat, vivat, cent fois vivat,*
> *Novus doctor qui tam bene parlat*!
> *Mille, mille annis, et manget, et bibat,*
> *Et seignet, et tuat*!

But the doctors were avenged. At the fourth performance of this gay comedy-ballet Molière, who was playing the imaginary invalid, was taken seriously ill, managed to stagger through his role and to get home, where, a few hours later, he died.

As he was only fifty-one, he might have given us many more delightful comedies, but, when he was on his deathbed, he had at least the satisfaction of knowing that he had accomplished much as actor, manager, and author of comedies.

As television had not been invented in his day, we cannot judge his acting except by the statements of his contemporaries. Even his enemies admitted that he was a great actor when they claimed that it was the acting of the *School for Wives* rather than its verses that made it succeed. The daughter of one of his comrades, herself at one time a member of his troupe, wrote of him as follows:

> He was neither too fat nor too thin; he was tall rather than short; he carried himself well, showed a fine leg. He had a large nose, a large mouth, thick lips, a swarthy complexion, black and heavy eyebrows, which he moved in such a way as to render his face extremely comical. He realized that nature had refused him the gifts required by a tragic actor and limited himself to comic roles, excelling both in farce and in high comedy, in such roles as those of Arnolphe, Orgon, and Harpagon, It is in them that he seduced the spectators to such an extent that they could no longer distinguish the actor from the character he represented.

I have referred to his success as a manager. As a dramatist he had certain limitations. He did not attempt tragedy. He avoided the sentimental type of play that was to develop in the eighteenth century and is not unknown today. He wrote one tragi-comedy, but, as it failed, he tried that kind of play no further and merely incorporated some of its lines in later plays. His genius led him to comedy of various kinds, from comedy of character and comedy of manners to comedy-ballet, farce, and comedy that emphasizes music and spectacle. In these he is the supreme master, with all respect to Aristophanes and Shakespeare.

He broke away from the tradition that comedy should have in its cast only persons of the middle and lower classes. *The Misanthrope* is essentially a comedy of high society, where entertainment, love affairs, duels, lawsuits, gossip, and dabbling in literature occupy men's minds rather than the business of making a living. Alceste, the Misanthrope, is an admirable member of society, but one who renders himself comic by his inability to make social compromises. The Truth always is his guide.

"What!" exclaims his friend Philinte, "would you go and tell old Emily that at her age it is unbecoming to pretend to be pretty, and that the powder she uses shocks everybody?"

"Certainly," answers Alceste.

"And would you tell Dorilas that everyone at court is bored by his constant talk about his own valor and the distinction of his family?"

"Certainly," repeats Alceste.

And this lover of truth, however disagreeable it. may be, of sincerity, of the accurate expression of one's feelings, is in love with a charming flirt, Célimène, a young widow to whom the truth has no meaning, and who is sought after by most of the men in the play.

Her admirers urge her to discuss her absent acquaintances. When she does so, she gives us a much larger picture of the society of the day than we could get from seeing only the characters in the play. There is Damon who says nothing at great length; Timante, who takes on mysterious airs, claims to have important secrets to tell, and ends by confiding in you something of no interest or importance; Géralde, who is constantly talking about horses and dogs and mentions no men and women except dukes, princes, and princesses; Cléon, who gets credit for his excellent table, but unfortunately serves there, not only delicious food, but himself.

Célimène's best scene is, perhaps, with the prude, Arsinoé, who is jealous of Célimène's youth, beauty, and attraction for men. She comes to tell Célimène of the trouble she has taken in her behalf. According to her, she had been the day before at the home of some excellent people where the conversation happened to fall upon Célimène. They said that the crowd of men who came to see her and the fact that she was much discussed caused her to be censured. Arsinoé, of course, came to her defense and said that her intentions were good, but she had to admit that Célimène did live in a way that was most unfortunate. There was nothing, of course, really immoral, but a woman should avoid the shadow of a suspicion. You understand that I'm telling you all this purely for your good.

Célimène smilingly thanks her for her kindness. "Far from taking it badly," she says, "I'm going to show how much I appreciate it by telling you something in return. The other day I was at the house of some admirable people who happened to talk about you. They said that, you were forever discussing honor and good behavior, always appearing shocked at any suggestion of indecency, continually criticizing others, but that you beat your servants and fail to pay them, make vain attempts to appear beautiful, and would be glad to be the heroine of a love affair. I defended you, but all were against me and pointed out that you would do well to look after your own conduct before showing so much interest in that of others.

The Misanthrope is a comedy of character, but it is not the first. Molière had already written the *School for Wives*, in which there is a dominant character, a person with whom we might sympathize were he not warped by one characteristic that renders him ridiculous. Molière might have called his play the *School for Husbands*, but he had already given this title to another play. The principal role, one that takes up a third of the text and one that he played himself, is that of Arnolphe, whose character is altered by his attitude towards women. He is now forty-two, about Molière's age at the time, but he has never married. His reason is that he fears his wife will not be faithful, but he thinks the trouble is with women's education. He has himself hit upon a plan that will, he is sure, solve his matrimonial problem.

Some eleven years before, he had secured possession of a girl who was only four years old and had put her in the care of two ignorant and stupid peasants in order that she should know nothing about the relations between the sexes until he could himself reveal them to her. When the play begins, he has just come home after an absence of some weeks. When he sees the girl, whom he calls Agnes, he is delighted by the childishness of her conversation and expresses his joy in a monologue filled with satisfaction over his educational experiment. Immediately afterwards the trouble begins. He has hardly finished his monologue when young Horace, son of an old friend, comes to greet him, to borrow money from him, and to tell him that he has fallen in love with a girl named Agnes whom he has seen on a balcony nearby and that he will use the money Arnolphe has loaned him in an effort to win her. When he has gone, Arnolphe has a second monologue differing in tone from the first. He expresses his agitation over the confidential information he has just received and decides upon an investigation.

In the interview with Agnes that follows he tries to be tactful and says that he has been told by gossips that a young man has come to see her, but that he couldn't believe it and was willing to bet. . . .

Agnes: Don't bet, you'll lose.
Arnolphe: What! Is it true that a young man . . . .
Agnes: Sure thing. He has hardly budged from our house.

Then she explains how it all happened.

I was on the balcony working in the fresh air when I saw passing by a handsome young man, who, catching my glance, bowed humbly; so I, not willing to be surpassed in politeness, made a bow to him. Then he bowed again and so did I. We kept this up till it grew dark. Next day an old woman came to tell me how deeply I had wounded the young man and how I could cure him only by letting him visit me. Of course I couldn't let him suffer, would you have done so?

Arnolphe hears of the visit, of kisses, of a ribbon the young man took. He is relieved to find that matters have gone no farther, but he thinks it advisable to marry Agnes himself as soon as possible. To prepare her for matrimony he reads her his Maxims of Marriage, which point out that a woman should seek to please her husband only, that she should receive no one unless her husband authorizes the visit, should accept no present, should never write letters, should avoid social gatherings, cards, picnics, etc. He sends her out with the programme in her hands and expresses in a new monologue the hope that, if he acts quickly, his plans may still succeed. But he gradually discovers that his method results in complete failure. He fails as a lover and as an educator. Young love triumphs over all his experience, over all the precautions that he takes. The plot is rendered comic by the fact that the two young innocents are constantly revealing to Arnolphe the progress of their love-affair. Whenever there is danger of our feeling sorry for Arnolphe, there are comic expressions or comic situations that keep us from becoming sentimental. And the monologues continue to emphasize the state of Arnolphe's emotions.

Another high comedy is *Tartuffe* in which the central character, Orgon, is so completely unable to tell the difference between a hypocrite and a really devout person that he lets himself be deceived by a deadbeat, who brings discord into his family, interferes with his daughter's marriage plans, and seeks to seduce his wife.

You may ask why *Tartuffe* was attacked by church organizations, though Molière made it plain that he is holding up to scorn hypocrites and their dupes, not really pious people and those who trust them. It was probably because there were in the Company of the Holy Sacrament and similar societies not only hypocrites who did not like to see themselves unmasked, but sincere people who, while they might not object to the play as a whole, were shocked by certain passages, such as those in which *Tartuffe* to make love uses the language of prayer and the arguments of the casuists whom Pascal had attacked in the *Provincial Letters*. Says Tartuffe to Elmire:

> The love that attaches us to beauty that is eternal does not stifle in us love for what is temporal. Our senses may readily be charmed by Heaven's perfect creations. The delights of Heaven are reflected in others, but they show in you their rarest marvels . . . . I have not been able to look upon you, perfect creature, without admiring in you the Author of nature and without feeling my heart fill with love when I contemplate the most beautiful portrait in which the Creator has painted Himself. At first I feared that this secret ardor was a clever trap set by the evil one, and, thinking that you were an obstacle to my salvation, I resolved to avoid you, but at last I came to understand that my feeling may not be guilty and that I can reconcile it with good conduct. That is why I allowed it to take possession of my heart. . . . And now in you is my hope, my welfare, my tranquility. Upon you depends my suffering or my beatitude.

Another comedy is *l'Avare* in which the central character is a wealthy business man, who is rendered highly amusing by his avarice. In the *Learned Ladies*, instead of having one central character, we have three women, a mother, her daughter, and her sister-in-law, who together represent the neglect of domestic duties for what they consider higher matters.

One of Molière's most interesting and most celebrated productions is the *Bourgeois Gentilhomme*. He apparently conceived it as a comedy of character in which the chief person, Monsieur Jourdain, was to be a merchant who would render himself ridiculous by his efforts to ape the nobility. While he was at work on this play, a Turkish mission visited Paris, was shown the splendors of the French court, but expressed no surprise or admiration. The court wished Molière to avenge it by burlesquing Turkish customs, and, for this purpose, put at his disposal a Frenchman who had traveled in North Africa, Syria, and Turkey. This man conferred with Molière and with Lulli, the opera composer, who was to write the music for the play. Molière arranged his plot in such a way that Jourdain would be deceived into thinking that he would be made a Turkish nobleman by a special ceremony, and it was in this ceremony that the knowledge the traveled Frenchman had of manners and of costumes could be employed. The ceremony and the ballets give the work the tone of an extravaganza, but much of it is nevertheless comedy of a high order.

Jourdain wishes to have an education, not for the sake of culture or the development of his powers, but in order that he may act the nobleman. He would practice writing in order to write courtly love-letters. He would learn to fence because noblemen fight duels. Whenever he learns something new, he loves to go and brag to his wife and his servant about his acquisition. Here are some samples of his conversation:

The professor of philosophy asks him what he wants to learn. Jourdain replies; "All I can. I am angry with my parents because they did not make me study all branches of knowledge when I was young."

The Professor of Philosophy: "That is a reasonable feeling. *Nam sine doctrina vita est quasi mortis imago.* You understand Latin of course." Jourdain; "Yes, but act as if I didn't. Explain what it means."

Then the professor tells how to make the vowels that Jourdain has been making ever since he learned to talk. Jourdain confides in him that he wishes to write a love letter he can drop at the feet of a certain noblewoman.

Professor: Do you want to write in verse?

Jourdain: No, no verses.

Professor: You want only prose?

Jourdain: No, I want neither prose, nor verse.

Professor: But it must be one or the other.

Jourdain: Why?

Professor: Because, sir, there are only these two ways of expressing oneself.

Jourdain: There is nothing but prose and verse?

Professor: No, sir. All that isn't prose is verse and all that isn't verse is prose.

Jourdain: And when one speaks, what is that?

Professor: Prose.

Jourdain: What! When I say, "Nicole, bring me my slippers and my night cap," it's prose?

Professor: Yes, sir.

Jourdain: In faith, I've been speaking prose for over forty years without ever knowing that I was doing it; and I am very much obliged to you for having told me that.

So much, indeed, that he hastens to show off his newly acquired learning. After talking to his wife of other matters, he says:

Do you know what you are saying?

Mme Jourdain: Yes, I know that what I am saying is well said and that you ought to live differently from the way you do.

Jourdain: I'm not talking about that. I'm asking you what are the words you are saying.

Mine Jourdain: They are words that are very wise and that's more than your conduct is.

Jourdain: I'm not talking about that, I tell you. I ask you what I am speaking with you, what I am saying at this time, what is it?

Mine Jourdain: Nonsense.

Jourdain: Oh, no; it's not that. What we are both saying, the language that we are speaking.

M me Jourdain: Well.

Jourdain: What is it called?

Mme Jourdain: Its called whatever one wishes to call it.

Jourdain: It's prose, ignorant woman.

Mme Jourdain: Prose?

Jourdain: Yes, prose. All that is prose is not verse; and all that is not verse is prose. That's what comes from studying!

Jourdain feels that to complete his role as a nobleman he must have a noblewoman as his mistress. He accordingly arranges to entertain a certain Dorimène, who is brought to his house by Dorante, an impecunious nobleman who for some time has been borrowing money from Jourdain. Dorante arranges to have an elegant meal brought in, for which, of course, Jourdain pays, the nobleman pretends to the young woman that he is giving her the dinner and has merely borrowed Jourdain's house for the occasion. The three sit down, after Jourdain has paid Dorimène elaborate compliments. Six cooks who have prepared the feast dance a ballet, then bring in the table covered with food. But in the middle of the dinner Mme Jourdain arrives and breaks up the party. Dorimène, shocked to find that she has been deceived, leaves in haste. Jourdain scolds his wife, who replies that all women will be on her side. Left alone, poor Jourdain laments: "She came in at a most unfortunate moment. I was in humor to say some very pretty things and I never before felt that I had so much wit."

Just think of all the clever things you were about to say when you were interrupted and give your sympathy to Monsieur Jourdain.

Molière is full of expressions like this that can easily be applied to our own experience. Take, for instance, the famous phrase in the *Fourberies de Scapin*, "What the devil was he going to do in that galley?" "*Que diable allait-il faire dans cette galère*?" A young man needs money. His valet tries to extract some for him from his miserly father. He pretends that the son was invited by a Turk on board his boat, was given delicious fruit, and, while they were eating, the galley put out to sea and the Turk now insists on the payment of 500 francs if the father does not want his son taken to Algiers. The father laments, tries to find a way out and every now and then repeats "What the devil was he going to do in this galley?" Of course, that is not the question. The important thing is to get the money and ransom the young man, but the miser is very human when he keeps asking the question.

The next time you lose your pocket-book, or break your glasses, or a plate you value, see if you do not ask yourself why you did something or went somewhere, though, if your question were answered, it would not find your pocket-book for you, or mend your glasses or your plate.

There is this permanent quality in Molière's work. There is also a picture of life in seventeenth-century France, drawn boldly and with comic effect. The king is, of course, referred to in flattering terms. Nothing else would have been possible in a play acted in Paris, but Molière had other reasons. He needed the king's protection and he probably had a high opinion of Louis XIV, who, up to the time of Molière's death, seemed to be an excellent young ruler. He had not yet revoked the Edict of Nantes, involved his country in lengthy wars, or ruined its financial structure.

Molière's nobles may be persons with whom we sympathize, or they may be held up to ridicule. When Molière first returned to Paris, he put on the stage, not a real marquis, but a valet disguised as one. A few years later he dramatized real marquises in all their finery and futility. Soon the young marquis became a conventional comic figure, especially amusing as he could be easily compared with the living marquises who were sitting as spectators on the stage.

Another type of aristocrat that Molière cartooned was the country nobleman, the fellow left high and dry by the tide that carried the capable and cultivated nobles to Versailles. M. and Mme de Sotenville, for instance, who appear in *George Dandin.* They make me think of a half-starved turkey-gobbler and his hen. They are still able to strut and to gobble about the achievements of their ancestors in the crusades, but they are forced to marry their daughter to a peasant, whose financial assistance they accept, but whom they keep at his social distance despite the fact that he has become their son-in-law.

The bourgeois constitute the largest class in Molière's comedies. One may, like Jourdain, be seeking to leave it, or he may, like Mme Jourdain, prefer to stay in it and to have a bourgeois son-in-law. He may be a miser like Harpagon, or a spendthrift like his son. Or he may be an excellent member of society.

And there are representatives of the workers, the clever valets and the peasants. Here again the character may be held up to ridicule, as is George Dandin, or he may be presented sympathetically as are the peasants in *Don Juan.*

Molière had a great gift for entering into his characters and making them live. He often distinguishes them from one another by their speech. He employed material supplied by the Romans, the Italians, the

Spaniards, by French dramatists and novelists, and by the life about him. Such material he made his own and presented in such a way as to produce highly comic scenes, sometimes at the expense of the plot. As someone said of Shakespeare, he is full of quotations. Here are some of them:

May propitious Heaven give us children of whom we are the fathers.

One dies only once and it's for such a long time,

Nice people know everything without studying.

Outside of Paris there is no salvation for gentlefolk.

Bolts and bars don't make the virtue of women and girls.

I should like to know if the great rule of all rules is not to please and if a play that has reached this goal has not followed a good route.

To esteem everybody is to esteem nobody.

It is true, my reason warns me every day, but reason is not what regulates love.

Age will bring anything, but at twenty it's no time to be a prude.

He who would drown his dog accuses him of being mad.

I live on good soup, not on fine talk.

In the good old days women thought only of their households. Their books were a thimble, thread and needles with which they prepared their daughters' trousseaux, but now they are far from such habits, they want to write and become authors . . . . And in this vain pursuit of knowledge, they know nothing about my dinner.

A learned fool is more of a fool than an ignorant fool.

When a shoemaker makes shoes, he can't spoil a piece of leather without having to pay for it, but a doctor can spoil a man without its costing him anything. It's always the fault of the man who dies. And among the dead there is the greatest discretion in the world, no one of them has ever been heard to complain of the doctor who killed him.

Molière impressed himself so deeply upon his countrymen that, twenty years after his death, an author of comedies declared that it was useless to try to excel in his profession. "If I imitate Molière, I am accused of plagiarism; if I write differently from him, my critics say, 'Ah! that is not Molière!'"

Let me close with a tribute from Austin Dobson:

True Comedy circum praecordia ludit—
It warms the heart's cockles. 'Twas thus that he viewed it,
That simple old Critic, who smote on his knee,
And named it no more than he knew it to be.
"True Comedy!"—Ah! there is this thing about it,
If it makes the House merry, you never need doubt it:
It lashes the vicious; it laughs at the fool;
And it brings all the prigs and pretenders to school.
To the poor it is kind; to the plain it is gentle;
It is neither too tragic, nor too sentimental;
Its thrust, like a rapier's, though cutting, is clean,
And it pricks Affectation all over the scene.
Its rules are the rules ARISTOTLE has taught us;
Its ways have not altered since TERENCE and PLAUTUS;
Its mission is neither to praise nor to blame;
Its weapon is Ridicule, Folly its game.

"True Comedy!"—such as our POQUELIN made it!
"True Comedy!"—such as our COQUELIN played it!
It clears out the cobwebs; it freshens the air;
And it treads in the steps of its Master, MOLIÈRE!

HENRY CARRINGTON LANCASTER

1953.

The School for Wives

[*L'École Des Femmes.*]

Translated by KATHARINE PRESCOTT WORMELEY

A COMEDY IN FIVE ACTS

Dramatis Personae

ARNOLPHE, *Otherwise called M. de la Souche.*
AGNES, *Innocent young girl, brought up by Arnolphe.*
HORACE, *Lover of Agnes.*
ALAIN, *Peasant, valet to Arnolphe.*
GEORGETTE, *Servant-woman to Arnolphe.*
CHRYSALDE, *Friend of Arnolphe.*
ENRIQUE, *Brother-in-law of Arnolphe.*
ORONTE, *Father of Horace and great friend of Arnolphe.*
A NOTARY.

The Scene is an Open Square of the Town.

Act I.

Scene I.

[CHRYSALDE, ARNOLPHE.]

CHRYSALDE. You have come back, you say, to give her your hand?

ARNOLPHE. Yes; I intend to conclude the matter now.

CHRYSALDE. Being quite alone, we can speak without fear. Will you let me, as a friend, lay open my heart? This project of yours makes me tremble with dread; no matter in what way you turn the affair, this taking a wife is, for you, a rash thing.

ARNOLPHE. I shall do so, my friend. Perhaps in your case you have reason for fears you bestow upon me; your forehead, I think, is expectant of horns,—the infallible dower most marriages bring.

CHRYSALDE. All that is a risk from which none are secure; and foolish, I think, are precautions against it. No, what I'm fearing for you is the satire you turn on a hundred poor husbands who suffer its sting. There are none, great or small, as you know very well, who have ever been safe from your critical tongue. Your greatest enjoyment, wherever you are, is to make an exposure of secret intrigues.

ARNOLPHE. So be it. But is there in all the world another town where husbands are as patient as in this? Do we not see every species of man putting up, in their homes, with all kinds of deception? One piles up wealth, which his wife is distributing to those who are busily giving him horns. Another, more happy, but none the less infamous, sees the presents that daily are made to his spouse, and no jealous thought ever enters his mind when she tells him, forsooth, they are gifts to her virtue! A third makes a fuss which profits him nothing; a fourth, with all sweetness, lets matters go on, and when the young gallant appears at his house takes his cloak and his gloves with a cordial smile. Some wives, clever females! confide false tales of pressing lovers to their faithful lords, who sleep in peace on that illusion and pity the poor gallants for wasting a devotion which is no waste at all! Others, to justify their splendor, say that they win at cards the sums they spend; and their booby husbands, not asking at what game they played, give thanks to God for such good luck! In short, there's everywhere such chance for satire, how can I help it if I have to laugh? If men are fools, shall I not—?

CHRYSALDE. Yes; but he who laughs at others must fear that in revenge they'll laugh at him. I hear the talk of the world and of those who idly run about to tell the things that happen; but, often as they divulge their secrets in my presence, I never yet was known to spread such gossip. I am reserved; and though on some occasions I may condemn a husband's tolerance and, in my own case, would not suffer what I see others bearing peaceably, I do not say so openly. We should always fear the rebound of satire; and we can never swear in any given case what we might do, or not do. So if my forehead, by fate which rules us all, should be disgraced, I may feel pretty certain that the world will be content to laugh in secret; nay, I might even have the comfort that some good folks would say it was a pity. But as for you, my friend, the case is different; and I say again, you run a devilish risk. If you would not be jeered at in your turn, you'll have to walk erect and straight among these husbands, whom for years your tongue has lashed until they think you in their hearts a devil let loose; for, if you give them but the slightest chance, beware the hue-and-cry they'll raise about you.

ARNOLPHE. Good heavens! my friend, don't worry about that. Adroit indeed would be the man who'd catch me there. I know the artful tricks and subtle plots the women use to fool us; and as so many men are duped by their dexterity, I have taken sure precautions in my case. The girl I marry has all the innocence I need to save my forehead from malignant influence.

CHRYSALDE. And do you think a little fool—?

ARNOLPHE. I wed a fool to be no fool myself. I think, as I am bound to do, your better half is virtuous, but an able woman is an ominous thing. I know the cost to some men of choosing wives with talent. What! saddle myself with a clever creature who could talk routs and *ruelle*, write prose and verse, receive the visits of choice wits and little marquises; while I, called by them all "the husband of madame," must play the part of saint whom no one worships? No, no, I do not want a mind so high; a wife who scribbles verses knows too much. Mine shall have less sublime illumination; she shall not even know what makes a rhyme, for if she plays at crambo she shall answer, when her turn comes, "Cream-tarts." In other words, I mean that she shall be extremely ignorant. It is enough for her if she can pray to God, love me, and sew and spin.

CHRYSALDE. Well, well! a stupid woman is your hobby, is she?

ARNOLPHE. So much so I would rather wed an ugly fool than take a handsome wife if clever.

CHRYSALDE. Mind and beauty—

ARNOLPHE. Virtue is enough.

CHRYSALDE. But how do you expect a fool to know what virtue is? Besides the weariness, as I conceive, of having all one's life a fool to live with, think you that you are wise to take her, and that the safety of your honor can rest upon this theory? A woman of mind may, certainly, betray her duty; but at least she does so by deliberate choice. A stupid fool may fail in hers without desire or even thought of doing so.

ARNOLPHE. To that fine argument and wise discourse I answer, as Pantagruel answered Panurge: Urge me to marry other than a fool, preach at me, argue on from now till Pentecost, and when 'tis done you will not have persuaded me one jot.

CHRYSALDE. Then I shall say no more.

ARNOLPHE. To each his own idea. About a wife, as in all else, I mean to follow mine. I am rich enough to choose a mate who will have nothing of her own but all from me; and whose submission and complete dependence will not oppose her wealth or birth to mine. Some time ago I saw with other children a child, then four years old, whose gentle quiet air inspired me with love. Her mother being in the utmost poverty, it came into my mind to ask her for her daughter; and the good peasant-woman, when she learned my wish, was glad enough to lay that burden down. In a little convent quite remote from life I have brought her up according to my policy; that is to say, I ordered that every means should be employed to make her mind as vacant as it can be. Success, thank God, has followed this design; and now, full grown, she is so simple-minded that I bless Heaven for granting what I want,—a wife who suits my wishes to a T. I have now removed her from the convent; but as my dwelling is open to all sorts of persons all day long, I keep her in this little house apart, where no one comes to see me; and, in order not to spoil her natural goodness, I have hired servants as simple as herself. Perhaps you'll say, "Why this narration?" It is that I may show you my precautions; and I now invite you, as my faithful friend, to sup with her to-night. I wish you to examine her a little and tell me if my choice is one to be condemned.

CHRYSALDE. I readily consent.

ARNOLPHE. You will be able at this interview to judge not only of her person but her innocence.

CHRYSALDE. As for that latter article, what you have told me cannot—

ARNOLPHE. The truth exceeds my statement. I am forced at every turn to admire her simplicity; sometimes she says a thing at which I die with laughter. The other day (if you'll believe it), she seemed to be in trouble, and asked me, with unequalled innocence, whether the children people made came through their ears.

CHRYSALDE. I am truly glad, Seigneur Arnolphe—

ARNOLPHE. There, there! why will you always call me by that name?

CHRYSALDE. In spite of me it comes upon my lips; I can't remember Monsieur de la Souche! But what the devil induced you, in your forty-second year, to be re-christened, and give yourself a title of nobility out of that poor old rotten farm?

ARNOLPHE. 'Tis the name of the house. But no matter for that, de la Souche to my ears is more pleasing than Arnolphe.

CHRYSALDE. What folly to give up the name of your fathers and try to take one which is based upon fancy! Most people will call it a morbid caprice. I once knew (not meaning to make a comparison) a peasant known to all by the name of Fat Peter, who owning a quarter of an acre of land dug a ditch all around it, and called himself pompously Lord of the Isle.

ARNOLPHE. Enough of such cases. De la Souche is the name that I hear. I have my own reasons; I find it agreeable; and to call me by any other name will simply displease me.

CHRYSALDE. Most people, I'm thinking, will hardly conform; in fact, all your letters I still see addressed—

ARNOLPHE. I bear it from persons not rightly informed; but from you—

CHRYSALDE. Oh! there's no need to squabble for that. I'll take care to accustom my mouth to the name, and Monsieur de la Souche I will call you henceforth.

ARNOLPHE. Adieu; I shall knock at my door just to say how d' ye do and announce my return.

CHRYSALDE. [*aside, as he walks away.*] Faith! he's crazy—crazy in every way.

ARNOLPHE. [*alone.*] He is a little annoyed at being opposed. Strange, with what passion people hold their own opinions! [*raps at the door.*] Holà!

SCENE II.

[ARNOLPHE; ALAIN; GEORGETTE, *within the house.*]

ALAIN. Who is knocking?

ARNOLPHE. Open the door. [*aside.*] There will be great joy, I think, at seeing me after my ten days' absence.

ALAIN. Who's there?

ARNOLPHE. I.

ALAIN. Georgette!

GEORGETTE. What?

ALAIN. Go and open the door.

GEORGETTE. Go yourself.

ALAIN. Go you.

GEORGETTE. Faith, I'll not go.

ALAIN. And I'll not go, either.

ARNOLPHE. A pretty state of things, to let me wait outside! Holà! ho! let me in.

ALAIN. Who knocks?

ARNOLPHE. Your master.

GEORGETTE. Alain!

ALAIN. What?

GEORGETTE. It is monsieur. Open the door, quick!

ALAIN. Open it yourself.

GEORGETTE. I am blowing the fire.

ALAIN. My bird will get out; I'm afraid of the cat.

ARNOLPHE. Whichever of you two who does not open the door *first* shall have nothing to eat for four days. Ha!

GEORGETTE. [*to* ALAIN.] What are you coming for? I've come.

ALAIN. Why you instead of me? a pretty trick!

GEORGETTE. Get out of my way.

ALAIN. No, get you out of mine.

GEORGETTE. I must open the door.

ALAIN. I must open it, I!

GEORGETTE. No, you sha'n't open it.

ALAIN. Nor you more than I.

GEORGETTE. Nor you, I say no.

ARNOLPHE. May I keep my soul in patience!

ALAIN. [*appearing at the door.*] At any rate, 'twas I, monsieur.

GEORGETTE. Beg pardon, monsieur, it was I.

ALAIN. Saving monsieur's presence, I'll—

ARNOLPHE. [*receiving a blow* ALAIN *aims at* GEORGETTE.] The devil!

ALAIN. Excuse me.

ARNOLPHE. What a dolt he is!

ALAIN. It was her fault, monsieur.

ARNOLPHE. Hold your tongues, both of you. Answer when I speak to you, and stop this silly talk.—Tell me, Alain, is everybody well?

ALAIN. Monsieur, we—[ARNOLPHE *takes the hat from* ALAIN'*s head.*] Monsieur, we—[ARNOLPHE *takes it off again.*] Thank God, we—

ARNOLPHE. [*taking off the hat for the third time and flinging it on the ground.*] Impertinent fool! who taught you to speak in my presence with a hat on your head?

ALAIN. You are right; I was wrong.

ARNOLPHE. [*to* ALAIN.] Tell Agnes to come down.

SCENE III.

[ARNOLPHE, GEORGETTE.]

ARNOLPHE. After my departure was Agnes sad?

GEORGETTE. Sad! No.

ARNOLPHE. No?

GEORGETTE. Oh, yes, she was.

ARNOLPHE. Why so?

GEORGETTE. I remember it now. She fancied all the time she saw you coming back. Nothing went past the house, horse, mule, or donkey, but she took it for you.

SCENE IV.

[ARNOLPHE, AGNES, ALAIN, GEORGETTE.]

ARNOLPHE. Her work in her hand—an excellent sign! Well, Agnes, you see that I've come back. Are you not glad?

AGNES. Yes, monsieur, thank God.

ARNOLPHE. And I am glad, too, to see you again. You have been, I suppose, quite well all the time?

AGNES. Except for the fleas, which plague me at night.

ARNOLPHE. Ah! you soon will have someone to chase them away.

AGNES. That will be a great pleasure.

ARNOLPHE. Yes; I think so too. What is that you are sewing?

AGNES. A frill for myself. Your shirts and your nightcaps are finished already.

ARNOLPHE. Ha, ha! that is well. Now return to your room. You must not feel lonely; I am coming back soon; for I've something important to say to you, Agnes.

SCENE V.

ARNOLPHE. [*alone.*] Ah! heroines of the period! women of parts! spouters of tenderness and all fine sentiments! I defy your romances, your verses, your billets-doux, your learning, your letters, to match the worth of chaste and honest ignorance. 'Tis not the gifts of mind that ought to dazzle us; and if our honor is—

SCENE VI.

[HORACE, ARNOLPHE.]

ARNOLPHE. What do I see? Is it? Yes. No, I am mistaken. Yes, yes, 'tis he himself, Horace.

HORACE. Seigneur Arnolphe!

ARNOLPHE. Ah! what joy! Since when are you here?

HORACE. For the last nine days.

ARNOLPHE. Is it possible!

HORACE. I went to your house at once, and heard you were gone.

ARNOLPHE. Yes, to the country.

HORACE. For more than ten days.

ARNOLPHE. Oh, how children grow up in a very few years! 'Tis surprising to see him the height he is now when I think how I knew him no higher than that.

HORACE. So you see.

ARNOLPHE. But tell me—your father, my dear and good friend Oronte, whom I love and esteem, where is he, and what is he doing? Is he still gay as ever? In all that concerns him he knows I take part; though 'tis more than four years since we met, and, what is more, since we have written to each other.

HORACE. He is still, Seigneur Arnolphe, the gayest of us all, and he charged me with a letter to give to you from him. Since then he has written to tell me that he himself is coming; but the reason for this step is still unknown to me. Are you aware that one of your fellow-citizens is returning hither with a large fortune, acquired in fourteen years spent in America.

ARNOLPHE. No. Were you told his name?

HORACE. Enrique.

ARNOLPHE. I do not know him.

HORACE. My father writes me of his return as though he ought to be well known to me. He says that they will come together, on some important business which he does not state.

[HORACE *gives* ARNOLPHE *Oronte's letter.*]

ARNOLPHE. It will be great joy to me to see your father; I shall do all that in me lies to entertain him. [*reads the letter.*] Between such friends these compliments are useless; he might have written me nothing and yet myself and all I have would be at your disposal.

HORACE. I am a man to take friends at their word; and I have instant need of a hundred pistoles.

ARNOLPHE. Faith, you oblige me truly by thus using me; I am rejoiced to have them in my pocket. Keep the purse also. [*gives him a purse.*]

HORACE. I must—

ARNOLPHE. No, let us drop the subject. Tell me, what think you of our town?

HORACE. Numerous in citizens, splendid in buildings, and, as I think, marvellous in its amusements.

ARNOLPHE. Each man takes his pleasure as he likes; but those who are dubbed with the title of gallant find much to content them, for the women of Paris are born to coquette. Dark or fair their humor is kind, and their husbands are also the mildest on earth. I find a princely pleasure in watching such affairs; the tricks I see are like a comedy played for my good. Perhaps you have already chosen your lady. Has any such good fortune come in your way? Young men who are made like you do better than win money; your face is one to entice away wives.

HORACE. Not wishing to hide the truth, I own to a love-affair found in this vicinity; friendship compels me to tell it to you.

ARNOLPHE. [*aside.*] Good! another wanton tale to put upon my tablets.

HORACE. But, I beg of you, pray keep the thing a secret.

ARNOLPHE. Oh!

HORACE. On such occasions, as you know, a blurted secret often ruins hopes.—Well, I will admit, with perfect frankness, that my soul is captive to a beauty here. My first attentions met with such return that I obtained at once sweet access to her presence. And now, without boasting, or disloyalty to her, I may say that my prospects are most excellent.

ARNOLPHE. [*laughing.*] And the lady is—

HORACE. [*pointing to* AGNES' *house.*] A young girl living in that house with the red walls you see from here. A simple girl, kept ignorant by the unheard-of error of a man who hides her from all intercourse with life; but she, amid that ignorance by which he is seeking to enslave her, shows sweet attractions capable of charm, a most engaging air, and something—I know not what—so tender that no heart could e'er withstand it. But it may be that you know already this young star of love, provided with so many choice attractions. Her name is Agnes.

ARNOLPHE. [*aside.*] Ah! I shall burst!

HORACE. The man, I think, is De la Zousse, or Source, or some such name; I did not pay attention to it. Rich, so they tell me; but as for judgment, none; in fact, they talk of him as most absurd. Do you not know him?

ARNOLPHE. [*aside.*] A sorry pill!

HORACE. You do not answer.

ARNOLPHE. Well, yes, I know him.

HORACE. Crazy, is he not?

ARNOLPHE. Hey!

HORACE. What say you? Hey! Does that mean yes? Jealous, is he, so that all men laugh at him? A fool? Ah! I see it is as others told me. Well, that most lovable Agnes has enslaved me. She's a sweet treasure, and I'd count it criminal if so rare a beauty were left in the power of that fantastic man. As for me, my efforts and my tenderest hopes are to make her mine in spite of his jealous care; and the money which I borrow with such frankness is to bring my enterprise to some safe end. You know, even better than I, that, whatever our efforts, gold is the pass-key that opens all locks. That precious metal, which affects all minds, in love as well as war, leads on to victory. But you seem grieved. Is it that you disapprove the plan I have made?

ARNOLPHE. No, no, I was dreaming.

HORACE. This talk has wearied you. Adieu. I shall go to your house before long, to thank you, I am sure, for my success.

ARNOLPHE. [*thinking himself alone.*] Ah! must I—

HORACE. [*returning.*] Once more, I beg you to be discreet. Do not, I pray you, let my secret out.

ARNOLPHE. [*thinking himself alone.*] What feelings in my soul!—

HORACE. [*returning.*] Above all to my father; who might, perhaps, make it a cause for anger.

ARNOLPHE. [*thinking* HORACE *still there.*] Oh!—

SCENE VII.

ARNOLPHE. [*alone.*] Oh, what tortures I have suffered in this interview! No trouble of mind has ever equaled this. What imprudence, and what headlong haste in telling this affair to me—myself! Although my name, of course, caused the mistake, did ever heedless youth show so much folly? But however much I suffered, I was forced to control myself, that I might know exactly what I had to fear. I heard to the end his thoughtless gabble to learn their secret commerce to its full extent. I'll follow him; he cannot have gone far, I think. 'Tis best to gain his confidence completely as to these facts. I tremble for the evil that may come of them; for often we seek more than we desire to find.

ACT II.

SCENE I.

ARNOLPHE. [*alone.*] When I reflect upon it, 'tis doubtless for the best that I have wasted my steps and missed finding his traces; the imperative trouble which fills my heart could not have been hidden wholly from his eyes; his presence must have forced out the anger that consumes me, and I do not desire he should know it as yet.—But I'm not a man to lick up his crumbs, and leave the field open to a puppy like him! I shall break up his scheme without further delay, and learn to what point the relations between them have ventured to go. My honor is concerned in a notable way; I regard her as a wife on the terms we are now; all she does is for my sake, and to fail in her duty is to cast shame on me. Ah! fatal departure! unfortunate journey! [*he raps at his door.*]

SCENE II.

[ARNOLPHE, ALAIN, GEORGETTE.]

ALAIN. There! monsieur, this time—

ARNOLPHE. Silence! Here, both of you. Stand there, I say.

GEORGETTE. Oh! you scare me; my blood's curdling.

ARNOLPHE. So this is the way you obey me when absent? You have laid your heads together, both of you, to betray me.

GEORGETTE. [*dropping on her knees.*] Oh! monsieur, oh! don't eat me up alive, I implore you.

ALAIN. [*aside.*] Some mad dog has bit him, I'm certain of that.

ARNOLPHE. [*aside.*] Ouf! I cannot speak, so angry am I. I suffocate; would I could tear my clothes off and go naked! [*to* ALAIN *and* GEORGETTE.] You have allowed, you cursed scum, a man to come here! [*to* ALAIN, *who tries to run away.*] You want to escape me, do you? Tell me at once—[*to* GEORGETTE.] If you stir, I'll—Now, I say, you must tell me—[*to* ALAIN *and* GEORGETTE, *who are both trying to escape.*] The first of you that stirs, by Death! I'll strike you down. How did that man get into my house? Speak! make haste! quick! hurry! No gaping now. Tell me, I say.

ALAIN and GEORGETTE. Aie! aie!

GEORGETTE. [*falling at* ARNOLPHE'*s feet.*] My heart's stopping!

ALAIN. [*falling at* ARNOLPHE'*s feet.*] I'm dying!

ARNOLPHE. [*aside.*] I'm wringing wet—let me get breath—I must have air, and walk about—Could I have guessed, when I first knew him, that small boy! that he would grow for this?—Heavens! how my heart beats! Had I not better from his own lips, gently, draw out the truth? I'll try to moderate my anger. Patience, my heart, go softly, softly. [*to* ALAIN *and* GEORGETTE.] Get up; go in; tell Agnes to come down. No, stop. [*aside.*] Her surprise would be less; I could not take her unawares if they should warn her; I'll go myself and bring her down. [*to* ALAIN *and* GEORGETTE.] Wait here.

Scene III.

[ALAIN, GEORGETTE.]

GEORGETTE. Heavens! isn't he terrible? His looks do frighten me with an awful fright; never did I see such a hideous mortal.

ALAIN. That monsieur vexes him; didn't I tell you so?

GEORGETTE. But why the deuce does he make us keep our mistress in the house in this harsh way? Why does he want to hide her from all the world, and never let a single soul come near her?

ALAIN. Because if they do it makes him jealous.

GEORGETTE. But what's the reason he has taken that notion?

ALAIN. The reason—well, the reason is he's jealous.

GEORGETTE. Yes, but *why* is he jealous? why does he get so angry?

ALAIN. Because jealousy—(Now you listen to what I say, Georgette.) jealousy is a thing—there, you know—makes people uneasy, drives folks away from coming round the house. I'll give you an instance, so you'll understand the thing. Tell me, isn't it true that if you had your broth and a hungry man wanted to eat it up, you'd get angry and drive him off?

GEORGETTE. Yes, I understand all that.

ALAIN. Well, this is just the same thing. A woman is, you may say, a man's broth; and when a man sees other men wanting to stick their fingers in his pot, he gets angry.

GEORGETTE. Well, if that's so why don't they all do alike? I am sure we see plenty who are very well pleased when their wives are with beaux.

ALAIN. That's because everyone isn't so greedy as to want to keep all for himself.

GEORGETTE. Unless my eyes deceive me, I see him coming back.

ALAIN. Your eyes are right; 'tis he.

GEORGETTE. How vexed he looks!
ALAIN. Something has worried him.

SCENE IV.

[ARNOLPHE, ALAIN, GEORGETTE.]

ARNOLPHE. [*aside.*] A certain Greek told the Emperor Augustus, as a piece of useful information, that when some incident had put him in a rage it was well to say the alphabet, in order that his bile might have time to subside and he himself do nothing he ought not to do. I practised that lesson just now upon Agues; and I shall take her out, on pretence of a walk, to let the doubts of my sick mind approach the mutter cautiously, and, by sounding her heart gently, gain the light they seek.

SCENE V.

[ARNOLPHE, AGNES, ALAIN, GEORGETTE.]

ARNOLPHE. Come, Agnes. [*to* ALAIN *and* GEORGETTE.] Return to the house.

SCENE VI.

[ARNOLPHE, AGNES.]

ARNOLPHE. A walk is pleasant.
AGNES. Very pleasant.
ARNOLPHE. The day is charming.
AGNES. Very charming.
ARNOLPHE. What is the news?
AGNES. The kitten is dead.
ARNOLPHE. That's a pity; however, we are all of us mortal, and each for himself. When I was in the country, did it rain about here?
AGNES. No.
ARNOLPHE. Were you dull?
AGNES. I am never dull.
ARNOLPHE. What were you doing those nine or ten days?
AGNES. Making six shirts, and six night-caps, I think.
ARNOLPHE. [*After some reflection.*] The world, dear Agnes, is a very strange thing. Consider its gossip, and how people talk! Some neighbors have told me that an unknown young man has been seen, in my absence, to enter this house; and that you yourself saw him and allowed him to talk to you. But I would not put faith in their

mischievous tongues, and I offered to bet that they falsely—

AGNES. Oh! goodness, don't bet, you will certainly lose.

ARNOLPHE. What! is it true that a man—

AGNES. Quite true, I assure you; he scarce stirred from the house.

ARNOLPHE. [*aside in a low voice.*] This confession—made with such sincerity—shows, at least, that she's ingenuous. [*aloud.*] But, Agnes, it seems to me, if I remember right, that I forbade you to see any one.

AGNES. Yes; but you don't know how it was I saw him. You would have done the same, no doubt, as I.

ARNOLPHE. Perhaps. But tell me the story of how it happened.

AGNES. It is quite surprising, and difficult to believe. I was on the balcony, sewing where it was cool, when I saw, passing under the trees nearby, a very well-made young man, who, catching my eye, made me at once a very humble bow. I, not to be lacking in civility, made him a bow myself; then he made me another, which I returned at once; then he a third, and I a third as quickly. He passed along, came back, and passed again, and each time made me a new bow. I, who watched his movements fixedly, returned them all; and should have done so longer if it had not grown dark rather than let him think I was less civil than he.

ARNOLPHE. Well?

AGNES. The next day, being at the door, an elderly woman came to me and said—something like this: "My child, may the good God bless you, and preserve your pretty looks. He has not made you such a handsome girl that you should make an ill use of his gifts; and you must know that you have wounded one who now is forced to make complaint."

ARNOLPHE. [*aside.*] Ha! tool of Satan! Execrable fiend!

AGNES. "I! wounded any one!" I said, amazed. "Yes," said she, "wounded, and wounded deeply. It is the man whom you saw yesterday beneath your balcony." "Alas!" I said, "how could I have done that? did I let something fall upon his head?" "No," she replied, "your eyes have given this fatal blow; it is their glance that did the harm." "Heavens!" I cried, "this is surprising. Have my eyes some evil in them which they cast on others?" "Yes," she replied, "your eyes possess a poison that you know not of, which made this wound. In short, he languishes, poor miserable man, and if," the charitable soul went on, "your cruelty refuses him relief, in a few days they'll take him to his grave." "Good God!" I said, "how I should grieve for that! What is it I must do to better him?" "My child," she said, "all that he asks is to come here and see and talk with you. Your eyes alone can remedy his trouble and be the medicine for the ill they've done."

ARNOLPHE. [*aside.*] Ha! you damned witch! you poisoner of souls!

may hell reward your charitable plots!

AGNES. That's how he came to see me and was cured. Do you not think yourself that I did right? Could I have had the conscience to let him die for want of such assistance,—I who am pitiful when others suffer, and cry to see them wring the chickens' necks?

ARNOLPHE. [*aside.*] All this must surely come from innocence of heart. I blame my lamentable absence, which left without a guide such ignorant goodness exposed to all the wiles of these seducers. I fear the villain with his lying vows has pushed his purpose farther than mere words.

AGNES. What is the matter? It seems to me that you are scolding just a little. Is there any harm in what I've told you?

ARNOLPHE. No. But tell me all that followed, and how the young man paid his visits.

AGNES. Ah! if you only knew how glad he was to come, and how his ills were cured the moment that he saw me, and the beauteous casket that he brought me, and the money that he gave to Alain and Georgette, you would love him, I know, and say with us—

ARNOLPHE. Yes, yes; but tell me what he did when quite alone with you.

AGNES. He said he loved me with incomparable love. Oh, he says the prettiest words in all the world, and things that nothing, I am sure, can equal; for every time I hear him say them I feel a gentle tingling, and something stirs within me, I don't know what.

ARNOLPHE. [*aside.*] Ah! cruel search into a fatal mystery in which the seeker suffers all the pain. [*aloud.*] Well, besides this talk and all this prettiness, did he not make you some caresses?

AGNES. Oh, yes, many! He took my hands and arms, and never tired of kissing them.

ARNOLPHE. Agnes, did he take nothing else? [*seeing her confusion.*] Ouf!

AGNES. Yes, he—

ARNOLPHE. What?

AGNES. Took—

ARNOLPHE. Ha!

AGNES. The—the—

ARNOLPHE. Go on.

AGNES. I dare not; you'll be angry with me.

ARNOLPHE. No.

AGNES. Yes, you will.

ARNOLPHE. Good God! no.

AGNES. Swear it, on your faith.

ARNOLPHE. By my faith, no.

AGNES. He took—oh, but you *will* be angry?

ARNOLPHE. No.

AGNES. Yes.

ARNOLPHE. No, no, no, no. The devil! what's this mystery? What did he take?

AGNES. He—

ARNOLPHE. [*aside.*] I suffer the tortures of the damned.

AGNES. He took the—ribbon that you gave me; to tell the truth, I was not able to prevent it.

ARNOLPHE. [*drawing a deep breath.*] Never mind the ribbon. But I wish to know what more he did to you than kiss your arms.

AGNES. How? what more do people do?

ARNOLPHE. Oh, nothing. But to cure the ills he said possessed him, did he ask you for no other remedy?

AGNES. No; but if he had, you may be sure to cure him I'd have granted all.

ARNOLPHE. [*aside.*] Thanks to heaven's mercy I am safe this time; and if I ever fall again into such danger, I give them leave to wrong me. But hush! [*aloud.*] Your innocence, Agnes, had its just effect. I shall say no more; what is done is done. I know that in thus flattering you this gallant meant to wrong you first and then to laugh at you—

AGNES. Oh, never, not at all; he told me so a score of times.

ARNOLPHE. Ah! you do not know the meaning of such pledges. But this I must teach you: to accept handsome caskets, to give ear to the nonsense of these fine gentlemen, and to let them kiss your hands and tingle your heart, is a mortal sin, and the worst you could commit.

AGNES. A sin, do you say? for mercy's sake, why?

ARNOLPHE. Because it is decreed such actions anger God.

AGNES. Anger him! But why should he be angry? it is so pleasing and so sweet a thing! I love the joy it gives me, for I knew nothing until now of what it was.

ARNOLPHE. Yes, such tendernesses, such pretty words and soft caresses, are indeed great pleasures; but we must take them honorably; marriage removes the crime.

AGNES. Then it is not a sin if we are married?

ARNOLPHE. No.

AGNES. Please marry me at once, I beg of you.

ARNOLPHE. If you wish that, I wish it too; in fact, I have come back to marry you.

AGNES. How glad I'll be!

ARNOLPHE. Yes; I have no doubt myself that marriage will please you.

AGNES. And you wish us—both of us—

ARNOLPHE. Assuredly I do.

AGNES. Ah! if that happens, how I will caress you!

ARNOLPHE. Ha! and on my part it will be reciprocal.

AGNES. But I never know, myself, when people are joking. Are you in earnest?

ARNOLPHE. Yes; can you not see it?

AGNES. We shall be married?

ARNOLPHE. Yes.

AGNES. But when?

ARNOLPHE. To-night.

AGNES. [*smiling.*] To-night?

ARNOLPHE. To-night—it makes you smile.

AGNES. Yes.

ARNOLPHE. To see you pleased is what I wish.

AGNES. Ah! how grateful I shall be to you! I know that with him I shall surely be happy.

ARNOLPHE. With whom?

AGNES. With—there!

ARNOLPHE. There!—*There* is not my intention. You are far too much in haste to choose a husband. 'Tis another whom I have ready for you; and as for Monsieur *There*, I intend, if you please, to bury the mischief he has put in your head and stop for the future all commerce between you. When he calls at this house to pay you a visit, you will order the door to be shut in his face; and if he still knocks you will fling, through the window, a stone to inform him he is not to return. Do you hear what I say? I shall hide in a corner and watch your behavior.

AGNES. Oh, la, la! he's so handsome; and—

ARNOLPHE. What language is that!

AGNES. I shall not have the heart—

ARNOLPHE. No more of this fuss. Go up to your room.

AGNES. But why? do you mean—?

ARNOLPHE. Enough! I'm your master; when I speak, you'll obey.

ACT III.

SCENE I.

[ARNOLPHE, AGNES, ALAIN, GEORGETTE.]

ARNOLPHE. Yes, all has gone right; my joy is extreme; you have followed my orders remarkably well. At all points the seducer is foiled; and you now see the use of a head to direct. Your innocence, Agnes, was being deceived. Look where you were thoughtlessly going—on the broad road to hell and eternal damnation! The morals of these fops are known to all; they wear fine breeches, ribbons, plumes; they sport long hair, white teeth, and make sweet speeches, but, as I told you, claws are underneath. They are veritable Satans, and their hungry jaws seek women's virtue for their prey. But, thanks to my command, you have escaped with honor. The air with which I saw you throw that stone which knocked his daring hopes to earth, confirms my will not to delay our wedding, for which I bid you now prepare. But, first of all, 'tis right that I should give you a little lesson as to marriage which will be salutary for you. [*to* ALAIN *and* GEORGETTE.] Bring me a seat out here. If either of you ever—

GEORGETTE. We shall remember monsieur's lessons. That other gentleman imposed upon us; but—

ALAIN. If he gets in again, may I never drink another drop! Besides which he's a cheat; didn't he give us the other day two coins that weren't full weight?

ARNOLPHE. Prepare for supper the dishes I prefer; and for the marriage-contract, as I said just now, go, one or other of you, for the notary who lodges at the corner of this square.

Scene II.

[ARNOLPHE, AGNES.]

ARNOLPHE. [*seated.*] Agnes, lay down your work, and listen to me. Lift up your head, and turn your face this way. [*putting his finger on his forehead.*] There, look at me during this interview; impress upon your mind my lightest word. I marry you, Agnes; and you ought, a hundred times a day, to bless the luck of such a destiny. Remembering the lowness of your birth, you should admire my goodness, which, from the vile condition of a village girl, has raised you to the station of an honorable bourgeoise, where you will enjoy the couch and the embraces of a man who hitherto has fled such ties—though to a score of women most capable of pleasing he has refused the honor he now bestows on you. You ought, I say, to keep before your eyes the humble place you hold without this splendid tie, in order that you may strive the more to merit the state of life to which I lift you, and, knowing what you were, act so that I be satisfied with what I do. Marriage is not a jest. The rank of wife involves stern duties; you are not, I must inform you, raised so high for libertine amusements and to take your pleasure. Your sex is here to be dependent; power is with the beard; although there are two sexes, two portions of society, those portions are not equal. One is supreme, the other is subordinate; one is, in all things, subject to the other, who governs. The soldier, trained to duty, obeys his leader, the valet obeys his master, the child its parents, the little boy his elder brother, but the obedience of them all does not approach the docile submissiveness, the humble and profound respect a wife must show her husband, her head, her lord, her master. When he casts a serious glance upon her, her duty is to drop her eyes and not to dare to look him in the face, unless, with a soft glance, he suffers it. This is a rule the women of these days neglect; but do not you be spoiled by such examples. Abstain from imitating vile coquettes whose capers ring throughout the town. Beware lest you be taken in the snares of Satan; that is, you must not listen to any fine young spark. Remember that in making you the half of my own person, Agnes, I place my honor in your keeping. That honor is a tender thing; a very little wounds it; on such a subject there must be no foolery. Hell has a boiling caldron in which are plunged forever ill-conducted wives. What I am telling you is no mere idle tale, and you must lay to heart these lessons. If your soul follows them and shuns all coquetry, it will be, like a lily, white and pure; but if it makes one false step as to honor, it will be black as coal. You then will seem to all a hideous object; and you will someday go, the devil's prey, to boil in hell to all eternity. God keep you from it in his heavenly mercy! Make your courtesy—Now, as a novice learns her rules by heart on entering a convent, so you on entering marriage must do likewise. Here, in my pocket, is a useful treatise which will instruct you on the duties of a wife. I do not know the author; he must be some worthy soul, and it is my wish that you shall make his words your only reading. [*rises.*] Take it; and let me hear if you can read it properly.

AGNES. [*reading aloud.*]

THE MAXIMS OF MARRIAGE

OR

THE DUTIES OF A MARRIED WOMAN, WITH A DAILY EXERCISE THEREIN.

FIRST MAXIM.

She who by virtuous tie
Enters a husband's bed,
Must fix it in her mind
That the man who takes her, takes her for himself.

ARNOLPHE. I'll explain to you later the meaning of that; at present you need only read the words.

AGNES. [*reading.*]

SECOND MAXIM.

She must adorn her person
As much, and no more,
As the man who possesses her wishes;
He alone is concerned in the care of her beauty,
And it is of no consequence
If others consider her ugly.

THIRD MAXIM.

Forbidden all study of glances,
All washes, all paints, all pomades,
And the thousand ingredients that make the skin bloom;
Such things are to virtue like poisonous drugs.
These cares for the person
To make it seem beautiful
Are taken too seldom for husbands.

FOURTH MAXIM.

When a wife walks abroad, her honor commands
That the glance of her eyes be concealed by a hood;
For to please her spouse well
She must please no one else.

FIFTH MAXIM.

Excepting those persons who visit the husband,
Good behavior forbids
The wife to receive a soul;
Those whose gallant humor
Cares only for madame
Do not suit monsieur.

SIXTH MAXIM.

She must refuse
All presents from men,
Because in these days
Nothing is given for nothing.

SEVENTH MAXIM.

In her apartments, no matter if she die of dulness,
There must be neither inkstand, ink, nor pens, nor paper;
The husband should, according to good customs,
Write all that must be written in his house.

EIGHTH MAXIM.

Those disorderly social routs,
So-called Assemblies,
Corrupt the minds of women daily;
Good policy demands they be suppressed;
'Tis there conspiracies are hatched
Against poor husbands.

NINTH MAXIM.

All women who to virtue vow themselves
Must forswear cards
As fatal snares;
For gambling, most insidious,
Often leads a wife
To stake her all.

TENTII MAXIM.

Excursions in fine weather,
Repasts given in the fields,
The wife must not accept;
For prudent brains declare
That husbands for these jaunts
Are those that pay.

ELEVENTH MAXIM—

ARNOLPHE. You can read the rest alone; and, step by step, as we go on, I will explain those maxims to you. I have just remembered a small matter I must attend to. Go in; and keep that little book most preciously. If the notary comes, let him wait till I return.

SCENE III.

ARNOLPHE. [*alone.*] I cannot do better than make her my wife. I can turn that soul every way that I wish. She's like wax in my hands, and will take any form it may please me to give her. How nearly inveigled she was through her innocence! But 'tis better, in truth, that the woman one marries should err on that side; the cure of such error is easy enough. A creature so simple is docile to lessons, and if for a moment she wanders astray, two words will suffice to recall her. But those women of parts are different animals! Our fate depends upon their heads, and what they once take into those no man can get out. Their wit is used to ridicule our maxims, and often to make virtues of their crimes; they find, to reach their guilty ends, all sorts of tricks that dupe the ablest men. To ward them off is wasted toil; a clever woman is a devil in wiles; and if her whims should doom our honor, we must submit and let her have her way. Many a worthy man, alas! knows that. But my young fop will have no chance to laugh; his chattering tongue has brought him his deserts. That is the common fault of Frenchmen; when they possess a love-affair, the secret always burns within them, and silly vanity has such attractions they'd rather lose their lives than hold their tongues. Oh! how the women are tempted of the devil when they go and choose such scatter-wits as these! and—But here he is. I'll hide my feelings well, and so discover how his defeat affects him.

SCENE IV.

[HORACE, ARNOLPHE.]

HORACE. I have just left your house; fate seems to say it has decreed that I shall never find you; but I mean to go so often that at last—

ARNOLPHE. A truce to compliments; nothing annoys me more than ceremony, and if I had my way it should be banished; these visits are a cursed custom on which two-thirds of people's time is wasted. Put on your hat. [*puts on his own.*] Well, about your love-affair? May I know, Seigneur Horace, how that is coming on? When you spoke to me lately my thoughts were much distracted. Since then I have reflected. I admire the rapidity with which you proceed, and in the result my mind takes an interest.

HORACE. Alas! since I showed you the state of my heart ill-luck has attended my love.

ARNOLPHE. Ho, ho! how is that?

HORACE. Cruel fortune has brought home the guardian of Agnes.

ARNOLPHE. A misfortune, indeed!

HORACE. Yes, and what's more, to my bitter regret he has heard of our secret relations.

ARNOLPHE. How the deuce did he hear it so soon?

HORACE. I don't know; but the thing is certain. I went, at my usual hour, to pay my little visit to her sweet attractions, when, changing totally in voice and visage, the valet and the maid both barred my way. "Be off," they said, "you trouble us;" and then they rudely slammed the door.

ARNOLPHE. They slammed the door?

HORACE. Yes, in my face.

ARNOLPHE. Well, that was rather strong.

HORACE. I tried to argue through the panels, but to all I said they answered: "You can't come in; Monsieur forbids it."

ARNOLPHE. They did not let you enter?

HORACE. No. Then Agnes from the window confirmed the fact of his return, and, telling me in haughty tones to go away, she flung a stone to emphasize her words.

ARNOLPHE. What! a stone?

HORACE. A stone—and not a small one either—cast by her hand, greeted my visit.

ARNOLPHE. The devil! stones are not plums. This is a grievous state of things.

HORACE. True; this return is fatally unlucky.

ARNOLPHE. I'm sorry for you—I protest I am.

HORACE. That man stops everything.

ARNOLPHE. Yes, for a time; but you will find some other way to come together.

HORACE. I shall try by some wise means to get the better of his jealous vigilance.

ARNOLPHE. To you that must be easy; and the girl? you say she loves you?

HORACE. Oh, assuredly.

ARNOLPHE. Then you must succeed.

HORACE. I hope to.

ARNOLPHE. But that stone that routed you? Did not that surprise you?

HORACE. Of course it did. At first I thought the man himself was there, and, hidden from sight, was prompting what she did. But what surprised me more, as it will you, was something else, which I will tell you,—a daring act done by my little beauty, which one could scarce expect of her simplicity. We must admit that Love is a great teacher; what we have never been, he teaches us to be; often a total change in all our being becomes, by his instruction, instantaneous. He smoothes the obstacles within our nature; and his effects seem miracles, so sudden are they. A miser is made generous, a hero a poltroon, a civil man a brute. Love makes the dullest soul alert and gives to innocence intelligence. Yes, this last miracle appeared in Agnes, for, driving me away with these harsh words, "Depart; your visits I renounce; I know the meaning of your speeches, and here's my answer," she threw the stone, and with it was—a letter! But oh! how charmed I was to find that letter interpreting the meaning of her words and the cast missile. Are you not surprised at such an act? And does not Love know well the art of sharpening wits? Can we deny that his all-potent flame can do amazing things within the soul? What think you of this little trick? and of her note? You must admire such cleverness of mind. Is it not droll to see the part our jealous guardian plays in this bamboozlement?

ARNOLPHE. Yes, very droll!

HORACE. Why don't you laugh? [ARNOLPHE *gives a forced laugh.*] 'Tis most amusing to see that man, in arms against my love, intrench himself within the house and fight with stones—as if I sought to enter by assault!—and, in his comic dread, set both his servants on me, while, before his very eyes, his machinations are being turned against him by her whom he has striven to keep a dunce. As for me, I own, though his return has brought great trouble to my love, I find it very funny, and I laugh with all my heart to think of it. But you don't laugh, my friend!

ARNOLPHE. Excuse me, I am laughing all I can.

HORACE. Now I must show you, as a friend, the letter. Her hand at least knows how to write all that her heart is feeling, in words most touching, full of goodness, innocent tenderness, and artless candor,—in short, the very way a pure young nature would express its earliest sense of love.

ARNOLPHE. [*aside.*] So! the minx! this is the use she makes of writing! 'Twas much against my will the art was taught her.

HORACE. [*reading.*] "I wish to write to you, but I am troubled how to do so. I have thoughts that I want you to know, but I do not feel able to say them; I distrust my words. As I have just begun to see how they have always kept me ignorant, I fear to write something that is not right, and to say more than I ought. To speak the truth, I do not know what you have done to injure me, but I know that I am sorry to death for what they are making me do against you; I shall suffer great pain in trying to do without you; and I should be very glad to be yours. Perhaps there is some harm in saying that, but indeed I cannot help saying it, and I hope I can do so without doing wrong. They tell me that all young men are deceivers; that I must not listen to them, and that all you have said was only said to harm me. But I do assure you I have not yet been able to think that of you; and I am so touched by your words that I know not how to believe they are deceitful. Tell me, frankly, how that is. I am so truly without suspicion that you would do me the greatest wrong in the world if you deceived me in this. I think I should die of that distress."

ARNOLPHE. [*aside.*] Ho! the slut.

HORACE. What is the matter?

ARNOLPHE. Nothing—I coughed.

HORACE. Did you ever hear sweeter expressions? In spite of the accursed care of unjust power, how beautiful the nature she reveals. Is it not a punishable crime to try, so wickedly, to spoil that soul and smother the natural light of such a mind in ignorance and stupidity? Love is beginning, as you see, to tear away the veil; and if, by the help of some good star I can, as I hope I may, give to that vile animal, that traitor, that brute, that scoundrel, that—

ARNOLPHE. Adieu.

HORACE. What, so soon?

ARNOLPHE. Yes, I have just bethought me of some pressing business.

HORACE. But cannot you tell me, as you live so near, of someone who has access to the house? I ask it without scruple, for between friends, 'tis not an unusual thing to do such service. There is no one now within the house but spies who watch me. The maid and valet, no matter how I try to soften them, won't hear a word. At first I employed a shrewd old woman, a genius in such matters, who served me well; but the poor thing died three days ago. Could you not point me to some other means?

ARNOLPHE. No, I cannot; you'll find them easily without me.

HORACE. Very well, adieu; you see I trust you.

Scene V.

ARNOLPHE. [*alone.*] How I was forced to curb myself before him! what pains I've borne to hide this smarting sorrow! Can innocence be so quick-witted? Did she feign innocence to me, the traitress? or did the devil breathe upon her soul? That fatal letter has destroyed me. I see the traitor has laid hold upon her mind and now, ejecting me, is anchored there. Oh! black despair and mortal pain! This robbery of her heart is double suffering, for love repines as well as honor. I am enraged to find my place usurped, enraged to see how she has foiled my prudence. I know well that to punish her wanton love I have but to leave her to her destiny; 'tis she herself who will avenge me. But it is very sorrowful to lose that which we love. Oh, Heaven! why, when I made my choice by true philosophy, why must I be so captive to her charms? She has no friends, no parents, no support; she has betrayed my care, my charity, my tenderness, and yet I love her! I love her after this base act so that I cannot live without her. Fool! are you not ashamed? Oh! I am mad, I burst with fury, I could beat my head a thousand times against that wall. I must go in; but only for a moment, just to see if, after this black deed, she keeps her countenance. Oh, Heaven! grant that my forehead he exempt from this disgrace. Or else, if it be written above that I must hear it, grant me at least, in these events, the firmness that I see in other men.

ACT IV.

SCENE I.

ARNOLPHE. [*alone.*] A thousand cares harass my mind. I cannot, I confess, control myself enough to form a plan which shall defeat, indoors and out, the efforts of that popinjay. With what an eye the traitress bore my glance! All she has done does not abash her; though she has brought me almost to my grave, one would think, to look at her, that she knew nothing of it. The more I watch her tranquil air, the more I feel the bile within me stirred; and yet those foaming transports which convulse my heart seem only to increase my amorous ardor. I was bitter, angry, desperate against her, and yet she never looked to mine so beautiful. Never did those eyes so shine to mine, and never did I feel for her such longing. I cannot live if my sad fate it is to bear this misery. What! shall I have trained her with all care and tenderness, shall I have kept her in my home since childhood, cherishing a precious hope, building my heart upon her budding charms, and forming her, for thirteen years, to suit me, only to see a puppy with whom she falls in love snatch her away beneath my very beard, when she is semi-married to me? No, *parbleu*! no! Young fool, my friend indeed! you shall not have the laugh on me; you may try all your tricks, but I will turn, my word upon it, all your hopes to ashes.

SCENE II.

[A NOTARY, ARNOLPHE.]

NOTARY. Ah! here he is. Good-day to you. I've come prepared to draw the contract you desire to make.

ARNOLPHE. [*not seeing the notary and thinking himself alone.*] But how can it be done?

NOTARY. In the usual form, of course.

ARNOLPHE. [*thinking himself alone.*] Let me reflect on my precautions—

NOTARY. I shall put nothing in against your interests.

ARNOLPHE. [*thinking himself alone.*] I must protect myself against all plots—

NOTARY. Suffice it that you place your interests in my hands; you need fear no deception.

ARNOLPHE. [*thinking himself alone.*] I fear, if I suffer this matter to transpire, that the whole town will gossip—

NOTARY. Well, 'tis easy enough to hinder that by signing the contract privately.

ARNOLPHE. [*thinking himself alone.*] But, in any case, how shall I treat her?

NOTARY. The jointure is regulated by the total of your property.

ARNOLPHE. [*thinking himself alone.*] I love her, and that love is my greatest hindrance.

NOTARY. 'Tis easy in all contracts to favor the wife.

ARNOLPHE. [*thinking himself alone.*] What treatment is best in this emergency?

NOTARY. The rule is that the husband should endow the wife with a third of her own *dot*; but that is not enforced; more can be given if desired.

ARNOLPHE. [*thinking himself alone.*] If—[*he sees the notary.*]

NOTARY. As for the benefit of the survivor, that must be arranged conjointly; I only say that the husband can, by the marriage contract, endow the wife as he sees fit.

ARNOLPHE. Hey?

NOTARY. If he loves her much and wants to please her he can favor her in various ways; either by jointure or by what is called "prefix,"—that is, a settlement reverting to the husband on the wife's decease; or without reversion, in which case it goes to her heirs; or by common law if both consent; or by donation in the contract which can be made either unconditional or reciprocal. Why do you shrug your shoulders? Am I talking like an ignoramus who does not know the forms of a marriage contract? Who can teach *me*, I'd like to know? No one, I presume. Don't I know that after marriage custom gives the parties equal rights in furniture and property, real or thereafter acquired, unless by deed they renounce them. Don't I also know that a third of the wife's *dot* becomes the common property of the husband in order to—

ARNOLPHE. Yes, yes; 'tis certain that you know all that; but who has said a word to you about it.

NOTARY. Why, you yourself, who are trying to make me out a fool, shrugging your shoulders and grimacing at me!

ARNOLPHE. A plague upon the fellow and his sluttish face! Adieu; to leave you is the only way to stop your mouth.

NOTARY. Did you not send for me to draw a contract?

ARNOLPHE. Yes, I did send for you; but the matter is now postponed.

They'll fetch you when the time is fixed. What a devil of a man for talk!

NOTARY. [*alone.*] I think he'll stick to that—and I always think right.

SCENE III.

[THE NOTARY, ALAIN, GEORGETTE.]

NOTARY. [*going up to them.*] Did you not fetch me by order of your master?

ALAIN. Yes.

NOTARY. I don't know what you think of him, but you can tell him from me that I say he is downright crazy.

GEORGETTE. We won't fail to do so.

SCENE IV.

[ARNOLPHE, ALAIN, GEORGETTE.]

ALAIN. Monsieur—

ARNOLPHE. Come here, the pair of you. You are my faithful, good, true friends; I know what you have done.

ALAIN. The notary—

ARNOLPHE. Never mind the notary; that's for another day. My honor is attacked by scurvy tricks; and what an injury to you, my children, if your master's honor is taken from him! You would not dare to show yourselves in any place; for even the people in the streets would point their ringers at you. Therefore, as this affair hurts you as well as me, you must keep so close a watch that this young gallant cannot, in any way—

GEORGETTE. You have already taught us how to do it.

ARNOLPHE. Yes; but beware lest his fine speeches get the better of you.

ALAIN. Pooh! they can't.

GEORGETTE. We shall know how to answer them.

ARNOLPHE. But suppose he softly says: "Alain, kind heart, comfort my trouble with a little help."

ALAIN. You are a fool.

ARNOLPHE. Right. [*to* GEORGETTE.] "Georgette, my dear, you seem to me so sweet and good a girl."

GEORGETTE. You are a booby.

ARNOLPHE. Good. [*to* ALAIN.] "What harm can you see in a plan so honest and all full of virtue?"

ALAIN. You are a knave and a cheat.

ARNOLPHE. Good, very good! [*to* GEORGETTE.] "My death is sure if you will not have pity on my pain."

GEORGETTE. You are an impudent jackass.

ARNOLPHE. Very good indeed! [*to* ALAIN.] "I'm not a man to ask nothing for nothing. I remember the services everyone does me; but, Alain, in advance, here's a trifle for drink; and here's for you, Georgette, to buy a new petticoat." [*they both put out their hands and take the money.*] "That's only a sample of what I will give you. All I ask in return is to see your young mistress."

GEORGETTE. [*pushing him.*] Talk that way to others.

ARNOLPHE. Ha! very good, that.

ALAIN. [*pushing him.*] Come, get out of here.

ARNOLPHE. Well done!

GEORGETTE. [*pushing him.*] Make haste and be off!

ARNOLPHE. Holà, that's enough.

GEORGETTE. Don't I do as I ought?

ALAIN. Isn't that what you meant!

ARNOLPHE. Yes—all but the money you ought not to have taken.

GEORGETTE. That's a part we forgot.

ALAIN. Do you wish us to do it again?

ARNOLPHE. No, once is enough. Return to the house.

ALAIN. You have only to say so.

ARNOLPHE. No, no; I say no! Return to the house as I tell you; I give you that money. Go in; keep an eye upon all, and second my efforts.

SCENE V.

ARNOLPHE. [*alone.*] I want a spy to watch the door. I'll take that cobbler at the corner of the street, and put him in my house; he'll keep good guard and drive away those sellers of ribbons, wigs, and handkerchiefs, perfumers, barbers, dealers in cast-off finery, who are always working underhand to help the schemes of lovers. I've seen the world; I know its wiles; and that young spark will be amazing clever if note or word from him enters my house.

SCENE VI.

[HORACE, ARNOLPHE.]

HORACE. How fortunate I am to meet you. I have just had a fine escape! As I passed along the street, not foreseeing this adventure, alone upon her balcony in the cool shadow of the trees, I saw Agnes. She made me a sign, and then she slipped into the garden and undid the gate. Scarcely, however, had we reached her room when she heard her jealous guardian on the stairs. All she could do, at such a pinch, was to put me in a closet. The man came in; I did not see him, but I heard him, striding up and down, fetching, from time to time, most pitiable sighs, giving great thumps upon the tables, striking a little dog that ran to him, and flinging violently round the room the clothes that lay there. He even broke, with furious hands, the vases with which my Agnes decked her mantel. No doubt some word had readied that rascally old ram about the trick she played in dropping me the letter. At last, after a hundred twists and turns, having discharged his wrath on everything, he left the room, and I my hiding-place. But fearing his return we did not dare remain together, it was too hazardous. However, this evening, late, I am to cough three times beneath her window to let her know I'm there, and, at the signal, I shall see her open it. Then with a ladder and the help of Agnes, my love will try to gain an entrance. As my one friend, I want to tell you this. The rapture of my heart increases if I can speak of it; though we may taste our perfect happiness a hundred times, we are not quite content if no one knows it. You will be glad, I think, at this good luck in my affairs. Adieu; for I must make my preparations.

SCENE VII.

ARNOLPHE. [*alone.*] So, then! the star that obstinately thwarts my hopes gives me no chance to breathe. Time after time am I to see their wits confound the prudence of my vigilant care? Am I, in my maturity, to be the dupe of a mere ignorant girl and a young featherhead—I, who am known for twenty years to meditate with sage philosophy upon the melancholy fate of husbands? Have I not studied carefully the dangers which bring misfortune to the wisest of them? The shame of others profiting my soul, I have sought means, wishing to take a wife, to guarantee my honor from affront; a noble purpose, for which I've put in practice the best, as I think, of all human policy; and yet,—as if fate willed that no one here below should be exempt!—after all the experience, all the light that I have gained upon this subject, after a score of years of meditation on the prudence of my conduct, am I to find myself with other husbands, in the same disgrace? Ah, cursèd destiny! how you have lied to me! But I hold possession of her still; although her heart be stolen from me by that malignant fop, at least I can prevent that he shall seize the rest. This night, selected for their daring exploit, shall not pass off as sweetly as he thinks. It is some pleasure in the midst of grief to have this warning of their plot and to find that giddy-pated fool who seeks my injury making a confidant of me, his rival!

SCENE VIII.

[CHRYSALDE, ARNOLPHE.]

CHRYSALDE. Well, shall we sup to-night before we take our walk?

ARNOLPHE. No; I fast this evening.

CHRYSALDE. What means that whim?

ARNOLPHE. I beg you to excuse me; I have much upon my mind.

CHRYSALDE. Will the marriage you intended not take place?

ARNOLPHE. You concern yourself too much in the affairs of others.

CHRYSALDE. Ho, ho! how trenchant! What's all this grief about? Tell me, old friend, has any tribulation happened to your love? I could almost swear it by the look upon your face.

ARNOLPHE. Whatever happens, I shall at least have this advantage, that I can never act like certain men who tolerate calmly the approach of gallants.

CHRYSALDE. 'Tis a strange fact that with so good a mind you make a bugbear of this matter; as if our sovereign happiness lay there, and you could not perceive in all the world another form of honor. To be a miser, brute, or cheat, wicked or cowardly, is nothing in your eyes compared to this disgrace. No matter, you think, what sort of life a man may lead, he is only a man of honor if he is not a cuckold. To go to the bottom of all this, why do you think our fame depends upon this casual chance, and that a well-born soul ought to reproach itself for unjust evils it cannot prevent? Why insist, I say, that by taking a wife a man involves himself in either praise or blame? Why make a scarecrow of the wrong her possible unfaithfulness may do him? Admit into your mind the thought that injured husbands may be gallant men; that, marriage being a game of chance, no one is safe; and, if the luck should go against him, a man should be indifferent, and reflect that all the harm, however people gossip, is in the way he takes the thing. The wisest conduct in such difficulty is—as in all things else—to avoid extremes. Not, on the one hand, to imitate those easy-going fellows who take a sort of vanity in such affairs, praise up the gallants of their wives, extol their talents, parade the closest intimacy, share in their parties and their gifts, and so conduct themselves that other men are forced to wonder at their barefaced coolness. Such behavior is most blamable. But on the other hand, the opposite extreme is much to be condemned. Although I disapprove these friends of lovers, I'm not ill favor of those turbulent folk whose growling and tempestuous grief imprudently attracts the eyes of all the world; and who, by such exposure, seem to wish that no one should be ignorant of their misfortune. Between these two extremes there is a better way, which, if the need occurs, a wise man should adopt; and when he takes it, he will find he does not have to blush for the worst actions that a wife can do. No matter what the world may say, husbands might easily regard this matter under less hideous aspects, and, as I said before, true wisdom lies in knowing how to turn the best side out.

ARNOLPHE. After this fine discourse, the whole fraternity of luckless husbands owes to your Grace, a vote of thanks; whoever listens to your words must surely wish to join that joyful band.

CHRYSALDE. I don't say that; for that is what I blame. But, as it is the fate which women bring us, I say we ought to take it as we throw the dice; if what we want does not turn up, we should play low, and with a humbler soul correct ill-fortune by our own good conduct.

ARNOLPHE. That is to say, eat and sleep well, and so persuade ourselves that nothing is amiss.

CHRYSALDE. You think you are making game of me. But let me tell you that I see a hundred things more to be dreaded, things that would be to me a greater misery, than this you fear. Think you that if I had to choose between the two, I would not rather bear the thing you speak of than be the husband of a shrew, whose nagging temper makes a fuss for naught; one of those dragons of virtue, spotless devils, who think they have the right to lord it over us and, on the ground of their fidelity, expect us to put up with all they do. Once more, old friend, I tell you truly, the fate you dread is only what you make it; and this disaster, like all other things, may have its pleasures and its compensations.

ARNOLPHE. If you've a temper that can thus content itself, so be it; as for me, I do not choose to risk that fate, and sooner than submit to such disgrace I swear—

CHRYSALDE. Oh, heavens!, don't swear, for fear of being perjured; if destiny decrees it, caution is superfluous; your counsel won't be taken in the matter.

ARNOLPHE. Well, enough of all this jesting; it annoys me; we'll stop it, if you please.

CHRYSALDE. You are angry; and I shall find out the cause. Adieu. Remember, although your honor prompts you in all this, he who makes oath he will not be the thing you fear is partly that already.

ARNOLPHE. Again I swear it; and I am going now to practise a sure remedy against it. [*he raps at his door.*]

Scene IX.

[ARNOLPHE, ALAIN, GEORGETTE.]

ARNOLPHE. Friends, I want your help. I am proud of your affection, but it must now shine forth in my defence; and if you serve me, as I think you will, you may be certain of your recompense. The man you know of (say no word of this) intends, as I have heard, to take us by surprise this very night, and enter Agnes' window by a ladder. We must, all three of us, prepare an ambush. I wish you each to take a stick and when he's near the top rung of the ladder, rain blows for my sake on him in such a way his back shall keep the memory of this night and teach him, once for all, he never can return. Be careful not to speak of me in any way, or let him know that I am close behind you. Shall you have sense enough to serve my anger?

ALAIN. If all that's needed is to strike, my goodness! we'll do that. When I strike, as you shall see, my hand ain't dead.

GEORGETTE. And mine, though it may look less strong, can hold its own in giving him a drubbing.

ARNOLPHE. Well, now go in; be careful not to gossip. [*alone.*] Now I can give a useful lesson to my neighbors. If all the husbands in this town received the gallants of their wives in this way the number of those cuckolds would diminish.

Act V.

Scene I.

[ARNOLPHE, ALAIN, GEORGETTE.]

ARNOLPHE. Wretches, what have you done by all this violence?

ALAIN. Just what you told us, monsieur.

ARNOLPHE. In vain you arm yourself with that excuse. My order was to beat him, not to kill him; to strike his back, but not rain blows upon his head. Good heavens! in what disaster fate involves me! how can I bear to look on that dead man! Go in at once, and say no word about the harmless order that I gave you. [*alone.*] The day is dawning; let me reflect how I had best conduct myself in such a dire mishap. Alas! what will become of me? what will the father say when he arrives and hears, on a sudden, of this sad affair.

SCENE II.

[HORACE, ARNOLPHE.]

HORACE. [*aside.*] I ought to reconnoitre who this is.

ARNOLPHE. [*thinking himself alone.*] How could I have foreseen—[*stumbles against* HORACE, *whom he does not recognize.*] Who's there, if you please?

HORACE. What, Seigneur Arnolphe, is this you?

ARNOLPHE. Yes, but who are you?

HORACE. I'm Horace, and I was going to your house to ask a favor. How early you are out!

ARNOLPHE. [*aside.*] 'Tis inconceivable! Is it enchantment? Is it illusion?

HORACE. I am, to tell the truth, in some anxiety, and I bless heaven for its sovereign kindness in allowing me to meet you here. I must tell you that my scheme succeeded even better than I dared to hope, and through an incident, moreover, which threatened to defeat it. I don't know how this assignation could have been suspected, but, at any rate, just as I reached the window several persons rushed upon me suddenly, so that I lost my balance and fell headlong from the ladder. But this fall saved me, at the cost of trifling bruises, from a score of blows; while those above (among them, I think, my enemy) believed the fall resulted from their blows, and, as the pain I felt kept me still lying on the ground, they thought they had killed me outright, and were much alarmed. I heard their talk amid the silence; each accused the other, and, in the darkness, quarrelling still, they all crept down to feel of me and see if I were dead. I leave you to imagine whether, it being pitch dark, I did not play the corpse. They soon departed, frightened, I think, to death, and I was just about to go myself when Agnes, who had heard these people talking of my death, came to me, trembling; for during this tumult, being less observed, she had been able easily to leave the house. Finding I was not really hurt, she yielded to a transport I cannot describe. How shall I tell you? This sweet young girl followed the counsels of her love; she would not enter that man's house again, and to my honor she commits her destiny. Think for a moment to what such innocence exposed her, and what grievous perils she might have run were I a man to treasure her less! But my soul is glowing with a love too pure; I'd rather die than wrong her. In all she does I see a grace that is deserving of a higher fate; and nothing now can part me from her until death. 'Tis true that I foresee my father's anger, but we must hope in time to appease his wrath. I yield myself to her sweet charms and know the value of content in life. What I have come to ask of you is this: that I may place my Agnes in your hands, and that your house may be her shelter for a day or two. Besides the fact that I must hide her flight and guard her from pursuit, you know that if a girl joins a young man in this way it will give rise to strange suspicions. And since to you, sure of your prudence, I have told my love, to you I now, as to a generous friend, confide this precious trust.

ARNOLPHE. I am, I pray do not doubt it, wholly at your service.

HORACE. Then you will really do me this kind office?

ARNOLPHE. Most willingly, I tell you. I am delighted with this chance to serve you, and I thank heaven that sends it to me; never have I done anything with so much joy.

HORACE. How grateful I am for all your kindness! I feared that you might make some difficulties. But you know life, and, in your wisdom, you can excuse the fire of youth. Agnes is here, close by; one of my servants guards her.

ARNOLPHE. Ah! how shall we manage it? 'Tis nearly daylight, and if I take her here I may be seen; yet if you come to me my servants might report it. The safest way would be to bring her to some dark place and give her to me there. The alley near my house is just the thing; I will await you there.

HORACE. Those are precautions you do well to take. As for me, I'll simply put her hand in yours and then return at once to my own house.

ARNOLPHE. [*alone.*] Ah, fortune! this propitious end repairs the wrongs your whims have done me.

SCENE III.

[AGNES, ARNOLPHE, HORACE.]

HORACE, *to Agnes*. Do not be troubled as to where I'm taking you; it is a safe retreat. To lodge you in my house would be to injure you. Enter this little gate, and let the person who will meet us lead you. [ARNOLPHE *takes* AGNES' *hand without her recognizing him.*]

AGNES. [*to* HORACE.] Why do you leave me?

HORACE. Dear Agnes, because I must.

AGNES. But come back soon, I beg you.

HORACE. My loving ardor urges it.

AGNES. When I do not see you I am not content.

HORACE. Away from you I, too, am sad.

AGNES. Alas! if that were so you'd stay with me.

HORACE. What! can you doubt my faithful love?

AGNES. No! you do not love me as I love you. [ARNOLPHE *pulls her.*] Ah! he pulls me from you.

HORACE. Because, dear Agnes, it is dangerous for you if we are seen together. My faithful friend whose hand holds yours obeys the prudent zeal he feels for us.

AGNES. But, to follow a stranger who—

HORACE. Fear nothing; in his hands you cannot but be safe.

AGNES. I'd rather be in those of Horace. [*to* ARNOLPHE, *who pulls her again.*] Ah! wait.

HORACE. Adieu; the daylight drives me from you.

AGNES. When shall I see you?

HORACE. Soon, soon, assuredly.

AGNES. How I shall weary for that moment!

HORACE. [*as he goes away.*] Thanks be to heaven, my happiness no longer fears a rival and I can sleep in peace.

Scene IV.

[ARNOLPHE, AGNES.]

ARNOLPHE. [*concealed by his cloak and disguising his voice.*] Come; it is not here that I shall lodge you. Your room has been prepared by me elsewhere. Come, I shall put your person now in some safe place. [*dropping his cloak.*] Do you know me now?

AGNES. Aie!

ARNOLPHE. My face, deceitful girl, may well alarm you; it vexes you to see me here; I thwart the scheming love that now possesses you. [AGNES *looks about, trying to see* HORACE.] You need not call your gallant with your eyes; he is too far off to give you any help. Ah! ah,! so young, and yet to play such tricks! Your artlessness, which seemed unparalleled—asking if children were not born through ears!—knows how to give a rendezvous by night and follow a lover slyly. *Tudieu*! I heard your tongue cajole him! He must have put you through a pretty schooling! But how the devil did you learn so fast? or did your gallant in a single night teach you this boldness? Ha, hussy! that *you* should come to this vile treachery! in spite of all my benefits, that *you* should form a scheme like this! Young serpent that I warmed within my bosom, who now, no longer numb, with base ingratitude seeks to do ill to him who cherished it!

AGNES. Why do you scold me thus?

ARNOLPHE. Ha! a great wrong I do you!

AGNES. I see no harm in what I do.

ARNOLPHE. To follow a lover is most infamous.

AGNES. He is a man who wants me for his wife. I have followed your lessons; you told me we should marry to avoid all sin.

ARNOLPHE. Yes, but I meant to take you for my wife; I think I made you understand that plainly.

AGNES. Yes, but to speak quite frankly, he is for that more to my taste than you. With you, marriage is cross and peevish, and all you say of it draws such a dreadful picture; but there! when he describes it, 'tis so full of pleasures he makes one wish to marry.

ARNOLPHE. Ha! you love him, treacherous girl!

AGNES. Yes, I love him.

ARNOLPHE. And you have the face to say it in my presence!

AGNES. Why, if it be true, should I not say it?

ARNOLPHE. Ought you to love him, jade?

AGNES. Ah! how can I help it? he is alone the cause. I never thought of it till the thing happened.

ARNOLPHE. You should have driven that amorous wish away.

AGNES. How can one drive away that which gives pleasure?

ARNOLPHE. Did you not know you were displeasing me?

AGNES. I? no, indeed. What harm could that do you?

ARNOLPHE. True, I have reason to rejoice! oh, yes! So then, you do not love me, it appears.

AGNES. You?

ARNOLPHE. Yes.

AGNES. No.

ARNOLPHE. What! you say no?

AGNES. No. Would you have me lie?

ARNOLPHE. And why, rebellious girl! do you not love me?

AGNES. It is not I you ought to blame. Why did not you, as he did, make yourself loved? I never, that I know of, hindered you.

ARNOLPHE. I strove with all my might to do so, but the pains I took have come to naught!

AGNES. Well, truly, he knows more of this than you; he did not find it hard to make me love him.

ARNOLPHE. [*aside.*] A plague upon her! how this wretched girl reasons and answers; no *précieuse* could say more. Ha! I have misconceived her; or else, by heaven! a silly girl knows more of these things than the ablest man. [*to* AGNES.] As your mind, it seems, has taken to reasoning, perhaps you can tell me whether 'tis likely I should have nourished you these many years, at my expense, for him?

AGNES. No; and he will pay you back to the last farthing.

ARNOLPHE. [*aside.*] Such speeches only double my vexation! [*aloud.*] Can he return, you hussy, with all his power, the obligations that you owe me?

AGNES. They are not so great as one would think.

ARNOLPHE. The care with which I brought you up from childhood,—it that nothing?

AGNES. Truly, how has that worked for me? What have you had me taught? Do you think I am deceived and in my mind I do not know that I am stupid? I am ashamed of it myself, and now that I am growing older I do not want to be a fool if I can help it.

ARNOLPHE. You want, at any rate, to escape your ignorance by learning something from that fair-haired dandy.

AGNES. Yes; for it is through him I now know what I could know. I think I owe to him far more than I owe to you.

ARNOLPHE. I don't know what prevents me from avenging this bravado with a slap; your saucy coolness is infuriating, and it would satisfy my heart to box your ears.

AGNES. Alas! you can do so, if you wish.

ARNOLPHE. [*aside.*] That answer and that look disarm me, and turn my heart again to tenderness. What a strange thing is love, that for these treacherous creatures men must be ever subject to such weakness! Who does not know their imperfections, made up of folly and extravagance? Their minds are wicked and their souls are frail; nothing on earth can be more feeble, imbecile, and faithless! And yet, in spite of that, all that we do in this world is for these animals. [*to* AGNES.] Well, Agnes, let us make it up. There, little traitress, I'll forgive you and grant you again my tenderness. Judge from that how much I love you; and seeing me so kind, you must in turn love me.

AGNES. With all my heart I wish that I could please you; if it were possible, I'm sure I would.

ARNOLPHE. Poor little heart! but you can love me if you will. Listen only to my tender sighs, look at my person, see my longing glances, and quit that silly fool, reject the sort of love he offers you. He has cast a spell upon you. You will be happier far with me. Your natural passion is to be smart and lively, and that you shall be, always—hear me! I promise it. Night and day I will caress you, pet you, kiss you; you shall do always as you wish in all things—[*aside in a low voice.*] Where will not passion lead us? [*aloud.*] In short, my love cannot be equaled. What proof can you desire, ungrateful girl? Would you have me weep? Would you see me smite myself? Shall I tear out my hair? expire at your feet? Speak! say what you wish, for I am ready, oh, cruel heart! to prove my love.

AGNES. But such talk does not touch my soul; Horace with two words can say more than you.

ARNOLPHE. Ha! this is braving me too much! you've dared my wrath too far. Unmanageable fool! I'll follow my first intent and send you from this town. You may reject my love and drive me to extremes, but a convent cell will amply punish all.

SCENE V.

[ARNOLPHE, AGNES, ALAIN.]

ALAIN. Monsieur, I don't know how it happened, but it seems to me that Agnes and the corpse have gone away together.

ARNOLPHE. Agnes is here. Take her, and lock her in my chamber. [*aside.*] He will not seek her there; besides, 'twill only be for half an hour; I'll get a coach at once and take her to safe retreat. [*to* ALAIN.] Lock the door secretly and do not let her, for one moment, out of your sight. [*alone.*] Perhaps her soul, if kept in solitude in some strange place, may yet be driven from this fatal love.

SCENE VI.

[ARNOLPHE, HORACE.]

HORACE. Ah! I seek you, overcome with grief. Heaven, Seigneur Arnolphe, is resolved upon my misery; and by a fatal act of deep injustice tears from my arms the woman whom I love. My father came last night; I found him stopping in a house nearby; and the reason of his coming, which, as I told you, was unknown to me, is that he plans my marriage, without a word to me, and comes here now to celebrate the tie. Imagine, you who have taken part in my anxieties, if any mischance could be as bad as this. Enrique, of whom I spoke to you, is the cause of it. He comes here with my father to complete my ruin; it is his only daughter to whom they marry me. At their first words I nearly fainted; then, unable to listen longer, and hearing my father speak of paying you a visit, I, with a mind distressed, have rushed here quickly to forestall him. For pity's sake, do not betray my love, which might incense him; and—because he has such confidence in you—try to dissuade him from this other marriage.

ARNOLPHE. Ho, yes, indeed!

HORACE. Advise him to postpone the thing awhile. Do, as a friend, this service to my love.

ARNOLPHE. Ha! I'll not fail to do it.

HORACE. My hope is all in you.

ARNOLPHE. So be it.

HORACE. I regard you as my true father. Tell him that my age—Ah! I see him coming. Step here with me, and listen to my reasons.

SCENE VII.

[ENRIQUE, ORONTE, CHRYSALDE, HORACE, ARNOLPHE.]

[HORACE *and* ARNOLPHE *retire to a corner and confer together*.]

ENRIQUE. [*to* CHRYSALDE.] The moment that I saw you enter, though nothing had been said to me, I knew you at once. I see in you the features of your lovely sister, of whom in marriage I was once possessed. Happy indeed, should I be now if cruel fate had let me bring my faithful partner back, to enjoy with me the pleasure of seeing our friends once more after our many sorrows. But, since the fatal power of destiny deprives us ever of her dear presence, let us endeavor to resign ourselves, and be content with the one pledge of love she left to me. This visit concerns you closely; I should do wrong to pledge my daughter's hand without consulting you. A marriage with Oronte's son is glorious in itself, but it must be your choice as well as mine.

CHRYSALDE. You have a poor opinion of my judgment if you doubt that I approve so wise a choice.

ARNOLPHE. [*aside to* HORACE.] Yes, I will serve you in the finest fashion.

HORACE. Pray be careful—

ARNOLPHE. Have no fear. [ARNOLPHE *leaves* HORACE *and comes forward to greet* ORONTE.]

ORONTE. [*to* ARNOLPHE.] Oh! how full of tenderness this greeting is!

ARNOLPHE. I feel, at the mere sight of you, the deepest joy.

ORONTE. I have come here to—

ARNOLPHE. I know already why you come.

ORONTE. Has someone told you?

ARNOLPHE. Yes.

ORONTE. So much the better.

ARNOLPHE. Your son resists this marriage; his heart, engaged elsewhere, sees only sadness in the prospect. He has even urged me to dissuade you from it. But as for that, the only counsel I shall give you is not to allow the least delay, and to enforce the authority of father. We ought to keep young men in place with vigor; we injure them by being too indulgent.

HORACE. [*aside*.] Oh, traitor!

CHRYSALDE. But if his heart feels some repugnance I do not think we ought to force it. My brother, I believe, will be of my opinion.

ARNOLPHE. What! would he let himself be governed by his son? Do you wish a father to be so timid as not to know how to make a son obey him? A fine thing truly it would be if fathers took the law from those whose duty 'tis to take the law from them. No, Oronte is my friend and his honor is mine; his word is given, and he must keep it. Let him show firmness now and force his son to yield obedience.

ORONTE. Yes, you say well. As for this marriage, I will myself be answerable for my son's obedience.

CHRYSALDE. [*to* ARNOLPHE.] I am surprised, for my part, at the eagerness you show about this new engagement. I can't imagine what motive you can have.

ARNOLPHE. I know what I am doing, and I say what I ought to say.

ORONTE. Yes, yes, Seigneur Arnolphe, it is—

CHRYSALDE. That name annoys him; call him, as I told you, Monsieur de la Souche.

ARNOLPHE. No matter for the name.

HORACE. [*aside.*] What do I hear?

ARNOLPHE. [*going up to* HORACE.] Yes, there's the whole mystery. You can judge now what I think right to do.

SCENE VIII.

[ENRIQUE, ORONTE, CHRYSALDE, HORACE, ARNOLPHE, GEORGETTE.]

GEORGETTE. Monsieur, if you don't come soon we can't keep Agnes in. She is trying to escape in every way; she may be jumping through the window now.

ARNOLPHE. Bring her to me. I am about to take her from this town. [*to* HORACE.] You need not feel distressed. Continual happiness makes men proud; to every man his turn, the proverb says.

HORACE. [*aside.*] Oh, heaven! what woes can equal mine! and what a gulf is this before me!

ARNOLPHE. [*to* ORONTE.] Hasten the wedding-day; I shall be back in time to take a part. You see I give myself an invitation.

ORONTE. It was my intention to invite you.

SCENE IX.

[AGNES, ORONTE, ENRIQUE, ARNOLPHE, HORACE, CHRYSALDE, ALAIN, GEORGETTE.]

ARNOLPHE. [*to* AGNES.] Come here, fair damsel, come, you whom they can't restrain, you are so headstrong. Here is your lover, and, to reward him, make him a sweet and humble curtsey. [*to*

HORACE.] Adieu; events are not exactly what you wished, but every lover can't be satisfied.

AGNES. Will you let me, Horace, be taken from you thus?

HORACE. I know not where I am, my anguish is so great.

ARNOLPHE. [*pulling* AGNES.] Come, chatterer, come.

AGNES. I wish to stay.

ORONTE. Tell us what all this mystery means. We are looking on, but cannot comprehend it.

ARNOLPHE. Later, when I have leisure, I'll explain. Till then, adieu.

ORONTE. Where are you going? You are not speaking to us as you ought to speak.

ARNOLPHE. I have advised you, much against his will, to conclude the marriage of your son.

ORONTE. Yes, but in order to conclude it, you surely know—if, as you say, they have told you all—that in your house you have the girl he is to marry,—the daughter whom Seigneur Enrique by a private marriage had of the charming Angelique. If you did not know this fact, on what was the advice you gave me founded?

CHRYSALDE. I thought his whole behavior most surprising.

ARNOLPHE. What!

CHRYSALDE. My sister by her secret marriage had a daughter, whose birth was hidden from the family—

ORONTE. A child, who under a feigned name was given by its father to a village foster-mother—

CHRYSALDE. Soon after which an adverse fate, bringing disaster on him, caused him to leave his native country—

ORONTE. And face a thousand perils in lands beyond the seas—

CHRYSALDE. Where his behavior won him the success that envy and detraction had denied him here—

ORONTE. On his return to France he sought at once the village-wife with whom he had left his daughter—

CHRYSALDE. And she, the peasant-woman, frankly told him that she had placed her in your hands when four years old—

ORONTE. Leaving her thus upon your charity because of her own excessive poverty—

CHRYSALDE. And he, with joy and eagerness of soul, has brought that woman to this town—

ORONTE. That you may see her. She comes to clear this mystery to the eyes of all.

CHRYSALDE. [*aside to* ARNOLPHE.] I can divine the torture you endure. But, after all, fate is, in this mischance, propitious to you; fearing so much the common fate of men, not to be married is your only safety.

ARNOLPHE. [*departing furious, and unable to speak.*] Ouf!

SCENE X.

[ENRIQUE, ORONTE, CHRYSALDE, AGNES, HORACE.]

ORONTE. Why does he rush away without a word?

HORACE. Ah, father! you must now be told in full this most surprising mystery. Chance had already brought about that which your wisdom has premeditated. I, in the gentle bonds of mutual love, had passed my word to marry this sweet girl. 'Tis she whom you have come to seek; she, whom I angered you by first refusing.

ENRIQUE. I cannot doubt it; from the moment that I saw her my soul has never ceased to be affected. Ah! my daughter, I yield me to the transports of this joy.

CHRYSALDE. And I, with all my heart, will do the same. But this is not the place for such emotions. Let us within the house clear up these mysteries, repay our friend the cost of his good care, and render thanks to heaven—which does all for the best!

[*curtain.*]

The School for Wives Criticized

[*La Critique De L'École Des Femmes*.]

Translated by KATHARINE PRESCOTT WORMELEY

A COMEDY IN ONE ACT

DRAMATIS PERSONAE

URANIE
ÉLISE
CLIMÈNE
THE MARQUIS
DORANTE, *the Chevalier.*
LYSIDAS, *poet.*
GALOPIN, *lacquey.*

The Scene is in Paris, at the House of Uranie.

ACT I.

SCENE I.

[URANIE, ÉLISE.]

URANIE. What! cousin, has no one come to visit you?

ÉLISE. No, not a soul.

URANIE. Really, it does surprise me that we both have been alone all day.

ÉLISE. Well, I'm surprised myself, for 'tis not customary; your house, thank God, is the usual refuge of all the idlers of the court.

URANIE. To tell the truth, to me the afternoon seemed *very* long.

ÉLISE. And I, I thought it short.

URANIE. Fine minds, they say, love solitude.

ÉLISE. Fine minds indeed! You know it was not that I meant.

URANIE. Well, as for me, I own that I like company.

ÉLISE. I like it too, but then I like it choice. The quantity of silly visits one has to endure among the rest is often the very reason why I like to be alone.

URANIE. Delicacy can only bear the presence of those who are refined.

ÉLISE. People are too compliant in tolerating with composure all sorts of persons.

URANIE. Well, I enjoy the wise, but I divert myself with all the silly ones.

ÉLISE. Yes, but the silly ones do not get far before they bore you; most of them are not amusing on their second visit. But, apropos of silly people, will you not rid me of your troublesome marquis! You can't expect to leave him on my hands forever, or that I will long endure his everlasting punning.

URANIE. Punning is all the fashion; they think it wit at court.

ÉLISE. Alas for those who strain all day to talk such empty jargon. A fine thing truly to drag old jokes, raked from the mud of markets and the Place Maubert, into the palace conversations! A pretty style of wit for courtiers! And what a mind a man displays when he remarks: "Madame, you may be in the Place Royale, but all the world, regarding you *de bon œil*, thinks you are three leagues out of Paris," simply because Bonneuil is a village three leagues distant. How very witty! and how gallant! No wonder those who invent such speeches boast of them.

URANIE. But they don't call it wit; for most of those who affect that style of language know 'tis silly.

ÉLISE. All the worse therefore to take such pains to be so silly and make themselves such sorry jesters knowingly. I think them the less excusable, and if *I* were judge of the world I know well to what I would condemn such punsters and their like.

URANIE. Well, let us drop the matter, which nettles you too much. Dorante is late, I think, for the supper we agreed to take together.

ÉLISE. Perhaps he has forgotten it, and—

SCENE II.

[URANIE, ÉLISE, GALOPIN.]

GALOPIN. Climène is here, madame, and asks to see you.

URANIE. Oh, heaven! what a visit!

ÉLISE. You grumbled because you were alone, and heaven has punished you.

URANIE. [*to* GALOPIN.] Quick! go and tell her I am not at home.

GALOPIN. She has been told already that you are.

URANIE. What fool said that?

GALOPIN. 'Twas I, madame.

URANIE. The deuced little wretch! I'll teach you to give answers from yourself.

GALOPIN. Then I'll go tell her, madame, that you say you are out.

URANIE. Stop, you little animal! let her come up; the mischief's done.

GALOPIN. She is talking still to someone in the street.

URANIE. [*to* ÉLISE.] Ah! cousin, how this visit does annoy me! Just at this moment, too!

ÉLISE. The lady is annoying in herself; I have always had a furious aversion to her, and, begging her quality's pardon, I think her the silliest fool that ever took to reasoning.

URANIE. Your epithets are rather strong.

ÉLISE. Well, she deserves them all, and more to boot if people did her justice. Is there a person more truly what is called a *précieuse*—giving the word, of course, its worst significance.

URANIE. She rejects that name, however.

ÉLISE. She rejects the name but not the thing: for that is what she is, from head to foot; the most affected creature in the world. It really seems as though the structure of her body were out of order, and that her hips, her head, her shoulders were jerked by springs. She affects that languid, silly tone of voice, purses her mouth to make you think it small, and rolls her eyes to make them larger.

URANIE. Oh! gently, please; suppose she heard you?

ÉLISE. No, she has not come up—I can't forget the night she wanted to see Damon, on the strength of his repute and the fine things the public say of him. You know the man, and his natural laziness in conversation. She invited him to supper as a wit, and never did he seem so stupid; the half-dozen persons she had gathered to enjoy his talk sat gazing at him with round eyes, as though he were a being not like others. They all considered he was there to feed them with bon-mots, and that every word that left his lips must be impromptu wit, if he but asked for drink. He fooled them all by silence, and my lady was as much displeased with him as I with her.

URANIE. Hush, hush! I am going to receive her at the door.

ÉLISE. Stay, one word more. I'd like to see her married to that marquis. What a pair 'twould be—a punster and a *précieuse*!

URANIE. Do be silent! here she comes.

SCENE III.

[URANIE, ÉLISE, CLIMÈNE, GALOPIN.]

URANIE. Really, 'tis very late—

CLIMÈNE. Oh! for pity's sake, my dear, give me a chair at once.

URANIE. [*to* GALOPIN.] An armchair, quick!

CLIMÈNE. Ah, heavens!

URANIE. What is it?

CLIMÈNE. I cannot bear it!

URANIE. But what's the matter?

CLIMÈNE. My heart is failing!

URANIE. Is it hysterics?

CLIMÈNE. Oh! no, no.

URANIE. Shall I unlace you?

CLIMÈNE. Good heavens, no—Ah!

URANIE. But where's the pain? when did it seize you?

CLIMÈNE. Three hours ago—at the Palais-Royal.[1]

URANIE. How?

CLIMÈNE. For my sins I went to see that wicked rhapsody "The School for Wives." I am fainting still from the nausea that it gave me—I think that I shall not recover for weeks.

ÉLISE. Just see how illness takes us unawares!

URANIE. I don't know what our constitutions are, my cousin's and mine, but we both went to see that very play last night, and came back gay and healthy.

CLIMÈNE. What! you have seen it?

URANIE. Yes, and heard it too, from end to end.

CLIMÈNE. My dear! and you did not go into convulsions?

URANIE. I am not so delicate, thank God! For my part, I thought the comedy more like to cure its hearers than to hurt them.

CLIMÈNE. Oh! how can you say so? How can a person with any revenue of common-sense put forth that proposition? You cannot, with impunity, fly in the face of reason. Come to the truth of things; is there a soul so eager for jocosity that it can relish the mawkish stuff with which that comedy is seasoned? For myself, I own I could not find a grain of spice in all of it. "Children by the ear" is odious in taste, it seems to me; "cream-tarts" have made me sick; and as for that "soup" I thought to vomit.

ÉLISE. Heavens! how elegantly that is said! I thought myself the play was good, but madame's eloquence is so persuasive, she turns things in a manner so delightful, that we must all agree in sentiment with her, no matter what our own opinion is.

URANIE. As for me, I am not so complying. To tell my honest thought, I think that comedy among the best the author has produced.

CLIMÈNE. Ah! when you say that you make me pity you; I can't endure that you should have such poor discernment. How can anyone, possessing virtue, find pleasure in a play which keeps our modesty forever in alarm and soils the imagination constantly.

ÉLISE. How charmingly she puts it! You are indeed a cruel critic, madame; I pity that poor Molière who has you for an enemy.

CLIMÈNE. [*to* URANIE.] Believe me, my dear, correct your judgment. For your own honor's sake, don't tell the world you liked that comedy.

URANIE. I do not see what you can find there to offend your modesty.

---

[1] Molière's troop was then playing at the Palais-Royal theatre.

CLIMÈNE. Alas! the whole of it. I do maintain no honest woman can see that play without confusion, such filth have I discovered in it.

URANIE. Then you have better eyes for filth than others; for my part, I saw none.

CLIMÈNE. Because you *would* not see it, most assuredly; for all this nastiness, thank God, is openly displayed. There's not the slightest veil to cover it; the boldest eyes are frightened at its nudity.

ÉLISE. Ah!

CLIMÈNE. He! he! he!

URANIE. But will you please to show me a single specimen of all this filth?

CLIMÈNE. Alas! can you really need to have it specified?

URANIE. Yes; I ask you to name a single point that shocks you.

CLIMÈNE. Can you want more than that scene with Agnes, when she tells Arnolphe what Horace has taken from her?

URANIE. You think that foul?

CLIMÈNE. Ah!

URANIE. But tell me.

CLIMÈNE. Fie!

URANIE. I ask you again.

CLIMÈNE. I can say nothing.

URANIE. For my part, I see no harm in it.

CLIMÈNE. So much the worse for you.

URANIE. So much the better, it seems to me. I look at things on the side they are shown to me; I do not twist them round to search for what I was not told to see.

CLIMÈNE. A woman's virtue—

URANIE. A woman's virtue is not in cant. It ill becomes her to assume to be more virtuous than those who are truly virtuous. Affectation is worse in this particular matter than in others. I know nothing so ridiculous as this super-sensitive virtue which finds evil everywhere, supposes criminal meaning in the most innocent words, and takes offence at shadows. Believe me, those who make this great ado are not considered better women. On the contrary, their whispering severity and their affected airs excite the censure of the world against the actions of their lives. People are charmed to find some blame to put upon them. To give you an example: opposite to the box in which we sat to see this comedy were certain women who, by their behavior throughout the play,—hiding their faces, turning away their heads affectedly,—excited men to say a hundred slighting things about their conduct which would not have been said without it: one man, in fact, among the lacqueys called out quite loud that their ears were more chaste than the rest of their bodies.

CLIMÈNE. Then people must be blind, or make believe they do not see the things that are in the play.

URANIE. They should not see the things that are not there.

CLIMÈNE. Well, I maintain once more, their nastiness affronts the eye.

URANIE. And I repeat that I do not agree with you.

CLIMÈNE. Is your modesty not wounded by what Agnes says in the scene I named?

URANIE. No, indeed not. She says no word that does not seem to me, most virtuous; and if you find some other meaning under it, 'tis you who make the filth, not she; she spoke and thought of a ribbon only.

CLIMÈNE. Ribbon indeed! but remember that the, on which she pauses—strange thoughts are in that *the*. That *the* is desperately scandalous, and, whatever you may say, you are not able to defend the insolence of that *the*.

ÉLISE. Cousin, 'tis very true. I am on madame's side against that *the*. That *the* is insolent to the last degree; you are very wrong to defend that *the*.

CLIMÈNE. It breathes an obscenity that to me is quite unbearable.

ÉLISE. How do you pronounce that word, madame?

CLIMÈNE. Obscenity, madame.

ÉLISE. Ah! obscenity. I don't know what the word may mean, but I think it very pretty.[2]

CLIMÈNE. [*to* URANIE.] There! you see how your own blood decides against you.

URANIE. Oh! she is only talking; she is not saying what she thinks. Believe me, do not trust her.

ÉLISE. How malicious, cousin, to try to make madame distrust me! Just see where I should be if she believed you! I am not, surely, so unfortunate, madame, that you should have such thoughts of me?

CLIMÈNE. No, no; I don't rely upon her words; I think you more sincere than she pretends.

ÉLISE. And you are right, madame; you do me justice when you think that I think you the most engaging person in the world; believe me, I understand your sentiments and am truly charmed with all the expressions that issue from your lips.

CLIMÈNE. Yes; what I say is wholly unaffected.

ÉLISE. We see that plainly, madame; all is so natural in you—your words, your tones, your looks, your step, your motions, even your attire; each has an air of quality enchanting to observers. I study you with my eyes and ears; in fact I am so full of you I'm like a monkey, and try to mimic you in various ways.

CLIMÈNE. But you are laughing at me, madame.

---

[2] The word [*obscénité.*] was doubtless a new one, created by *les précieuses.* [Fr. ed.]

ÉLISE. Pardon me, madame; pray who would dream of laughing at you?

CLIMÈNE. I am not a perfect model, madame.

ÉLISE. Oh! yes, indeed you are!

CLIMÈNE. You flatter me, madame.

ÉLISE. No, not at all.

CLIMÈNE. Spare me such praises, I entreat.

ÉLISE. If I spare you I leave the half of what I think unsaid.

CLIMÈNE. Ah! heavens! say no more; you cast me into unutterable confusion. [*to* URANIE.] Now we are two against you, and obstinacy doth so ill become a clever woman that—

SCENE IV.

[THE MARQUIS, CLIMÈNE, URANIE, ÉLISE, GALOPIN.]

GALOPIN. [*at the door.*] Stop, if you please, monsieur.

THE MARQUIS. I presume you do not know me.

GALOPIN. Oh, yes, I know you; but you can't go in.

THE MARQUIS. What nonsense is all this, you little lacquey.

GALOPIN. It isn't right to enter in spite of people's wishes.

THE MARQUIS. I wish to see your mistress.

GALOPIN. She is not at home, I tell you.

THE MARQUIS. But there she is; I see her in the room.

GALOPIN. There she is, truly, but she is not at home.

URANIE. What is all this?

THE MARQUIS. Your lacquey, madame, who plays the fool.

GALOPIN. I tell him that you are not at home, madame, but he insists on coming in.

URANIE. Why did you tell monsieur that I was not at home?

GALOPIN. You scolded me just now for having said you were.

URANIE. Saucy fellow! I beg you, monsieur, to pay no heed to him. He is a giddy boy who took you for someone else.

THE MARQUIS. So I supposed, madame; and but for your presence I should have taught him to know a man of quality.

ÉLISE. My cousin is greatly obliged for that forbearance.

URANIE, *to Galopin.* A chair, at once, impertinent boy.

GALOPIN. There's one.

URANIE. Bring it nearer.

[GALOPIN *pushes the chair roughly and goes out.*]

SCENE V.

[THE MARQUIS, CLIMÈNE, URANIE, ÉLISE.]

THE MARQUIS. Your little lacquey, madame, is contemptuous of my person.

ÉLISE. He is very wrong, no doubt.

THE MARQUIS. [*adjusting his collar.*] Perhaps I'm paying interest on my poor *stock*—ha! ha! ha! ha!

ÉLISE. Age will enlighten him as to people's merits.

THE MARQUIS. What were you talking of, ladies, when I entered?

URANIE. Of the new comedy, "The School for Wives."

THE MARQUIS. I have just come from there.

CLIMÈNE. Well, monsieur, what think you of it, if you please?

THE MARQUIS. Most impertinent.

CLIMÈNE. Ah! I am delighted.

THE MARQUIS. The most disgusting thing in the world. The devil! I could scarcely get a place. I was almost smothered at the door, and everybody trod upon my toes. Just see how shockingly my ruffles and my ribbons have been crushed.

ÉLISE. Yes, they cry vengeance on "The School for Wives;" you condemn that comedy with justice.

THE MARQUIS. A more wretched comedy, I think, was never made.

URANIE. Ah! here comes Dorante, for whom we are waiting.

SCENE VI.

[DORANTE, CLIMÈNE, URANIE, ÉLISE, THE MARQUIS.]

DORANTE. Don't move, I beg of you; go on with what you were saying. You are talking of a matter which for the last four days has been the topic of every house in Paris. Nothing was ever more amusing than the diversity of the judgments expressed upon it. I have heard certain persons condemn that comedy for the very things that others value most.

URANIE. Here is the marquis saying all sorts of evil of it.

THE MARQUIS. Yes, truly. I think it detestable; *morbleu*! de-test-a-ble; most detestable.

DORANTE. And I, dear marquis, think that judgment of yours detestable.

THE MARQUIS. What! chevalier, do you pretend to support that play?

DORANTE. Yes, undoubtedly, I do intend to support it.

THE MARQUIS. *Parbleu*! I swear it is detestable.

DORANTE. But, marquis, for what reason is it what you say?

THE MARQUIS. Why it is detestable?

DORANTE. Yes.

THE MARQUIS. It is detestable because it *is* detestable.

DORANTE. After that, of course, there's nothing to be said; the verdict's rendered. But still, you might instruct us, and show us the defects.

THE MARQUIS. How should I know them? I did not even take the trouble to listen. But I know, God save me, I never saw a play that was half so bad, and Dorillas, with whom I went, agreed with me.

DORANTE. A fine authority! You are well sustained!

THE MARQUIS. It was enough to hear the laughter in the pit; I don't want other proof the play was worthless.

DORANTE. Ah! you belong to those young stylish fellows who deny the pit has common-sense, and are ashamed to laugh with it, even though the play were the best in the world. I saw a friend of ours the other night, who made himself ridiculous in just that way. He listened throughout the piece with a gloomy air, and frowned at all that made the others gay. At every burst of laughter he shrugged his shoulders and looked at the pit with scorn; sometimes his glance was spiteful, and he said aloud: "Oh! *you* can laugh, you pit!" He was a second comedy himself, poor man; and he performed it for the whole assembly, who all agreed it could not have been better played. Learn, marquis, I implore you (and others too), that judgment and good sense have no exclusive place in theatres. Standing or seated, men may have poor opinions, but, as a general thing, I'd rather trust the approbation of the pit; for the reason, that among those who fill it are many who are capable of judging a play by rules of art, and others who judge by the best method of judging, which is by its effect on them,—not by blind prejudice, or silly complaisance, or foolish prudery.

THE MARQUIS. So you defend the pit, chevalier? *Parbleu*! I am delighted; I will not fail to let it know your friendship, ha! ha! ha!

DORANTE. Laugh if you like. I'm for good sense where'er I meet it; I cannot stand the frothy brains of our Mascarille marquises. It makes me furious to see such men, in spite of their quality, prove themselves ridiculous; men who give opinions and boldly talk of things about which they know nothing; applauding at a play the poorest parts and ignorant of the good ones; when they see a picture or listen to a concert, praise and blame in the wrong places, and seize the terms of art only to misapply them. Hey! *morbleu*, messieurs, hold your tongues, I want to say to them. If God has not bestowed the knowledge of a thing upon you, don't make yourself a laughing-stock by talking of it. Reflect that if you do not talk the world, perhaps, may think you clever.

THE MARQUIS. *Parbleu*! chevalier, you are—

DORANTE. 'Tis not to you I'm speaking, marquis; 'tis to a dozen of those young seigneurs who dishonor other courtiers by their foolish manners, and make the people think that we are all alike. As for me, I vindicate myself as often as I can; I jeer them and their folly wherever I encounter them, hoping perhaps to make them wiser.

THE MARQUIS. Tell me, chevalier, do you think Lysandre has wit?

DORANTE. Yes, no doubt; and a great deal of it.

URANIE. That is a thing that no one could deny.

THE MARQUIS. Then ask him what *he* thinks of "The School for Wives;" you'll find he'll tell you that he does not like it.

DORANTE. Well, there are many men whom too much wit has spoiled; they see things falsely from mere force of light; and sometimes they dislike to share the ideas of others, in order to have the credit of deciding all themselves.

URANIE. Yes, that is true. Our friend is of that class no doubt. He wants to be the first of his opinion, and have his verdict waited with respect. All approbation which precedes his own is an attack on his intelligence, for which he takes revenge by contrary opinion. He wishes to be consulted on matters of the intellect, and I am certain that had our author shown him that comedy before he let the public see it, Lysandre would have thought it the finest ever written.

THE MARQUIS. [*to* DORANTE.] What will you say to the Marquise Araminti, who everywhere declares it is most dreadful, and says she cannot bear the nastiness of which 'tis full.

DORANTE. I say that such a speech is worthy of the character she takes. There are many persons who make themselves ridiculous by assuming to have too much virtue. Though she is clever, certainly, she follows the bad example of those women who, as their years advance, strive to replace the thing they see they've lost by something else, and so imagine that the grimaces of a squeamish prudery will take the place of youth and beauty. The marquise pushes that idea farther than most; and her qualms of decency discover nastiness where others see it not. Those qualms, they say, have gone so far as even to distort the language; and there are scarcely any words from which this austere lady does not lop the heads or tails because she thinks those syllables indecent.

URANIE. Chevalier, you are savage!

THE MARQUIS. In fact, chevalier, you defend your comedy by satirizing those who blame it.

DORANTE. Not so. But I do say that lady takes offence at nothing.

ÉLISE. Gently, chevalier! there may be others present who share those sentiments.

DORANTE. I am sure that *you* do not, at any rate; for when you saw that play performed—

ÉLISE. Quite true; but I have changed my mind. [*motioning to* CLIMÈNE.] Madame supports the opposite opinion with such convincing reasons that she has drawn me over to her side.

DORANTE. [*to* CLIMÈNE.] Ah! madame, I beg your pardon; and, if you choose, I will unsay, for love of you, all I have said.

CLIMÈNE. I do not wish it done for love of me, but for love of reason; for really, this play, to take it at its best, is indefensible, and I can't conceive—

URANIE. Ah! here comes Lysidas, the writer. His arrival is most timely. Monsieur Lysidas, pray take a chair and sit you there.

SCENE VII.

[LYSIDAS, CLIMÈNE, URANIE, ÉLISE, DORANTE, THE MARQUIS.]

LYSIDAS. Madame, I have come a little late, but I was forced to read my play in the salon of that marquise of whom I told you, and the praises there bestowed upon it kept me a full hour longer than I expected.

ÉLISE. Praises have spells to hold an author.

URANIE. Be seated, Monsieur Lysidas; we'll hear your play when we have taken supper.

LYSIDAS. Those who were present have all agreed to attend the first performance; they promised me to do their duty properly.

URANIE. I can believe it. But now sit down, I beg of you. We are talking on a subject that I desire to continue.

LYSIDAS. I presume, madame, that you will take a box on that occasion?

URANIE. I'll see about it. Allow us to continue now what we were saying.

LYSIDAS. I warn you, madame, that they are mostly taken.

URANIE. Very good. I really needed you when you came in, for everyone here present is against me.

ÉLISE. No, Dorante was at first on your side; but since he knows that madame [*motioning to* CLIMÈNE.] leads the opposite party, I fear you must indeed seek other help.

CLIMÈNE. No, no; I will not have him court your cousin so ill; and I permit his mind to go where his heart is.

DORANTE. With that permission, madame, I shall make bold to defend my views.

URANIE. But first, I wish to hear the sentiments of Monsieur Lysidas.

LYSIDAS. On what, madame?

URANIE. On this new play, "The School for Wives."

LYSIDAS. Ah! ah!

URANIE. What do you think of it?

LYSIDAS. I have nothing to say of it. You know that authors should always speak with circumspection of one another's works.

DORANTE. But still, between ourselves, what think you of that comedy?

LYSIDAS. I, monsieur?

URANIE. Come, in confidence, give us your opinion.

LYSIDAS. I think it very fine.

DORANTE. What! really?

LYSIDAS. Undoubtedly. Why not? It is, in fact, the finest of all plays.

DORANTE. Ho, ho! malicious demon, you are not saying what you think.

LYSIDAS. Pardon me—

DORANTE. Heavens! I know you; don't dissimulate.

LYSIDAS. I, monsieur!

DORANTE. 'Tis plain to see your praises of that play are mere civility, and in your heart you agree with those who think it had.

LYSIDAS. Ha, ha, ha!

DORANTE. Come, own it is a poor affair, this comedy.

LYSIDAS. 'Tis true that connoisseurs do not approve it.

THE MARQUIS. I' faith, chevalier, now you have caught it! You are well paid off for all your satire. Ha, ha, ha!

DORANTE. Laugh on, dear marquis, laugh away!

THE MARQUIS. You see we have the *savants* on our side.

DORANTE. True. The judgment of Monsieur Lysidas is much to be considered. But Monsieur Lysidas must permit me not to yield on that account; and since I have the audacity to defend my side against the opinions of madame, [*bowing to* CLIMÈNE.] he will not take it ill that I should combat his.

ÉLISE. What! when you see madame, the marquis, and Monsieur Lysidas against you, do you still dare resist? Fie, what bad grace!

CLIMÈNE. But what confounds me is that reasonable beings should take it into their heads to protect the follies of that play.

THE MARQUIS. God bless me! madame, it is abject from beginning to end.

DORANTE. That is soon said, marquis. Nothing is easier than to cut a matter short in that way; and I know nothing that is sheltered from the tyranny of such dicta.

THE MARQUIS. *Parbleu*! the other comedians who were there to see it said all the harm in the world of it.

DORANTE. Ah! then I say no more: you are right, dear marquis. If the other comedians said harm of it, we must, assuredly, believe them. They are such enlightened people, and have no selfish motives in what they say. There's nothing further to be said, and I surrender.

CLIMÈNE. Surrender, or not, as you please, I know one thing: I shall never be persuaded to endure the immodesty of that comedy, nor the insulting satire that it casts on women.

URANIE. Well, as for me, I am not insulted by it; I do not take to my account all that is said. Such satire falls upon our manners and customs; it strikes at persons only by the way. Let us not fix upon ourselves the shafts of a general censure; we may profit by the lesson if we can, but not behave as though 'twere meant for us. All those ridiculous pictures which the stage presents should be regarded without prejudice by everyone. They are public mirrors, in which we never ought to show we see ourselves; to be so scandalized at such reproofs is openly confessing our defects.

CLIMÈNE. I do not speak of these things as if I had a part in them. I live in the world in such a style that I need not fear to be depicted among those women who are ill-behaved.

ÉLISE. Assuredly, madame, you never will be sought in that direction. Your conduct is well-known; 'tis of a kind that nobody disputes.

URANIE. [*to* CLIMÈNE.]And nothing I have said, madame, applies to you: my speeches, like the satire of the comedy, remain in generalities.

CLIMÈNE. I do not doubt it, madame. But let us quit this topic—I am not aware how you receive the insults offered to our sex in certain portions of that play, but for myself I own that I am furiously angry when its impertinent author calls us "animals."

URANIE. But do you not see that he makes a ridiculous person say so?

DORANTE. Besides, madame, you surely know that a lover's insults are not insulting. Some loves are vehement, others gentle; and there are times when the strangest words, and something worse, are taken by the ladies who receive them as proofs of strong affection.

ÉLISE. Say what you please, I never can digest that speech, nor the "soup," nor the "cream-tarts" madame mentioned.

THE MARQUIS. Faith! yes, *cream*-tarts! I noticed that; "cream-tarts"! I thank you, madame, for reminding me of those "cream-tarts." Are there apples enough in Normandy to pelt "cream-tarts"! "Cream-tarts," *morbleu*! "cream-tarts"!

DORANTE. Well, cream-tarts; what then?

THE MARQUIS. *Parbleu*! *cream-tarts*, chevalier.

DORANTE. Yes, what of them?

THE MARQUIS. *Cream-tarts*!

DORANTE. Give us your reasons.

THE MARQUIS. Why, *cream-tarts*!

URANIE. But people should explain their thoughts, it seems to me.

THE MARQUIS. *Cream-tarts*, madame!

URANIE. What do you find to say against them?

THE MARQUIS. I?—*cream-tarts*!

URANIE. Oh! I give up.

ÉLISE. Monsieur le marquis has the best of it and foils you finely. But I could wish that Monsieur Lysidas would take those cream-tarts up and give them a few pats after his fashion.

LYSIDAS. 'Tis not my custom to find fault; I am known to be indulgent to the work of others. Still, without offending the regard which Monsieur le chevalier exhibits for the author, I must acknowledge that comedies of this sort are not real comedies; there is a mighty difference between such trifles and the beauties of a serious play. Yet all the world in these days is taken in by them! society runs after them, and after nothing else! Noble works are left in frightful solitude, while flimsy folly rules all Paris. I own to you that often my heart bleeds; it is a shame to France.

CLIMÈNE. The public taste is strangely spoilt of late; our present age is horribly given to *s'encanailler*.

ÉLISE. *S'encanailler*! why, there's another pretty word. Did you invent it, madame?

CLIMÈNE. Eh—er—

ÉLISE. I thought as much.

DORANTE. So you think, Monsieur Lysidas, that intellect and beauty are only to be found in serious poems, and that comic plays are silly trifles which deserve no praise?

URANIE. Those are not my sentiments, at any rate. Tragedy, no doubt, is something grand when it is rightly handled; but comedy has many charms; and I think 'tis no less difficult to write than tragedy.

DORANTE. You are right, madame; and as for difficulty, you would not be wrong if you should add a little to the scale of comedy. I think myself 'tis easier to be grand over grand sentiments, brave adverse fortune, challenge destiny, and hurl defiance at the gods than to exhibit in a proper spirit the absurdities of men and show their failings pleasantly upon the stage. When you depict a hero you can make him what you choose. Such portraits follow fancy, and no one seeks resemblance; you trust the pinions of imagination, which often soars from truth to attain the marvellous. But when you picture men you must paint from nature. Those portraits must be likenesses; and if you do not make them recognized as the men and women of our day you have done nought. In a word, it is enough in serious works to say sound things in choicely written language; but in comedy we must be comic; and 'tis indeed a curious enterprise to make the honest public laugh.

CLIMÈNE. I count myself among that honest public, and I could not find one word to laugh at in that comedy.

THE MARQUIS. Nor I, upon my word.

DORANTE. As for you, marquis, I am not surprised; you found no puns to please you.

LYSIDAS. And what there is to find is scarcely better; the jokes, I thought, were very dry.

DORANTE. The court thought otherwise.

LYSIDAS. Oh, monsieur! the court indeed!

DORANTE. Continue, Monsieur Lysidas; I see you long to say the court knows nothing of such matters. The usual refuge of all authors when their works do not succeed is to blame the injustice of the age and the dull intellect of courtiers. But let me tell you, Monsieur Lysidas, that courtiers have eyes as good as others; a man may be intelligent in Venice point and plumes as well as in a bob-tail wig and muslin collar; and the great test of all your comedies is the court judgment. 'Tis the court taste you ought to study to find the art of pleasing; there's no tribunal where the decisions are so just. Without considering the many men of intellect who belong to it, the simple, natural good sense and manners of the great world form a habit of mind which, without comparison, judges with greater delicacy than all the rusty wisdom of the pedants.

URANIE. It is very true that, however little one may live at court, so many things pass daily before our eyes that we acquire a certain habit of judging, especially of all relating to good or evil pleasantry.

DORANTE. That the court has some absurdities I readily admit, for I have been, as you well know, the first to laugh at them. But, faith! there's plenty of that sort of thing among the most noted *beaux esprits*, and if we sometimes laugh at marquises there is greater reason still to show up authors. 'Twould be a most amusing thing to put upon the stage their learned humbug, their finical absurdities, their vicious custom of stabbing others through their works, their greediness of praise, their compromise with thoughts, their traffic in reputation, their leagues, offensive and defensive, as well as their wars of mind and their battles of prose and verse.

LYSIDAS. Molière is lucky, monsieur, to have so warm a patron as yourself. But still, to come to facts, the question is whether his play is good, and I'll engage to show you at least a hundred visible defects.

URANIE. 'Tis a strange thing that all you poets condemn the plays that people rush to see, and say no good of any but of those that no one cares for. To the first you show a hatred quite invincible, to the others a tenderness that's almost inconceivable.

DORANTE. Because he is generous and takes the side of all neglected persons.

URANIE. But Monsieur Lysidas, I beg of you, show us those defects which I have been unable to perceive.

LYSIDAS. Those who know Aristotle and Horace, madame, can see at once that Molière's comedy transgresses all the rules of art.

URANIE. I own I am not intimate with the gentlemen you name, and I know nothing of the rules of art.

DORANTE. You *savants* are so amusing with your "rules of art," by which you puzzle ignorant people and stun us daily. To hear you talk, one would really think those "rules of art" were mysteries; whereas they are only simple observations, made by common-sense, on things that may affect the pleasure people take in poems of that sort. And the same good sense which made these observations in the olden time makes them as easily in our day, without the help of Horace or of Aristotle. I would like to ask if the great rule of rules is not—*to please*; and if a play which attains that end upon the stage is not upon the high-road of good art. Do you think the public is mistaken in such matters? or that each member cannot judge of the pleasure he receives?

URANIE. I have remarked one thing in authors; those who talk most of rules, and know them best, write comedies that no one considers beautiful or goes to see.

DORANTE. A fact which shows us, madame, we need not pay attention to such abstruse disputes. For, after all, if plays that follow rules don't please, and those that please don't follow rules, the reason must be, of necessity, the rules are bad. 'Tis best to laugh at all such quibbling criticism, to which these writers seek to subject the public taste. Let us enjoy in simple faith the things that please our inmost souls, and seek no arguments to spoil our pleasure.

URANIE. For my part, when I see a comedy I care for nothing but the effect it has on me. If it amuses me I do not ask if I am wrong, and whether the rules of Aristotle forbid my laughing.

DORANTE. Like the man who, finding a sauce good, does not examine to see if it follows precisely the receipt in the "Frenchman's Cook-book."

URANIE. True. I wonder often at the hypercriticism of certain persons on matters about which we ought to *feel* within us.

DORANTE. You are right, madame, to think such finical refinements strange. If they prevailed we could have no belief in our own selves; our very senses would be slaves; even to eating and drinking we should not dare to think things good without the sanction of milord the expert.

LYSIDAS. In short, chevalier, your only reason for liking "The School for Wives" is that it pleases; you do not mind its violating rules, because—

DORANTE. Stop, Monsieur Lysidas; I cannot grant you that. I said, indeed, that the great rule of art was to know how to please; and that this comedy, having pleased the public for whom the author wrote it, I thought he need not care for all the rest. But, further than that. I do maintain it does not violate the rules you mention. I have read them all, thank God, as often as any one, and I could show you, easily, we have no comedy upon the stage more regulated by those rules than this one.

ÉLISE. Courage, Monsieur Lysidas; we are lost if you retreat.

LYSIDAS. But monsieur! consider the *protasis*, the *epitasis*, the *katastrophe*.

DORANTE. Ha! Monsieur Lysidas, you are trying to crush me with grand words; but don't, for heaven's sake, assume such learning. Bring your discourse to earth and speak to be understood. Greek adds no weight to argument; and don't you think 'twould be as fine to say: "the explanation of the subject" in place of the *protasis*, or "plot" for *epitasis*, and "the end" for the *katastrophe*?

LYSIDAS. Those are terms of art which it is well to use. But since they wound your ears I will explain myself in other ways: and I request you to answer plainly certain questions which I wish to put. First: can a play be suffered to defy its very name? The words "dramatic poem" come from a Greek word signifying "to act," in order to show that the nature of that poem consists of action. Now, in this comedy there is no action; it all consists of narratives, told either by Horace or by Agnes.

THE MARQUIS. Ha! ha! chevalier.

CLIMÈNE. Most wittily remarked; you have gone to the root of things in that.

LYSIDAS. Was ever anything less witty, or rather I should say, more vulgar, than certain words at which the audience laughs; more especially those of "children by the ear"?

CLIMÈNE. Good, very good!

ÉLISE. Ha!

LYSIDAS. That scene within the house between the valet and the maid, is it not tiresome, and far too long, and quite uncalled-for?

THE MARQUIS. True.

CLIMÈNE. Yes, true indeed!

ÉLISE. He is right.

LYSIDAS. And does not Arnolphe give that money to Horace much too freely. Being, as he is, the ridiculous personage of the piece, he ought not to be made to do a handsome action.

THE MARQUIS. Good; that remark is good.

CLIMÈNE. Yes, admirable.

ÉLISE. Wonderful!

LYSIDAS. Arnolphe's sermon and those maxims, are they not ridiculous, and even shocking to the respect we owe the Mysteries!

THE MARQUIS. Well said!

CLIMÈNE. You put it as you ought.

ÉLISE. Nothing could possibly be better.

LYSIDAS. And this Monsieur de la Souche, who after all is really a man of intellect, and seems, in certain parts, most serious, does he not descend to something far too comic, too burlesque, in that fifth act, where he explains to Agnes the violence of his love with rolling eyes, and those ridiculous sighs and silly tears that make the audience laugh?

THE MARQUIS. *Morbleu*! you are marvellous.

CLIMÈNE. Miraculous!

ÉLISE. Vivat Monsieur Lysidas!

LYSIDAS. I drop a thousand other points, lest I be wearisome.

THE MARQUIS. *Parbleu*! chevalier, you are worsted now.

DORANTE. That's to be seen.

THE MARQUIS. You have found your match, i' faith.

DORANTE. Perhaps.

THE MARQUIS. But answer, answer, answer, answer.

DORANTE. Most willingly. It—

THE MARQUIS. Answer, I say.

DORANTE. Well, let me do so. If—

THE MARQUIS. *Parbleu*! I challenge you to make an answer.

DORANTE. I can't if you keep talking.

CLIMÈNE. Pray let us listen to his reasons.

DORANTE. In the first place, it is not true that all the play is narrative. Much action is performed upon the stage. The narratives themselves are actions, and follow the formation of the subject. They are all made naively, those narratives, to the person interested; who is thrown, as each is told him, into a confusion that delights the audience, and takes his measures, which carry on the play, to avoid the evil that he fears.

URANIE. I think the beauty of the play consists in these perpetual confidences; and what is most amusing, it seems to me, is that a man of Arnolphe's mind, warned by an innocent girl who is in his power, and by a giddy youth who is his rival, is yet unable to avoid the fate that overtakes him.

THE MARQUIS. Nonsense, nonsense!

CLIMÈNE. A feeble answer.

ÉLISE. Wretched reasons!

DORANTE. As to those "children by the ear," they are only droll, of course, as they relate to Arnolphe. The author did not put them there as wit, but solely to characterize the man and paint his folly by showing how he relates a trivial silliness of Agnes as a fine thing which gives him wondrous pleasure.

THE MARQUIS. That's a bad answer.

CLIMÈNE. It does not satisfy me.

ÉLISE. There's nothing in it.

DORANTE. As for money which he gives so liberally, besides the fact that the letter of his dearest friend was certainly security enough, it is not incompatible that a person who is ridiculous in many ways should be a worthy man in others. The scene between Alain and Georgette within the house, which some have thought too long, is surely not unnecessary; for Arnolphe, foiled by the innocence of his mistress and kept at his door by the ignorance of his servants, receives his punishment on all sides through the very means he took to make himself secure.

THE MARQUIS. Such arguments amount to nothing.

CLIMÈNE. They are all mere whitewash.

ÉLISE. And most pitiable!

DORANTE. As for the moral lecture, which you call a sermon, truly pious persons who have heard it found nothing there to shock them, as you say. "Hell" and the "boiling caldrons" they thought justified by Arnolphe's raving passion and by the ignorance of her to whom he spoke. As for the lover's transport in the last act, which you accuse of being too comic and grotesque, I would like to ask if lovers are not fair game, and whether worthy persons, even solemn ones, do not on such occasions do things—

THE MARQUIS. Upon my word, chevalier, you had better hold your tongue.

DORANTE. Well, well; but if we look at home when we are much in love—

THE MARQUIS. I will not even listen to you.

DORANTE. Listen you must. I say that in the violence of passion—

THE MARQUIS. [*sings*.] La la, la, la la-ré la, la, la, la, la!

DORANTE. What?

THE MARQUIS. La, la, la, la, la-ré, la, la, la, la, la!

DORANTE. I don't know whether—

THE MARQUIS. La, la, la, la, la-ré, la, la, la, la, la!

URANIE. It seems to me that—

THE MARQUIS. La, la, la, la, la-ré, la, la, la, la, la, la, la, la, la!

URANIE. Our dispute is certainly amusing; I think 'twould make a little comedy that would not come amiss as an appendix to "The School for Wives."

DORANTE. You are right.

THE MARQUIS. *Parbleu*! chevalier, you would play a part but little to your credit.

DORANTE. A true part, marquis.

CLIMÈNE. As for me, I should like to have it done, provided the affair were told just as it happened.

ÉLISE. I'll furnish my particular role with all my heart.

LYSIDAS. Mine I shall not refuse, I think.

URANIE. As we are all so well content, make notes, chevalier, of the whole affair, and carry them to Molière, whom you know, and tell him to put them in a comedy.

CLIMÈNE. He will not consent to that, of course, as these are not verses in his honor.

URANIE. You are mistaken. I know his humor. He does not care who blames his play, provided always that they go to see it.

DORANTE. Yes, but what finale can we give to this affair? There is neither a marriage nor yet a recognition; in fact I see no way to make a fitting end to this dispute.

URANIE. We must reflect, and find some incident.

[*enter* GALOPIN.]

GALOPIN. Madame is served.

DORANTE. Ha! here's precisely the conclusion that we want; nothing could be more natural. They shall dispute on both sides, hard and firm, as we have done; no one shall yield; a little lacquey shall come in and say that madame is served; then all shall rise and go to supper.

URANIE. No better ending could be found; we shall do well to make it ours.

[*curtain.*]

The Impromptu At Versailles

[*L'impromptu De Versailles.*]

Translated by HENRI VAN LAUN

A COMEDY IN ONE ACT

DRAMATIS PERSONAE

MOLIÈRE, *a ridiculous Marquis.*
BRÉCOURT, *a man of Quality.*
LA GRANGE, *a ridiculous Marquis.*
DU CROISY, *a poet.*
LA THORILLIÈRE, *a fidgetty Marquis.*
BÉJART, *a busybody.*
FOUR BUSYBODIES.

MADEMOISELLE DUPARC, *a ceremonious Marchioness.*
MADEMOISELLE BÉJART, *a prude.*
MADEMOISELLE DEBRIE, *a sage coquette.*
MADEMOISELLE MOLIÈRE, *a satirical wit.*
MADEMOISELLE DU CROISY, *a whining plague.*
MADEMOISELLE HERVÉ, *a conceited chambermaid.*

ACT I.

[*Scene.—Versailles, in the King's Antechamber.*]

SCENE I.

[MOLIÈRE, BRÉCOURT, LA GRANCE, DU CROISY, MADEMOISELLE DUPARC, MADEMOISELLE BÉJART, MADEMOISELLE DEBRIE, MADEMOISELLE MOLIÈRE, MADEMOISELLE DU CROISY, MADEMOISELLE HERVÉ.]

MOLIÈRE. [*alone, speaking to his fellow-actors behind the scenes.*] Come, ladies and gentlemen, is this delay meant for a joke? Are you never coming here? Plague take the people! I say, Brécourt!
BRÉCOURT. [*behind.*] What?
MOLIÈRE. La Grange!
LA GRANGE. [*behind.*] What is it?
MOLIÈRE. Du Croisy!

DU CROISY. [*behind.*] Who calls?

MOLIÈRE. Mademoiselle Duparc!

MADEMOISELLE DUPARC. [*behind.*] Well?

MOLIÈRE. Mademoiselle Béjart!

MADEMOISELLE BÉJART. [*behind.*] What is the matter?

MOLIÈRE. Mademoiselle Debrie!

MADEMOISELLE DEBRIE. [*behind.*] What do you want?

MOLIÈRE. Mademoiselle Du Croisy!

MADEMOISELLE DU CROISY. [*behind.*] Whatever is it?

MOLIÈRE. Mademoiselle Hervé!

MADEMOISELLE HERVÉ. [*behind.*] I am coming.

MOLIÈRE. I think I shall go mad with these people. Listen to me! [*enter* BRECOURT, LA GRANGE, DU CROISY.] Deuce take me! gentlemen, will you drive me out of my wits today?

BRÉCOURT. What would you have us do? We do not know our parts, and you will drive us out of our wits, if you force us to play in this style.

MOLIÈRE. Oh, what an awkward team to drive are actors! [*enter* MESDEMOISELLES BEJART, DUPARC, DEBRIE, MOLIERE, DU CROISY, *and* HERVE.]

MADEMOISELLE BÉJART. Well, here we are. What do you mean to do?

MADEMOISELLE DUPARC. What is your idea?

MADEMOISELLE DEBRIE. What is to be done?

MOLIÈRE. Pray, let us take our positions; and, since we are ready dressed, and the King will not come for a couple of hours, let us employ the time in rehearsing our piece, and see how we are to play our parts.

LA GRANGE. How are we to play what we do not know?

MADEMOISELLE DUPARC. As for me, I declare that I do not remember a word of my part.

MADEMOISELLE DEBRIE. I am sure I shall have to be prompted from beginning to end.

MADEMOISELLE BÉJART. And I just mean to hold mine in my hand.

MADEMOISELLE MOLIÈRE. So do I.

MADEMOISELLE HERVÉ. For my part, I have not much to say.

MADEMOISELLE DU CROISY. Nor I either; but, for all that, I would not promise not to make a slip.

DU CROISY. I would give ten pistoles to be out of it.

BRÉCOURT. I would stand a score of good blows with a whip to be the same, I assure you.

MOLIÈRE. You are all just disgusted at having parts that do not please you. What would you do if you were in my place, I should like to know.

MADEMOISELLE BÉJART. Who, you? You are not to be pitied; for having written the piece, you need not be afraid of tripping.

MOLIÈRE. And have I nothing to fear but want of memory? Do you reckon the anxiety as to our success, which is entirely my own concern, nothing? And do you think it a trifle to provide something comic for such an assembly as this; to undertake to excite laughter in those who command our respect, and who only laugh when they choose? Must not any author tremble when he comes to such a test? Would it not be natural for me to say that I would give everything in the world to be quit of it?

MADEMOISELLE BÉJART. If that makes you tremble, you should have been more careful, and not have undertaken what you have done in eight days

MOLIÈRE. How could I refuse the command of a King?

MADEMOISELLE BÉJART. How? By a respectful excuse, based on the impossibility of the thing in the short time that was allowed you. Anyone else in your place would have thought more of his reputation, and would have taken care not to expose himself, as you are doing. What will you do, pray, if the thing fails? Think what advantage all your enemies will take of it.

MADEMOISELLE DEBRIE. Ay, to be sure! You ought to have respectfully excused yourself to the King, or required more time.

MOLIÈRE. Oh! Mademoiselle, Kings like nothing better than a ready obedience, and are not at all pleased to meet with obstacles. Things are not acceptable, save at the moment when they desire them; to try to delay their amusement is to take away all the charm. They want pleasures that do not keep them waiting; and those that are least prepared are always the most agreeable to them. We ought never to think of ourselves in what they desire of us; our only business is to please them; and, when they command us, it is our part to respond quickly to their wish. We had better do amiss what they require of us, than not do it soon enough; if we have the shame of not succeeding, we always have the credit of having speedily obeyed their commands. But now, pray, let us set about our rehearsal.

MADEMOISELLE BÉJART. What would you have us do, if we do not know our parts?

MOLIÈRE. I tell you, you shall know them; even if you do not quite know them, can you not fill in out of your own heads, as it is in prose, and you know your subject?

MADEMOISELLE BÉJART. Thank you for nothing! Prose is worse than verse.

MADEMOISELLE MOLIÈRE. Shall I tell you what it is? You ought to write a comedy in which you could act all alone.

MOLIÈRE. Be quiet, wife. What a dunce you are!

MADEMOISELLE MOLIÈRE. Thanks, dear husband. That just shows how strangely marriage alters people. You would not have said that to me eighteen months ago.

MOLIÈRE. Pray be quiet.

MADEMOISELLE MOLIÈRE. It is an odd thing that a trifling ceremony deprives us of all our good qualities, and that a husband and a lover regard the same woman with such different eyes.

MOLIÈRE. Here is a sermon!

MADEMOISELLE MOLIÈRE. Upon my word, if I were to write a comedy, that should be my subject; I would justify women in many things of which they are accused, and I would make husbands afraid of the contrast between their abrupt manners and the civility of lovers.

MOLIÈRE. Well, let it pass. We cannot chatter now; we have something else to do.

MADEMOISELLE BÉJART. But, since you were ordered to work on the subject of the criticism that is passed on you, why not write that comedy of actors[3] that you have talked about so long? It was a ready-made notion, and would have come quite pat; the more so, as, having undertaken to delineate you, they gave you an opportunity to delineate them; it might have been called their portrait, far more justly than all their productions can be called yours. For, to try to mimic a comedian in a comic part is not to describe himself, but only after him the characters he represents, and making use of the same touches, and the same hues which he is obliged to employ in the various ridiculous characters that he draws from nature. But to mimic an actor in serious parts is to describe him by faults which are entirely his own, since characters of this kind do not carry either the gestures or ridiculous tones by which the actor is recognized.

MOLIÈRE. It is true; but I have my reasons for not doing it; between ourselves, I did not think it would be worth the trouble; and, besides, I should want more time to work out the idea. As their days for acting are the same as our own,[4] I have hardly seen them three or four times since we have been in Paris; I have caught nothing of their style of delivery, but what was at once apparent to the eye; I should have to study them more, to make my portraits very like them.[5]

---

[3] See *The School for Wives Criticized*, where Dorante throws out this idea: "It would be amusing to put them [the actors.] on the stage, with their learned antics and ridiculous refinements," &c.

[4] By "their," is meant the comedians of the hotel de Bourgogne, who, as well as Molière's troupe, played on Tuesdays, Fridays and Sundays.

[5] A clever side hit at the rival comedians who had been satirizing our poet, and who had no better opportunity of studying Molière, than he of studying them.

MADEMOISELLE DUPARC. I must say I have recognized some of them in your imitations.

MADEMOISELLE DEBRIE. I never heard this talked of.

MOLIÈRE. I had the idea once in my head, but I dismissed it as a trifle, a jest, which might have raised a laugh.

MADEMOISELLE DEBRIE. Give me a specimen, as you have given it to others.

MOLIÈRE. We have no time now.

MADEMOISELLE DEBRIE. Just a word or two!

MOLIÈRE. I thought of a comedy in which there should have been a poet, whose part I would have taken myself, coming to offer a piece to a strolling company fresh from the provinces. "Have you actors and actresses," he was to say, "capable of doing justice to a play? For my play is a play . . ." "Oh, sir," the comedians were to answer, "we have ladies and gentlemen who have passed muster wherever we have been." "And who plays the Kings amongst you?" "There is an actor who sometimes undertakes it." "Who? That well-made young man? Surely you jest. You want a King who is very fat, and as big as four men. A king, by Jove, well stuffed out. A king of vast circumference, who could fill a throne handsomely.[6] Only fancy a well-made king! There is one great fault to begin with; but let me hear him recite a dozen lines." Then the actor should repeat for example, some lines of the king in Nicomède:[7]

"I say, Araspus," &c.

"Do you see this attitude? Observe that well. There, lay the proper stress on the last line; that is what elicits approbation, and makes the public applaud you." "But, sir," the actor was to answer, "methinks a King who is conversing alone with the captain of his guards talks a little more mildly, and hardly uses this demoniacal tone." "You do not understand it. Go and speak in your way, and see if you get an atom of applause." "Ah, let us hear a scene

---

[6] An allusion to Montfleury, an actor of the hôtel de Bourgogne who was very stout, and of whom one of his contemporaries said: "He is so fat, that it takes several days to give him a sound beating."

[7] Nicomède is a tragedy of Corneille. These lines are said by Prusias, and the passage is Act ii., Scene I.

"I say, Araspus, he has too well served me,
Has raised my power. . ."

and so on, in the most natural manner he could. Then the poet:—"What? Call you that reciting? You are joking. You should say things with an emphasis. Listen to me." [*He imitates Montfleury, a comedian of the hotel de Bourgogne.*]

between a lover and his mistress." On which an actor and actress should have played a scene together —that of Camilla and Curiatius:—[8]

"Dost go, dear soul, and does this fatal honour
So charm thee at the cost of all our bliss?
Ah! now too well I see, etc . . . ."

—like the other, as naturally as they could. And the poet would break out: "You are joking; that is good for nothing. This is how you ought to recite it:" [*imitating* MADEMOISELLE DE BEAUCHATEAU, *an actress of the hotel de Bourgogne.*]

"Dost go, dear soul, &c.
"Nay, but I know the better, etc. . .[9]

"See how natural and impassioned this is. Admire the smiling face she maintains in the deepest affliction." There, that was my idea; and my poet should have run through all the actors in the same manner.

MADEMOISELLE DEBRIE. I like the notion; and I recognized some of them by the very first lines. Do go on.

MOLIÈRE. [*imitating* BEAUCHATEAU *in some lines from Cid.*][10]

"Pierced to the centre of my heart," &c.

And do you know this man in *Sertorius's* Pompey? [*imitating* HAUTEROCHE, *a comedian of the hotel de Bourgogne.*][11]

"The enmity which either faction sways
Engenders here no honour," &c.

---

[8] Personages from *Les Horaces*, a tragedy by P. Corneille.

[9] Madeleine de Bouget, the wife of Beauchateau, the actor, a very handsome and clever actress, played the princesses in tragedy, as well as the *ingénues* in comedy. She died at Versailles, on the 6th of January, 1683. The first two lines, "Dost go," are from *les Horaces* [Act ii., Scene 5.]; the third is the answer of Curiatius, to whom Camilla replies in a speech beginning with, "Nay, but I know thee better." Molière probably imitated the actor Beauchateau as Curiatius.

[10] *The Cid and Sertorius* were two tragedies by P. Corneille.

[11] Noel de Breton, sieur de Hauteroche, born in Paris 1617, was of very good family, and became a comedian against their wish. After many adventures he came to Paris, where he played, first at the théatre du Marais, and afterwards at the hôtel du Bourgogne, chiefly the confidants of the tragic heroes. Hauteroche was of lofty stature, and remarkably lean; he was also an author, and died 1707, at the age of ninety years.

MADEMOISELLE DEBRIE. I think I know him a little.

MOLIÈRE. And this one? [*imitating* DE VILLIERS, *another comedian of the hotel de Bourgogne.*][12]

"My lord, Polybius is dead," &c.[13]

MADEMOISELLE DEBRIE. Yes, I know who he is; but I fancy there are some amongst them whom you would find it hard to mimic.

MOLIÈRE. Good Heavens! there is not one that cannot be had somewhere, if I had studied them well.[14] But you make me lose precious time. Pray, let us think of ourselves, and not amuse ourselves any longer with talking. [*to* LA GRANGE.] Take care how you act the part of Marquis with me.

MADEMOISELLE MOLIÈRE. Marquises again?

MOLIÈRE. Yes, Marquises again. What the deuce would you have me hit on for a character acceptable to the audience? The Marquis in these days is the funny character in a comedy; and as, in all the old comedies, there was always a clownish servant to make the spectators laugh, so now, in all our pieces, there must be always a ridiculous Marquis to divert the company.

MADEMOISELLE BÉJART. It is true, that cannot be left out.

MOLIÈRE. As to you, Mademoiselle . . .

MADEMOISELLE DUPARC. Nay, as to me, I shall act wretchedly; I do not know why you have given me this ceremonious part.

MOLIÈRE. Good Heavens! Mademoiselle, that is what you said when you had your part in *The School for Wives Criticized*;[15] yet you acquitted yourself admirably, and everyone agreed that it could not be better done. Believe me, this will be the same; you will play it better than you think.

MADEMOISELLE DUPARC. How can that be? There is no one in the world less ceremonious than I.

MOLIÈRE. True; and that is how you prove yourself to be an excellent actress, representing well a character which is opposed to your mood. Try then, all of you, to catch the spirit of your parts aright, and to imagine that you are what you represent. [*to* DU CROISY.] You play a poet, and you ought to be taken up with your part; to mark the pedantic air which is maintained amidst the converse of the fashionable world; that sententious voice and precision of pronunciation, dwelling on every syllable, and not letting a letter

---

[12] De Villiers answered Molière in *la Vengeance des Marquis*.

[13] This is taken from the third scene of the fifth act of *Œdipe*, a tragedy by Corneille, but it ought to be "King Polybius is dead."

[14] The only actor of the hotel de Bourgogne whom Molière does not imitate is Floridor, who was really excellent.

[15] Madame Duparc played the part of Climène in *The School for Wives Criticized.*

drop from the strictest spelling. [*to* BRÉCOURT.] As for you, you play a courtier, as you have already done in *The School for Wives Criticized*; that is, you must assume a sedate air, and a natural tone of voice, and gesticulate as little as possible. [*to* LA GRANGE.] As for you, I have nothing to say to you. [*to* MADEMOISELLE BÉJART.] You represent one of those women who, provided they are not making love, think everything else is permitted to them; who are always proudly entrenched in their prudery, looking up and down on everyone, holding all the good qualities that others possess as nothing in comparison with a miserable honour which no one cares about. Keep this character always before your eyes, that you may show all its tricks. [*to* MADEMOISELLE DEBRIE.] As for you, you play one of those women who think they are the most virtuous persons in the world, so long as they save appearances; who believe that the sin lies only in the scandal; who would quietly carry on their intrigues in the style of an honourable attachment, and call those friends whom others call lovers. [*to* MADEMOISELLE MOLIÈRE.] You play the same character as in *The School for Wives Criticized*, and I have nothing more to say to you than to Mademoiselle Duparc. [*to* MADEMOISELLE DU CROISY.] As for you, you represent one of those people who are sweetly charitable to everyone, who always give a passing sting with their tongues, and who would be very sorry if they let their neighbours be well spoken of. I believe you will not acquit yourself badly in this part. [*to* MADEMOISELLE HERVÉ.] For you, you are the maid of the *précieuse*, who is always putting her spoke into the conversation, and picks up all her mistress' expressions, as well as she can. I tell you all your characters, that you may impress them strongly on your minds. Let us now begin to rehearse, and see how it will do. Oh, here comes a bore. This is all we wanted!

Scene II.

[LA THORILLIÈRE, MOLIÈRE, BRÉCOURT, LA GRANGE, DU CROISY, MADEMOISELLE DUPARC, MADEMOISELLE BÉJART, MADEMOISELLE DEBRIE, MADEMOISELLE MOLIÈRE, MADEMOISELLE DU CROISY, MADEMOISELLE HERVÉ.]

LA THORILLIÈRE. Good day, Molière.

MOLIÈRE. Sir, your servant. [*aside.*] Plague take the man.

LA THORILLIÈRE. How goes it?

MOLIÈRE. Very well. What can I do for you? [*to the actresses.*] Ladies, do not . . .

LA THORILLIÈRE. I come from a place where I have been praising you up.

MOLIÈRE. I am obliged to you. [*aside.*] The devil take you! [*to the actors.*] Pray take care . . .

LA THORILLIÈRE. You play a new piece to-night?

MOLIÈRE. Yes, sir. [*to the actresses.*] Do not forget . . .

LA THORILLIÈRE. The King got you to do it?

MOLIÈRE. Yes, sir. [*to the actors.*] Pray remember . . .

LA THORILLIÈRE. What do you call it?

MOLIÈRE. Yes, sir.

LA THORILLIÈRE. I ask what you call it?

MOLIÈRE. Oh! Upon my word I do not know. [*to the actresses.*] You must, if you please . . .

LA THORILLIÈRE. How are you going to be dressed?

MOLIÈRE. As you see. [*to the actors.*] I beg you . . .

LA THORILLIÈRE. When do you begin?

MOLIÈRE. When the King comes. [*aside.*] The deuce take him and his questions.

LA THORILLIÈRE. When do you think he will come?

MOLIÈRE. May the quinsy choke me if I know, sir!

LA THORILLIÈRE. Do you not know . . .

MOLIÈRE. Look here, sir; I am the most ignorant man in the world. I swear I know nothing of anything about what you may ask. [*aside.*] I am going mad. This wretch comes cross-examining me in his cool way, never dreaming that I may have other things to attend to.

LA THORILLIÈRE. Ladies, your servant.

MOLIÈRE. Ah good! now he is on the other side.

LA THORILLIÈRE. [*to* MADEMOISELLE DU CROISY.] You are as handsome as a little angel. Do you both play to-day? [*looking at* MADEMOISELLE HERVÉ.]

MADEMOISELLE DU CROISY. Yes, sir.

LA THORILLIÈRE. Without you, the comedy would not be worth much.[16]

MOLIÈRE. [*whispering to the actresses.*] Can you not send that man about his business?

MADEMOISELLE DEBRIE. Sir, we have a rehearsal on.

LA THORILLIÈRE. Oh, Zounds, I shall not prevent you; you have only to go on.

MADEMOISELLE DEBRIE. But . . .

LA THORILLIÈRE. Nay, nay, I should be sorry to trouble any one. Do what you have to do without scruple.

---

[16] This compliment is addressed to Mesdemoiselles Du Croisy and Hervé, two of the weakest actresses in Molière's troupe.

MADEMOISELLE DEBRIE. Yes; but . . .

LA THORILLIÈRE. I assure you, I am a man of no ceremony; and you can rehearse what you like.

MOLIÈRE. Sir, these ladies hesitate to tell you that they would much prefer that no one should be present during this rehearsal.

LA THORILLIÈRE. But why? You have nothing to fear from me.

MOLIÈRE. Sir, it is their custom; you will be the better pleased when the thing takes you by surprise.

LA THORILLIÈRE. Then I shall go and tell them you are ready.

MOLIÈRE. By no means, sir; do not be in a hurry, pray.

SCENE III.

[MOLIÈRE, BRÉCOURT, LA GRANGE, DU CROISY, MADEMOISELLE DUPARC, MADEMOISELLE BÉJART, MADEMOISELLE DEBRIE, MADEMOISELLE MOLIÈRE, MADEMOISELLE DU CROISY, MADEMOISELLE HERVÉ.]

MOLIÈRE. Oh dear, this world is full of impertinent people! But now come, let us begin. In the first place, then, imagine that the scene is in the King's antechamber; for it is a place where plenty of amusing things go on every day. It is easy to introduce there whomsoever we please; and reasons can even be found to explain the appearance of the ladies whom I bring in. The comedy opens with the meeting of two Marquises. [*to* LA GRANGE.] Be sure and do not forget to come from that side, as I told you, with what they call a distinguished air, combing your wig, and humming a tune between your teeth. La, la, la, la, la, la, la! Just move aside, the rest of you; for a couple of Marquises require room, and they are not the sort of persons to be satisfied with a small space. [*to* LA GRANGE.] Now then, speak.

LA GRANGE. "Good day, Marquis."

MOLIÈRE. Oh dear! That is not the way in which Marquises talk. It must be a little higher. Most of these gentlemen affect a special tone to distinguish themselves from the vulgar. "Good day, Marquis." Try again.

LA GRANGE. "Good day, Marquis."

MOLIÈRE. "Ah, Marquis, your most obedient."

LA GRANGE. "What are you doing there?"

MOLIÈRE. "'Sdeath, you may see. I am waiting until all these persons have cleared away from the door, that I may show my face there."

LA GRANGE. "Zounds! what a crowd! I do not care to go and push myself through, I had rather wait till the last."

MOLIÈRE. "There is a score there who have no chance of getting in, but they take good care to press forward, and occupy all the approaches to the door."

LA GRANGE. "Let us call out our names to the door-keeper, so that he may summon us."

MOLIÈRE. "That may do for you; but I do not wish Molière to take me off."

LA GRANGE. "Yet I think, Marquis, that it is you he takes off in *The School for Wives Criticized.*"

MOLIÈRE. "Me? Most mighty potentate! it is your very self."

LA GRANGE. "Ah! upon my word, you are kind, to fit me with your own character."

MOLIÈRE. "Death, you are amusing, to give me what belongs to yourself."

LA GRANGE. [*laughing.*] "Ah, ha! How entertaining!"

MOLIÈRE. [*laughing.*] "Ah, ha! How comical!"

LA GRANGE. "What! you mean to maintain that it is not you who are exhibited in the Marquis of *The School for Wives Criticized*?"

MOLIÈRE. "Just so; it is I. 'Detestable; egad! detestable! Cream tart!' Oh, it is I, it is I, assuredly it is I!"

LA GRANGE. "Yes, it is you. You need not jest; and we shall lay a wager, if you like, and see which of us is right."

MOLIÈRE. "Well then, what will you bet?"

LA GRANGE. "I bet a hundred pistoles that it is you."

MOLIÈRE. "And I bet a hundred it is you."

LA GRANGE. "Money down!"

MOLIÈRE. "Money down! Ninety on Amyntas, and ten cash."

LA GRANGE. "Content!"

MOLIÈRE. "Done, then.

LA GRANGE. "Your money runs a great risk."

MOLIÈRE. "Yours is in danger."

LA GRANGE. "Who shall be umpire?"

MOLIÈRE. "Here is a gentleman who shall decide. Chevalier!"

BRÉCOURT. "What is it?"

MOLIÈRE. Good. Here is the other who assumes the tone of a Marquis. Did I not tell you that you were playing a part in which you had to speak naturally?

BRÉCOURT. So you did.

MOLIÈRE. Now then. "Chevalier. . ."

BRÉCOURT. "What is it?"

MOLIÈRE. "Just decide betwixt us on a wager we have made."

BRÉCOURT. "What wager?"

MOLIÈRE. "We cannot agree who is the Marquis in Molière's *School for Wives Criticized.* He bets that it is I, and I bet that it is he."

BRÉCOURT. "Well, I decide that it is neither the one nor the other. You are fools, both of you, to wish that these caps should fit; this is just what I heard Molière complaining of the other day, when he was talking to some people who charged him with the same thing. He said that nothing annoyed him so much as to be accused of animadverting upon anyone in the portraits he drew; that his design is to paint manners without striking at individuals, and that all the characters whom he introduces are imaginary—phantoms, so to speak, which he clothes according to his fancy in order to please his audience; that he would be much vexed to have hit any one through them; and that if aught could sicken him of writing comedies, it would be the resemblances that people always insisted on finding, and on which his enemies maliciously tried to fix attention, in order to do him an injury with certain persons of whom he had never thought. And, indeed, I think he is right; for why, pray, should you apply all his actions and words, and seek to draw him into quarrels by publicly declaring that he is showing up so-and-so, when the facts are such as will fit a hundred people? As the business of comedy is to represent in a general way all the faults of men, and especially of the men of our day, it is impossible for Molière to create any character not to be met with in the world; and if he must be accused of thinking of everyone in whom are to be found the faults which he delineates he must, of course, give up writing comedies."[17]

MOLIÈRE. "Upon my word, Chevalier, you wish to justify Molière, and spare our friend here."

LA GRANGE. "Not at all. It is you he spares; and we shall find another umpire."

MOLIÈRE. "So be it. But tell me, Chevalier, do you not think that Molière is exhausted by this time, and that he will find no more subjects for . . .?"

BRÉCOURT. "No more subjects? Ah, dear Marquis, we shall always go on providing him with plenty; and we are scarcely taking the course to grow wise, for all that he can do or say."

MOLIÈRE. Stay. You must be more emphatic with this passage. Just listen to me for a moment.[18] "And that he will find no more subjects for . . .—No more subjects? Ah, dear Marquis, we shall always go on providing him with plenty, and we are scarcely taking the course to grow wise, for all that he can do or say. Do

---

[17] This is an intentional and very forcible self-defence upon the part of the author, to which the nature of the comedy lends itself admirably. No doubt Molière had much ado to keep himself out of an endless series of personal quarrels with those whom his satire affected; and though one object of *The School for Wives Criticized* was to lay stress on the general meaning of his delineations, its immediate effect was, doubtless, to aggravate the annoyance of his lay-figures. The *Impromptu* could not fail to allay these grievances, and to conciliate the author's contemporaries.

[18] This is very skilful; Molière now takes up his own argument in his proper person, thus challenging the closer attention of his audience.

you imagine that he has exhausted in his comedies all the follies of men; and without leaving the Court, are there not a score of characters which he has not yet touched upon? For instance, has he not those who profess the greatest friendship possible, and who, when they turn their backs, think it a piece of gallantry to tear each other to pieces? Has he not those unmitigated sycophants, those vapid flatterers, who never give a pinch of salt with their praises, and whose flatteries have a sickly sweetness which nauseate those who hear them? Has he not the craven courtiers of favorites, the treacherous worshippers of fortune, who praise you in prosperity, and run you down in adversity? Has he not those who are always discontented with the Court, those useless hangers-on, those troublesome, officious creatures, those people who can count up no services except importunities, and who expect to be rewarded for having laid a ten years' siege to the King? Has he not those who fawn on all the world alike, who hand their civilities from left to right, who run after all whom they see, with the same salutations, and the same professions of friendship? 'Sir, your most obedient. Sir, I am entirely at your service. Consider me wholly yours, dear sir. Reckon me, sir, as the warmest of your friends. Sir, I am enchanted to embrace you. Ah! sir, I did not see you. Oblige me by making use of me; be assured I am wholly yours. You are the one man in the world whom I most esteem. There is no one whom I honour like you. I entreat you to believe it. I beg of you not to doubt it. Your servant. Your humble slave.' Oh, Marquis, Marquis, Molière will always have more subjects than he needs; and all that he has aimed at as yet is but a trifle to the treasure which is within his reach." That is something of the style in which it should be played.

BRÉCOURT. It is sufficient.

MOLIÈRE. Go on.

BRÉCOURT. "Here are Climène and Eliza."

MOLIÈRE. [*to* MADEMOISELLES DUPARC *and* MOLIÈRE.] Hereupon you two are to come up. [*to* MADEMOISELLE DUPARC.] Be sure, you, to attitudinize well, and observe a good many formalities. That will constrain you a little; but it cannot be helped. One must sometimes do violence to oneself.

MADEMOISELLE MOLIÈRE. "Madam, I easily recognized you a long way off, and perceived from your bearing that it could be no other than you."

MADEMOISELLE DUPARC. "You see, I have come to wait for a man with whom I have a little matter of business."

MADEMOISELLE MOLIÈRE. "That is just my case."

MOLIÈRE. Ladies, these boxes will serve you for arm-chairs.

MADEMOISELLE DUPARC. "Come, Madam, I beg you to be

seated."

MADEMOISELLE MOLIÈRE. "After you, Madam."

MOLIÈRE. Good. After these little dumb shows, let each take a seat, and speak sitting, whilst the Marquises must sometimes get up and sometimes sit down again, in accordance with their natural restlessness. "'Sdeath, Chevalier, you ought to physic your rolls."

BRÉCOURT. "How so?"

MOLIÈRE. "They look ill.'

BRÉCOURT. "I salute your punstership."

MADEMOISELLE MOLIÈRE. "Heavens, Madam, I do think your complexion dazzling white, and your lips of a marvellous flame-colour."

MADEMOISELLE DUPARC. "Ah! what is that you say, Madam? Do not look at me; I am frightfully ugly to-day."

MADEMOISELLE MOLIÈRE. "Do, Madam, just raise your hood."

MADEMOISELLE DUPARC. "Fie! I am frightful, I tell you, and shock even myself."

MADEMOISELLE MOLIÈRE. "You are so lovely."

MADEMOISELLE DUPARC. "No, no."

MADEMOISELLE MOLIÈRE. "Show yourself."

MADEMOISELLE DUPARC. "Oh, pray do not."

MADEMOISELLE MOLIÈRE. "Please do."

MADEMOISELLE DUPARC. "Heavens, no!"

MADEMOISELLE MOLIÈRE. "Yes, do."

MADEMOISELLE DUPARC. "How troublesome you are!"

MADEMOISELLE MOLIÈRE. "Just for an instant."

MADEMOISELLE DUPARC. "Ah!"

MADEMOISELLE MOLIÈRE. "You positively shall show yourself. We cannot do without seeing you."

MADEMOISELLE DUPARC. "Good gracious, what an odd creature you are! What you wish you wish so desperately."

MADEMOISELLE MOLIÈRE. "Ah, Madam, I am sure you need not dread the broad daylight. How wicked people are to say that you use any paint! I shall certainly be able to contradict them now."

MADEMOISELLE DUPARC. "Lackaday, I do not so much as know what you mean by using paint! But where are those ladies going?"

MADEMOISELLE DEBRIE. "Permit us, ladies, to give you in passing the most agreeable news conceivable. Here is Mr. Lysidas, who has just told us that someone has made a play against Molière, which the grand company are going to act."

MOLIÈRE. "It is true, they wished to read it to me. A certain Br . . . Brou . . . Brossaut has written it."

DU CROISY. "Sir, it is advertised under the name of Boursault; but, to let you into the secret, many people have contributed to this piece, and one is disposed to form pretty high expectations of it. Since all authors and actors look on Molière as their greatest enemy, we all unite against him to do him an ill turn. Each of us has added a stroke to his portrait; but we have taken good care not to put our names to it. It would have been too much honour for him to succumb, before the eyes of the world, to the efforts of a combined Parnassus; and so, to make his discomfiture more ignominious, we thought of picking out on purpose an author without repute."

MADEMOISELLE DUPARC. "For my part, I confess that I am greatly rejoiced at it."

MOLIÈRE. "And so am I. Gad, the mocker shall be mocked; upon my word, he shall have a rap over the knuckles."

MADEMOISELLE DUPARC. "That will teach him to satirize everybody. What! This impertinent fellow will have it that women have no wit. He condemns all our lofty modes of expression, and makes out that we are always speaking in a humdrum way."

MADEMOISELLE DEBRIE. "Speech matters nothing; but he blames all our intimacies, however harmless they may be; and according to him, it is criminal to possess merit."

MADEMOISELLE DU CROISY. "It is unbearable. Women can do nothing henceforth. Why cannot he let our husbands be at peace, without opening their eyes and making them notice things of which they never thought?"

MADEMOISELLE BÉJART. "All this is a trifle; but he satirizes even virtuous women; the wicked buffoon styles them 'respectable she-devils.'"[19]

MADEMOISELLE MOLIÈRE. "He is an impertinent wretch. He deserves all he gets."

DU CROISY. "This play, Madam, must needs be supported: and the comedians of the hotel . . ."

MADEMOISELLE DUPARC. "Oh, let them have no fear. I will lay my life on the success of this piece."

MADEMOISELLE MOLIÈRE. "You are right, Madam. Too many people are interested in thinking it good. You may judge whether all those who believe themselves to have been satirized by Molière will not take the opportunity of avenging themselves on him by applauding this comedy."

BRÉCOURT. [*ironically.*] "No doubt; and for my part I can answer for a dozen Marquises, six *précieuses*, a score of coquettes, and thirty victimized husbands, who will not fail to applaud."

MADEMOISELLE MOLIÈRE. "Exactly so. Why should he go and offend all these people, and especially the victimized husbands,

---

[19] See *The School for Wives*, Act iv., Scene 8.

who are the best people in the world?"[20]

MOLIÈRE. "Gad, I have been told that they will have a rub both at him and at all his plays, in fine style, and that actors and authors, from great to small, are deucedly savage against him."

MADEMOISELLE MOLIÈRE. "That just serves him right. Why does he write wicked pieces that all Paris goes to see, and in which he paints people so well, that everybody knows himself? Why does he not make plays like those of Mr. Lysidas? He would have no one against him, and all the authors would speak well of him. It is true that such plays do not draw large audiences; but, on the other hand, they are always well written; nobody writes against them, and all who see them are desperately anxious to think them fine."

DU CROISY. "It is true that I have the advantage of making no enemies, and that all my works are approved of by the learned."[21]

MADEMOISELLE MOLIÈRE. "You are justified in being satisfied with yourself. That is worth more than all the applause of the public, and than all the money that Molière's pieces may draw. What does it matter to you whether people come to see your plays, so long as they are praised by your professional friends?"

LA GRANGE. "But when will *The Painter's Portrait* be acted?"

DU CROISY. "I do not know; but I intend to appear in the front seat, and cry, This is something like a play!"

MOLIÈRE. Gad, and I too."

LA GRANGE. "And so do I, as I hope to be saved."

MADEMOISELLE DUPARC. "For my part, I shall show myself there, as I ought; and I will answer for a round of applause which shall drown all adverse opinion. It is really the least we can do, to assist with our approbation the avenger of our cause."

MADEMOISELLE MOLIÈRE. "Well said!"

MADEMOISELLE DEBRIE. "That is what we must all do."

MADEMOISELLE BÉJART. "Assuredly."

MADEMOISELLE DU CROISY. "Undoubtedly."

MADEMOISELLE HERVÉ. "No quarter to this mimic."

MOLIÈRE. "Upon my word, Chevalier, your Molière must hide his head."

BRÉCOURT. "Who? He? I promise you, Marquis, that he intends to take a seat upon the stage, and laugh with the rest at the portrait they have drawn of him."[22]

---

[20] One of the commentators of Molière says that the proof that our author was not jealous is to be found in the words he puts into his wife's mouth. I imagine Mademoiselle Molière spoke ironically.

[21] Earlier Molière, in answer to Mademoiselle Debrie's remarks, replies for Lysidas, here it is Du Croisy; this seems a contradiction.

[22] "De Villiers, in the *Vengeance des Marquis*, mentions that Molière took one day a seat on the stage of the hotel de Bourgogne to listen to Boursalt's *Painter's Portrait*.

MOLIÈRE. "Gad, then, he will laugh on the wrong side of his face."

BRÉCOURT. "Come, come; perchance he will find more cause for laughter than you think. I was shown the play; and as everything amusing in it was exactly taken from Molière, the pleasure which this will afford, will not be likely to offend him; for, as to the parts where they set themselves to blacken him, I am very much mistaken if this is applauded by any one. And as for all the people whom they have tried to set against him, of whom, it is said, he had drawn too faithful likenesses, not only is it in bad taste, but I never saw anything more ridiculous, or worse done; I never yet thought that it was a reproach to a dramatic author to depict men too well."

LA GRANGE. "The actors told me they expected a rejoinder from him, and that . . ,"

BRÉCOURT. "A rejoinder? Verily, I should think him a great fool if he took the trouble to reply to their invectives. Everyone knows well enough from what motives they must be acting; and the best answer which he can make them is a comedy which will succeed like all the others. This is the true plan of being avenged on them; and judging from what I know of their disposition, I am sure that a new play, which will take their audiences from them, will annoy them much more than all the satires which could be written against them individually."

MOLIÈRE. "But, Chevalier . . .?"

MADEMOISELLE BÉJART. Let me interrupt the rehearsal for a moment. [*to* MOLIÈRE.] May I make a suggestion? If I had been you, I should have treated the thing in another way. Everyone expects a vigorous rejoinder from you; and, after the way in which they tell me you have been treated in this comedy, you were justified in saying anything against the actors; and you ought not to spare one of them.

MOLIÈRE. I am annoyed to hear you speak thus. This is just the way with you ladies. You would have me fire up against them, and follow their example by rushing into invectives and insults. A great deal of honour I should get from it, and a vast deal of vexation I should bring them! Are they not quite prepared for that kind of thing? And, when they were discussing whether they should play *The Painter's Portrait*, for fear of a rejoinder, did not some of them say: "Let him abuse us as much as he likes, so long as we get money?"—Is not that the mark of a soul very sensitive to shame; and should I not be well avenged by giving them what they greatly long to receive?

MADEMOISELLE DEBRIE. They complained strongly of three or four words you said of them in *The School for Wives Criticized*, and *The Pretentious Young Ladies*.

MOLIÈRE. It is true that these three or four words are very offensive; and they have great reason to quote them. Come, come, it is not that. The greatest harm I have done them is that I have been fortunate enough to please a little more than they would have liked; their whole conduct since we came to Paris has too clearly shown what pricks them. But let them do what they will, all their efforts cannot disturb me. They criticize my plays, so much the better; and Heaven forbid that I should ever do aught that pleased them! It would be a bad business for me.

MADEMOISELLE DEBRIE. Still there is not much pleasure in seeing one's works pulled to pieces.

MOLIÈRE. What does it matter to me? Have I not got from my comedy all that I wished, since it had the good fortune to please those lofty personages whom I specially aim at pleasing? Have I not cause to be content with my lot, and are not all their censures a little too late? Does that affect me now, pray? When they attack a piece which has been successful, do they not attack the judgment of those who praised it, rather than the skill of him who wrote it?

MADEMOISELLE DEBRIE. Upon my word, I should have had a hit at that little scribe, who is rash enough to write against people who do not trouble their heads about him.

MOLIÈRE. How silly you are. A fine subject for diversion monsieur Boursault would be! I should like to know how he could be tricked out to make him amusing; and whether, if he were ridiculed on the stage, he would be fortunate enough to make any one laugh. It would be too much honour for him, to be represented, before an august assembly. He would ask nothing better; and he attacks me wantonly in order to make himself known in any way. He is a man who has nothing to lose, and the actors have let him loose on me only in order to engage me in a foolish quarrel, and turn me aside, by this dodge, from other works which I have on hand; and yet you are simple enough to fall into the trap. But I shall make a public declaration on this point. I do not mean to make any reply to all their criticisms and counter-criticisms. Let them say all the evil they can of my pieces; I am quite willing. Let them take our leavings, and turn them inside out like a coat, to bring them on their own stage, and try to profit by any pleasant thing they find in them, and by a little of my good fortune; I give them leave; they have need of it, and I shall be happy to contribute to their necessities, provided they will be satisfied with what I can decently grant them. Courtesy must have its limits; and there are some things which can make neither spectators laugh, nor him of whom they are spoken. I gladly leave to them my works, my figure, my attitudes, my words, the tone of my voice, and my style of recitation, to make and say whatever they will of them, if they can snatch some profit from them. I have nothing to say against all this, and shall be delighted if this can please people; but whilst I give them all this, they must do me the favour to leave me the remainder, and not to touch on things of the nature of those upon which, I hear, they attack me in their comedies.[23] This I shall politely request of the honourable gentleman who undertakes to write for them; and this is all the answer they shall have from me.

MADEMOISELLE BÉJART. But, in a word . . .

MOLIÈRE. But, in a word, you will drive me mad. Let us say no more of this. We amuse ourselves by talking when we ought to be rehearsing our comedy. Where were we? I do not remember.

MADEMOISELLE DEBRIE. You were at the very place . . .

MOLIÈRE. Good Heavens, what noise do I hear? Surely the King is come! I can plainly see we shall have no time to get through it. That is what comes of our gossiping. Oh, well, you must do the best you can with the rest.

MADEMOISELLE BÉJART. On my word, I am in such a fright, I shall never be able to play my part unless I rehearse it all.

MOLIÈRE. What! You will not be able to play your part.

MADEMOISELLE BÉJART. No.

MADEMOISELLE DUPARC. Nor I mine.

MADEMOISELLE DEBRIE. No more shall I.

MADEMOISELLE MOLIÈRE. Nor I.

MADEMOISELLE HERVÉ. Nor I.

MADEMOISELLE DU CROISY. Nor I.

MOLIÈRE. What on earth do you mean to do? Are you all mocking me.

Scene IV.

[BÉJART, LA THORILLIÈRE, MOLIÈRE, BRÉCOURT, LA GRANGE, DU CROISY, MADEMOISELLE DUPARC, MADEMOISELLE BÉJART, MADEMOISELLE DEBRIE, MADEMOISELLE MOLIÈRE, MADEMOISELLE DU CROISY, MADEMOISELLE HERVÉ.]

BÉJART. Gentlemen, I come to inform you that the King has arrived, and waits for you to begin.

MOLIÈRE. Ah, sir, you see me in a terrible strait. I am distracted as I speak to you. These ladies are frightened, and say they must rehearse their parts before commencing. We beg the favour of

---

[23] Most likely Boursault's *le Portrait du Pointre*, Montfleury's *Impromptu de l'hotel de Condé*, and De Villier's *la Vengeance des Marquis*, contained some personal attacks, either against Molière, his wife, or his friends, which were suppressed when those plays were printed.

another moment. The King is kind, and he knows well that the piece has been done hurriedly.

SCENE V.

[LA THORILLIÈRE, MOLIÈRE, BRÉCOURT, LA GRANGE, DU CROISY, MADEMOISELLE DUPARC, MADEMOISELLE BÉJART, MADEMOISELLE DEBRIE, MADEMOISELLE MOLIÈRE, MADEMOISELLE DU CROISY, MADEMOISELLE HERVÉ.]

MOLIÈRE. Oh, pray try and recover yourselves. Take courage, I entreat you.

MADEMOISELLE DUPARC. You must go and excuse yourself.

MOLIÈRE. How can I excuse myself?

SCENE VI.

[A BUSYBODY, LA THORILLIÈRE, MOLIÈRE, BRÉCOURT, LA GRANGE, DU CROISY, MADEMOISELLE DUPARC, MADEMOISELLE BÉJART, MADEMOISELLE DEBRIE, MADEMOISELLE MOLIÈRE, MADEMOISELLE DU CROISY, MADEMOISELLE HERVÉ.]

FIRST BUSYBODY. Gentlemen, begin.

MOLIÈRE. At once, sir. I believe I shall go out of my mind over this precious business . .

SCENE VII.

[A SECOND BUSYBODY, LA THORILLIÈRE, MOLIÈRE, BRÉCOURT, LA GRANGE, DU CROISY, MADEMOISELLE DUPARC, MADEMOISELLE BÉJART, MADEMOISELLE DEBRIE, MADEMOISELLE MOLIÈRE, MADEMOISELLE DU CROISY, MADEMOISELLE HERVÉ.]

SECOND BUSYBODY. Gentlemen, begin!

MOLIÈRE. In a moment, sir. [*to his fellow-actors*.] What, would you have me affronted . . .

SCENE VIII.

[A THIRD BUSYBODY, LA THORILLIÈRE, MOLIÈRE, BRÉCOURT, LA GRANGE, DU CROISY, MADEMOISELLE DUPARC, MADEMOISELLE BÉJART, MADEMOISELLE DEBRIE, MADEMOISELLE MOLIÈRE, MADEMOISELLE DU CROISY, MADEMOISELLE HERVÉ.]

THIRD BUSYBODY. Gentlemen, begin!

MOLIÈRE. Yes, sir, that is what we are about to do. How officious these gentry are, coming and bidding us begin, when the King did not order them!

SCENE IX.

[A FOURTH BUSYBODY, LA THORILLIÈRE, MOLIÈRE, BRÉCOURT, LA GRANGE, DU CROISY, MADEMOISELLE DUPARC, MADEMOISELLE BÉJART, MADEMOISELLE DEBRIE, MADEMOISELLE MOLIÈRE, MADEMOISELLE DU CROISY, MADEMOISELLE HERVÉ.]

FOURTH BUSYBODY. Gentlemen, begin!

MOLIÈRE. It is done sir. [*to his fellow-actors.*] What! must I be covered with confusion . . .

SCENE X.

[BÉJART, LA THORILLIÈRE, MOLIÈRE, BRÉCOURT, LA GRANGE, DU CROISY, MADEMOISELLE DUPARC, MADEMOISELLE BÉJART, MADEMOISELLE DEBRIE, MADEMOISELLE MOLIÈRE, MADEMOISELLE DU CROISY, MADEMOISELLE HERVÉ.]

MOLIÈRE. Sir, you come to bid us begin, but . . .

BÉJART. No, gentlemen, I come to say that the King has heard of the trouble you are in, and that, in the kindness which distinguishes him, he defers your new comedy to another time, and will be satisfied to-day with the first you can give him.

MOLIÈRE. Oh, sir, you give me new life. The King bestows on us the greatest possible favour in giving us time for that which he desired; we shall all go and thank him for the extreme goodness which he displays towards us.[24]

[*curtain.*]

[24] A flattery to the Grand Monarque, heightened by what had previously been said by Molière of the impatience of Kings to taste the pleasures on which they have set their minds. [Scene I, *ad init.*]

Tartuffe

[*Tartuffe, ou l'Imposteur.*]

A COMEDY IN FIVE ACTS

Translated by CURTIS HIDDEN PAGE

DRAMATIS PERSONAE

MADAME PERNELLE, *mother of Orgon.*
ORGON, *husband of Elmire.*
ELMIRE, *wife of Orgon.*
DAMIS, *son of Orgon.*
MARIANE, *daughter of Orgon, in love with Valere.*
CLEANTE, *brother-in-law of Orgon.*
TARTUFFE, *a hypocrite.*
DORINE, *Mariane's maid.*
M. LOYAL, *a bailiff.*
A Police Officer
FLIPOTTE, *Madame Pernelle's servant.*

The Scene is at Paris.

ACT I.

SCENE I.

[MADAME PERNELLE *and* FLIPOTTE, *her servant*; ELMIRE, MARIANE, CLEANTE, DAMIS, DORINE.]

MADAME PERNELLE. Come, come, Flipotte, and let me get away.
ELMIRE. You hurry so, I hardly can attend you.
MADAME PERNELLE. Then don't, my daughter-in law. Stay where you are.
I can dispense with your polite attentions.
ELMIRE. We're only paying what is due you, mother.
Why must you go away in such a hurry?
MADAME PERNELLE. Because I can't endure your carryings-on,
And no one takes the slightest pains to please me.
I leave your house, I tell you, quite disgusted;
You do the opposite of my instructions;
You've no respect for anything; each one
Must have his say; it's perfect pandemonium.

DORINE. If . . .

MADAME PERNELLE. You're a servant wench, my girl, and much
Too full of gab, and too impertinent
And free with your advice on all occasions.

DAMIS. But . . .

MADAME PERNELLE. You're a fool, my boy—f, o, o, l
Just spells your name. Let grandma tell you that
I've said a hundred times to my poor son,
Your father, that you'd never come to good
Or give him anything but plague and torment.

MARIANE. I think . . .

MADAME PERNELLE. O dearie me, his little sister!
You're all demureness, butter wouldn't melt
In your mouth, one would think to look at you.
Still waters, though, they say . . . you know the proverb;
And I don't like your doings on the sly.

ELMIRE. But, mother . . .

MADAME PERNELLE. Daughter, by your leave, your conduct
In everything is altogether wrong;
You ought to set a good example for 'em;
Their dear departed mother did much better.
You are extravagant; and it offends me,
To see you always decked out like a princess.
A woman who would please her husband's eyes
Alone, wants no such wealth of fineries.

CLEANTE. But, madam, after all . . .

MADAME PERNELLE. Sir, as for you,
The lady's brother, I esteem you highly,
Love and respect you. But, sir, all the same,
If I were in my son's, her husband's, place,
I'd urgently entreat you not to come
Within our doors. You preach a way of living
That decent people cannot tolerate.
I'm rather frank with you; but that's my way—
I don't mince matters, when I mean a thing.

DAMIS. Mr. Tartuffe, your friend, is mighty lucky . . .

MADAME PERNELLE. He is a holy man, and must be heeded;
I can't endure, with any show of patience,
To hear a scatterbrains like you attack him.

DAMIS. What! Shall I let a bigot criticaster
Come and usurp a tyrant's power here?
And shall we never dare amuse ourselves
Till this fine gentleman deigns to consent?

DORINE. If we must hark to him, and heed his maxims,
There's not a thing we do but what's a crime;

He censures everything, this zealous carper.
MADAME PERNELLE. And all he censures is well censured, too.
He wants to guide you on the way to heaven;
My son should train you all to love him well.
DAMIS. No, madam, look you, nothing—not my father
Nor anything—can make me tolerate him.
I should belie my feelings not to say so.
His actions rouse my wrath at every turn;
And I foresee that there must come of it
An open rupture with this sneaking scoundrel.
DORINE. Besides, 'tis downright scandalous to see
This unknown upstart master of the house—
This vagabond, who hadn't, when he came,
Shoes to his feet, or clothing worth six farthings,
And who so far forgets his place, as now
To censure everything, and rule the roost!
MADAME PERNELLE. Eh! Mercy sakes alive! Things would go better
If all were governed by his pious orders.
DORINE. He passes for a saint in your opinion.
In fact, he's nothing but a hypocrite.
MADAME PERNELLE. Just listen to her tongue!
DORINE. I wouldn't trust him,
Nor yet his Lawrence, without bonds and surety.
MADAME PERNELLE. I don't know what the servant's character
May be; but I can guarantee the master
A holy man. You hate him and reject him
Because he tells home truths to all of you.
'Tis sin alone that moves his heart to anger,
And heaven's interest is his only motive.
DORINE. Of course. But why, especially of late,
Can he let nobody come near the house?
Is heaven offended at a civil call
That he should make so great a fuss about it?
I'll tell you, if you like, just what I think;

[*pointing to* ELMIRE.]

Upon my word, he's jealous of our mistress.
MADAME PERNELLE. You hold your tongue, and think what you are saying.
He's not alone in censuring these visits;
The turmoil that attends your sort of people,
Their carriages forever at the door,
And all their noisy footmen, flocked together,

Annoy the neighbourhood, and raise a scandal.
I'd gladly think there's nothing really wrong;
But it makes talk; and that's not as it should be.
CLEANTE. Eh! madam, can you hope to keep folk's tongues
From wagging? It would be a grievous thing
If, for the fear of idle talk about us,
We had to sacrifice our friends. No, no;
Even if we could bring ourselves to do it,
Think you that everyone would then be silenced?
Against backbiting there is no defence
So let us try to live in innocence,
To silly tattle pay no heed at all,
And leave the gossips free to vent their gall.
DORINE. Our neighbour Daphne, and her little husband,
Must be the ones who slander us, I'm thinking.
Those whose own conduct's most ridiculous,
Are always quickest to speak ill of others;
They never fail to seize at once upon
The slightest hint of any love affair,
And spread the news of it with glee, and give it
The character they'd have the world believe in.
By others' actions, painted in their colours,
They hope to justify their own; they think,
In the false hope of some resemblance, either
To make their own intrigues seem innocent,
Or else to make their neighbours share the blame
Which they are loaded with by everybody.
MADAME PERNELLE. These arguments are nothing to the purpose.
Orante, we all know, lives a perfect life;
Her thoughts are all of heaven; and I have heard
That she condemns the company you keep.
DORINE. O admirable pattern! Virtuous dame!
She lives the model of austerity;
But age has brought this piety upon her,
And she's a prude, now she can't help herself.
As long as she could capture men's attentions
She made the most of her advantages;
But, now she sees her beauty vanishing,
She wants to leave the world, that's leaving her,
And in the specious veil of haughty virtue
She'd hide the weakness of her worn-out charms.
That is the way with all your old coquettes;
They find it hard to see their lovers leave 'em;
And thus abandoned, their forlorn estate
Can find no occupation but a prude's.

These pious dames, in their austerity,
Must carp at everything, and pardon nothing.
They loudly blame their neighbours' way of living,
Not for religion's sake, but out of envy,
Because they can't endure to see another
Enjoy the pleasures age has weaned them from.

MADAME PERNELLE. [*to* ELMIRE.] There! That's the kind of rigmarole to please you,
Daughter-in-law. One never has a chance
To get a word in edgewise, at your house,
Because this lady holds the floor all day;
But none the less, I mean to have my say, too.
I tell you that my son did nothing wiser
In all his life, than take this godly man
Into his household; heaven sent him here,
In your great need, to make you all repent;
For your salvation, you must hearken to him;
He censures nothing but deserves his censure.
These visits, these assemblies, and these balls,
Are all inventions of the evil spirit.
You never hear a word of godliness
At them—but idle cackle, nonsense, flimflam.
Our neighbour often comes in for a share,
The talk flies fast, and scandal fills the air;
It makes a sober person's head go round,
At these assemblies, just to hear the sound
Of so much gab, with not a word to say;
And as a learned man remarked one day
Most aptly, 'tis the Tower of Babylon,
Where all, beyond all limit, babble on.
And just to tell you how this point came in . . .

[*to* CLEANTE.]

So! Now the gentlemen must snicker, must he?
Go find fools like yourself to make you laugh
And don't . . .

[*to* ELMIRE.]

Daughter, good-bye; not one word more.
As for this house, I leave the half unsaid;
But I shan't soon set foot in it again,

[*cuffing* FLIPOTTE.]

Come, you! What makes you dream and stand agape,
Hussy! I'll warm your ears in proper shape!
March, trollop, march!

SCENE II.

[CLEANTE, DORINE.]

CLEANTE. I won't escort her down,
For fear she might fall foul of me again;
The good old lady . . .
DORINE. Bless us! What a pity
She shouldn't hear the way you speak of her!
She'd surely tell you you're too "good" by half,
And that she's not so "old" as all that, neither!
CLEANTE. How she got angry with us all for nothing!
And how she seems possessed with her Tartuffe!
DORINE. Her case is nothing, though, beside her son's!
To see him, you would say he's ten times worse!
His conduct in our late unpleasantness[25]
Had won him much esteem, and proved his courage
In service of his king; but now he's like
A man besotted, since he's been so taken
With this Tartuffe. He calls him brother, loves him
A hundred times as much as mother, son,
Daughter, and wife. He tells him all his secrets
And lets him guide his acts, and rule his conscience.
He fondles and embraces him; a sweetheart
Could not, I think, be loved more tenderly;
At table he must have the seat of honour,
While with delight our master sees him eat
As much as six men could; we must give up
The choicest tidbits to him; if he belches,

['*tis a servant speaking*.][26]

Master exclaims: "God bless you!"—Oh, he dotes
Upon him! he's his universe, his hero;
He's lost in constant admiration, quotes him

[25] Referring to the rebellion called La Fronde, during the minority of Louis XIV.

[26] Moliere's note, inserted in the text of all the old editions. It is a curious illustration of the desire for uniformity and dignity of style in dramatic verse of the seventeenth century, that Moliere feels called on to apologize for a touch of realism like this. Indeed, these lines were even omitted when the play was given.

On all occasions, takes his trifling acts
For wonders, and his words for oracles.
The fellow knows his dupe, and makes the most on't,
He fools him with a hundred masks of virtue,
Gets money from him all the time by canting,
And takes upon himself to carp at us.
Even his silly coxcomb of a lackey
Makes it his business to instruct us too;
He comes with rolling eyes to preach at us,
And throws away our ribbons, rouge, and patches.
The wretch, the other day, tore up a kerchief
That he had found, pressed in the *Golden Legend*,
Calling it a horrid crime for us to mingle
The devil's finery with holy things.

Scene III.

[ELMIRE, MARIANE, DAMIS, CLEANTE, DORINE.]

ELMIRE. [*to* CLEANTE.] You're very lucky to have missed the speech
She gave us at the door. I see my husband
Is home again. He hasn't seen me yet,
So I'll go up and wait till he comes in.
CLEANTE. And I, to save time, will await him here;
I'll merely say good-morning, and be gone.

Scene IV.

[CLEANTE, DAMIS, DORINE.]

DAMIS. I wish you'd say a word to him about
My sister's marriage; I suspect Tartuffe
Opposes it, and puts my father up
To all these wretched shifts. You know, besides,
How nearly I'm concerned in it myself;
If love unites my sister and Valere,
I love his sister too; and if this marriage
Were to . . .
DORINE. He's coming.

SCENE V.

[ORGON, CLEANTE, DORINE.]

ORGON. Ah! Good morning, brother.
CLEANTE. I was just going, but am glad to greet you.
Things are not far advanced yet, in the country?
ORGON. Dorine . . .

[*to* CLEANTE.]

Just wait a bit, please, brother-in-law.
Let me allay my first anxiety
By asking news about the family.

[*to* DORINE.]

Has everything gone well these last two days?
What's happening? And how is everybody?

DORINE. Madam had fever, and a splitting headache
Day before yesterday, all day and evening.
ORGON. And how about Tartuffe?
DORINE. Tartuffe? He's well;
He's mighty well; stout, fat, fair, rosy-lipped.
ORGON. Poor man!
DORINE. At evening she had nausea
And could't touch a single thing for supper,
Her headache still was so severe.
ORGON. And how
About Tartuffe?
DORINE. He supped alone, before her,
And unctuously ate up two partridges,
As well as half a leg o' mutton, deviled.
ORGON. Poor man!
DORINE. All night she couldn't get a wink
Of sleep, the fever racked her so; and we
Had to sit up with her till daylight.
ORGON. How
About Tartuffe?
DORINE. Gently inclined to slumber,
He left the table, went into his room,
Got himself straight into a good warm bed,
And slept quite undisturbed until next morning.

ORGON. Poor man!
DORINE. At last she let us all persuade her,
And got up courage to be bled; and then
She was relieved at once.
ORGON. And how about
Tartuffe?
DORINE. He plucked up courage properly,
Bravely entrenched his soul against all evils,
And to replace the blood that she had lost,
He drank at breakfast four huge draughts of wine.
ORGON. Poor man!
DORINE. So now they both are doing well;
And I'll go straightway and inform my mistress
How pleased you are at her recovery.

SCENE VI.

[ORGON, CLEANTE.]

CLEANTE. Brother, she ridicules you to your face;
And I, though I don't want to make you angry,
Must tell you candidly that she's quite right.
Was such infatuation ever heard of?
And can a man to-day have charms to make you
Forget all else, relieve his poverty,
Give him a home, and then . . . ?
ORGON. Stop there, good brother,
You do not know the man you're speaking of.
CLEANTE. Since you will have it so, I do not know him;
But after all, to tell what sort of man
He is . . .
ORGON. Dear brother, you'd be charmed to know him;
Your raptures over him would have no end.
He is a man . . . who . . . ah! . . . in fact . . .a man
Whoever does his will, knows perfect peace,
And counts the whole world else, as so much dung.
His converse has transformed me quite; he weans
My heart from every friendship, teaches me
To have no love for anything on earth;
And I could see my brother, children, mother,
And wife, all die, and never care—a snap.
CLEANTE. Your feelings are humane, I must say, brother!
ORGON. Ah! If you'd seen him, as I saw him first,
You would have loved him just as much as I.
He came to church each day, with contrite mien,

Kneeled, on both knees, right opposite my place,
And drew the eyes of all the congregation,
To watch the fervour of his prayers to heaven;
With deep-drawn sighs and great ejaculations,
He humbly kissed the earth at every moment;
And when I left the church, he ran before me
To give me holy water at the door.
I learned his poverty, and who he was,
By questioning his servant, who is like him,
And gave him gifts; but in his modesty
He always wanted to return a part.
"It is too much," he'd say, "too much by half;
I am not worthy of your pity." Then,
When I refused to take it back, he'd go,
Before my eyes, and give it to the poor.
At length heaven bade me take him to my home,
And since that day, all seems to prosper here.
He censures everything, and for my sake
He even takes great interest in my wife;
He lets me know who ogles her, and seems
Six times as jealous as I am myself.
You'd not believe how far his zeal can go:
He calls himself a sinner just for trifles;
The merest nothing is enough to shock him;
So much so, that the other day I heard him
Accuse himself for having, while at prayer,
In too much anger caught and killed a flea.

CLEANTE. Zounds, brother, you are mad, I think! Or else
You're making sport of me, with such a speech.
What are you driving at with all this nonsense . . . ?

ORGON. Brother, your language smacks of atheism;
And I suspect your soul's a little tainted
Therewith. I've preached to you a score of times
That you'll draw down some judgment on your head.

CLEANTE. That is the usual strain of all your kind;
They must have every one as blind as they.
They call you atheist if you have good eyes;
And if you don't adore their vain grimaces,
You've neither faith nor care for sacred things.
No, no; such talk can't frighten me; I know
What I am saying; heaven sees my heart.
We're not the dupes of all your canting mummers;
There are false heroes—and false devotees;
And as true heroes never are the ones
Who make much noise about their deeds of honour,

Just so true devotees, whom we should follow,
Are not the ones who make so much vain show.
What! Will you find no difference between
Hypocrisy and genuine devoutness?
And will you treat them both alike, and pay
The self-same honour both to masks and faces
Set artifice beside sincerity,
Confuse the semblance with reality,
Esteem a phantom like a living person,
And counterfeit as good as honest coin?
Men, for the most part, are strange creatures, truly!
You never find them keep the golden mean;
The limits of good sense, too narrow for them,
Must always be passed by, in each direction;
They often spoil the noblest things, because
They go too far, and push them to extremes.
I merely say this by the way, good brother.

ORGON. You are the sole expounder of the doctrine;
Wisdom shall die with you, no doubt, good brother,
You are the only wise, the sole enlightened,
The oracle, the Cato, of our age.
All men, compared to you, are downright fools.

CLEANTE. I'm not the sole expounder of the doctrine,
And wisdom shall not die with me, good brother.
But this I know, though it be all my knowledge,
That there's a difference 'twixt false and true.
And as I find no kind of hero more
To be admired than men of true religion,
Nothing more noble or more beautiful
Than is the holy zeal of true devoutness;
Just so I think there's naught more odious
Than whited sepulchres of outward unction,
Those barefaced charlatans, those hireling zealots,
Whose sacrilegious, treacherous pretence
Deceives at will, and with impunity
Makes mockery of all that men hold sacred;
Men who, enslaved to selfish interests,
Make trade and merchandise of godliness,
And try to purchase influence and office
With false eye-rollings and affected raptures;
Those men, I say, who with uncommon zeal
Seek their own fortunes on the road to heaven;
Who, skilled in prayer, have always much to ask,
And live at court to preach retirement;
Who reconcile religion with their vices,

Are quick to anger, vengeful, faithless, tricky,
And, to destroy a man, will have the boldness
To call their private grudge the cause of heaven;
All the more dangerous, since in their anger
They use against us weapons men revere,
And since they make the world applaud their passion,
And seek to stab us with a sacred sword.
There are too many of this canting kind.
Still, the sincere are easy to distinguish;
And many splendid patterns may be found,
In our own time, before our very eyes
Look at Ariston, Periandre, Oronte,
Alcidamas, Clitandre, and Polydore;
No one denies their claim to true religion;
Yet they're no braggadocios of virtue,
They do not make insufferable display,
And their religion's human, tractable;
They are not always judging all our actions,
They'd think such judgment savoured of presumption;
And, leaving pride of words to other men,
'Tis by their deeds alone they censure ours.
Evil appearances find little credit
With them; they even incline to think the best
Of others. No caballers, no intriguers,
They mind the business of their own right living.
They don't attack a sinner tooth and nail,
For sin's the only object of their hatred;
Nor are they over-zealous to attempt
Far more in heaven's behalf than heaven would have 'em.
That is my kind of man, that is true living,
That is the pattern we should set ourselves.
Your fellow was not fashioned on this model;
You're quite sincere in boasting of his zeal;
But you're deceived, I think, by false pretences.

ORGON. My dear good brother-in-law, have you quite done?

CLEANTE. Yes.

ORGON. I'm your humble servant.

[*starts to go.*]

CLEANTE. Just a word.
We'll drop that other subject. But you know
Valere has had the promise of your daughter.

ORGON. Yes.

CLEANTE. You had named the happy day.

ORGON. 'Tis true.
CLEANTE. Then why put off the celebration of it?
ORGON. I can't say.
CLEANTE. Can you have some other plan
In mind?
ORGON. Perhaps.
CLEANTE. You mean to break your word?
ORGON. I don't say that.
CLEANTE. I hope no obstacle
Can keep you from performing what you've promised.
ORGON. Well, that depends.
CLEANTE. Why must you beat about?
Valere has sent me here to settle matters.
ORGON. Heaven be praised!
CLEANTE. What answer shall I take him?
ORGON. Why, anything you please.
CLEANTE. But we must know
Your plans. What are they?
ORGON. I shall do the will
Of Heaven.
CLEANTE. Come, be serious. You've given
Your promise to Valere. Now will you keep it?
ORGON. Good-bye.
CLEANTE. [*alone.*] His love, methinks, has much to fear;
I must go let him know what's happening here.

ACT II.

SCENE I.

[ORGON, MARIANE.]

ORGON. Now, Mariane.
MARIANE. Yes, father?
ORGON. Come; I'll tell you
A secret.
MARIANE. Yes . . . What are you looking for?
ORGON. [*looking into a small closet-room.*]
To see there's no one there to spy upon us;
That little closet's mighty fit to hide in.
There! We're all right now. Mariane, in you
I've always found a daughter dutiful
And gentle. So I've always love you dearly.
MARIANE. I'm grateful for your fatherly affection.
ORGON. Well spoken, daughter. Now, prove you deserve it

By doing as I wish in all respects.
MARIANE. To do so is the height of my ambition.
ORGON. Excellent well. What say you of—Tartuffe?
MARIANE. Who? I?
ORGON. Yes, you. Look to it how you answer.
MARIANE. Why! I'll say of him—anything you please.

SCENE II.

[ORGON, MARIANE, DORINE.]

[*coming in quietly and standing behind* ORGON, *so that he does not see her*.]

ORGON. Well spoken. A good girl. Say then, my daughter,
That all his person shines with noble merit,
That he has won your heart, and you would like
To have him, by my choice, become your husband.
Eh?
MARIANE. Eh?
ORGON. What say you?
MARIANE. Please, what did you say?
ORGON. What?
MARIANE. Surely I mistook you, sir?
ORGON. How now?
MARIANE. Who is it, father, you would have me say
Has won my heart, and I would like to have
Become my husband, by your choice?
ORGON. Tartuffe.
MARIANE. But, father, I protest it isn't true!
Why should you make me tell this dreadful lie?
ORGON. Because I mean to have it be the truth.
Let this suffice for you: I've settled it.
MARIANE. What, father, you would . . . ?
ORGON. Yes, child, I'm resolved
To graft Tartuffe into my family.
So he must be your husband. That I've settled.
And since your duty . .

[*seeing* DORINE.]

What are you doing there?
Your curiosity is keen, my girl,
To make you come eavesdropping on us so.

DORINE. Upon my word, I don't know how the rumour
Got started—if 'twas guess-work or mere chance
But I had heard already of this match,
And treated it as utter stuff and nonsense.
ORGON. What! Is the thing incredible?
DORINE. So much so
I don't believe it even from yourself, sir.
ORGON. I know a way to make you credit it.
DORINE. No, no, you're telling us a fairly tale!
ORGON. I'm telling you just what will happen shortly.
DORINE. Stuff!
ORGON. Daughter, what I say is in good earnest.
DORINE. There, there, don't take your father seriously;
He's fooling.
ORGON. But I tell you . . .
DORINE. No. No use.
They won't believe you.
ORGON. If I let my anger . . .
DORINE. Well, then, we do believe you; and the worse
For you it is. What! Can a grown-up man
With that expanse of beard across his face
Be mad enough to want . . .?
ORGON. You hark me:
You've taken on yourself here in this house
A sort of free familiarity
That I don't like, I tell you frankly, girl.
DORINE. There, there, let's not get angry, sir, I beg you.
But are you making game of everybody?
Your daughter's not cut out for bigot's meat;
And he has more important things to think of.
Besides, what can you gain by such a match?
How can a man of wealth, like you, go choose
A wretched vagabond for son-in-law?
ORGON. You hold your tongue. And know, the less he has,
The better cause have we to honour him.
His poverty is honest poverty;
It should exalt him more than worldly grandeur,
For he has let himself be robbed of all,
Through careless disregard of temporal things
And fixed attachment to the things eternal.
My help may set him on his feet again,
Win back his property—a fair estate
He has at home, so I'm informed—and prove him
For what he is, a true-born gentleman.
DORINE. Yes, so he says himself. Such vanity

But ill accords with pious living, sir.
The man who cares for holiness alone
Should not so loudly boast his name and birth;
The humble ways of genuine devoutness
Brook not so much display of earthly pride.
Why should he be so vain? . . . But I offend you:
Let's leave his rank, then,—take the man himself:
Can you without compunction give a man
Like him possession of a girl like her?
Think what a scandal's sure to come of it!
Virtue is at the mercy of the fates,
When a girl's married to a man she hates;
The best intent to live an honest woman
Depends upon the husband's being human,
And men whose brows are pointed at afar
May thank themselves their wives are what they are.
For to be true is more than woman can,
With husbands built upon a certain plan;
And he who weds his child against her will
Owes heaven account for it, if she do ill.
Think then what perils wait on your design.

ORGON. [*to Mariane.*] So! I must learn what's what from her, you see!

DORINE. You might do worse than follow my advice.

ORGON. Daughter, we can't waste time upon this nonsense;
I know what's good for you, and I'm your father.
True, I had promised you to young Valere;
But, first, they tell me he's inclined to gamble,
And then, I fear his faith is not quite sound.
I haven't noticed that he's regular
At church.

DORINE. You'd have him run there just when you do.
Like those who go on purpose to be seen?

ORGON. I don't ask your opinion on the matter.
In short, the other is in Heaven's best graces,
And that is riches quite beyond compare.
This match will bring you every joy you long for;
'Twill be all steeped in sweetness and delight.
You'll live together, in your faithful loves,
Like two sweet children, like two turtle-doves;
You'll never fail to quarrel, scold, or tease,
And you may do with him whate'er you please.

DORINE. With him? Do naught but give him horns, I'll warrant.

ORGON. Out on thee, wench!

DORINE. I tell you he's cut out for't;
However great your daughter's virtue, sir,

His destiny is sure to prove the stronger.

ORGON. Have done with interrupting. Hold your tongue.
Don't poke your nose in other people's business.

DORINE. [*she keeps interrupting him, just as he turns and starts to speak to his daughter.*] If I make bold, sir, 'tis for your own good.

ORGON. You're too officious; pray you, hold your tongue.

DORINE. 'Tis love of you . . .

ORGON. I want none of your love.

DORINE. Then I will love you in your own despite.

ORGON. You will, eh?

DORINE. Yes, your honour's dear to me;
I can't endure to see you made the butt
Of all men's ridicule.

ORGON. Won't you be still?

DORINE. 'Twould be a sin to let you make this match.

ORGON. Won't you be still, I say, you impudent viper!

DORINE. What! you are pious, and you lose your temper?

ORGON. I'm all wrought up, with your confounded nonsense;
Now, once for all, I tell you hold your tongue.

DORINE. Then mum's the word; I'll take it out in thinking.

ORGON. Think all you please; but not a syllable
To me about it, or . . . you understand!

[*turning to his daughter.*]

As a wise father, I've considered all
With due deliberation.

DORINE. I'll go mad
If I can't speak.

[*she stops the instant he turns his head.*]

ORGON. Though he's no lady's man,
Tartuffe is well enough . . .

DORINE. A pretty phiz!

ORGON. So that, although you may not care at all
For his best qualities . . .

DORINE. A handsome dowry!

[ORGON *turns and stands in front of her, with arms folded, eyeing her.*]

Were I in her place, any man should rue it
Who married me by force, that's mighty certain;

I'd let him know, and that within a week,
A woman's vengeance isn't far to seek.

ORGON. [*to* DORINE.] So—nothing that I say has any weight?
DORINE. Eh? What's wrong now? I didn't speak to you.
ORGON. What were you doing?
DORINE. Talking to myself.
ORGON. Oh! Very well. [*aside.*] Her monstrous impudence
Must be chastised with one good slap in the face.

[*he stands ready to strike her, and, each time he speaks to his daughter, he glances toward her; but she stands still and says not a word.*][27]

ORGON. Daughter, you must approve of my design. . . .
Think of this husband . . . I have chosen for you. . .

[*to* DORINE.]

Why don't you talk to yourself?

DORINE. Nothing to say.
ORGON. One little word more.
DORINE. Oh, no, thanks. Not now.
ORGON. Sure, I'd have caught you.
DORINE. Faith, I'm no such fool.
ORGON. So, daughter, now obedience is the word;
You must accept my choice with reverence.
DORINE. [*running away.*]
You'd never catch me marrying such a creature.
ORGON. [*swinging his hand at her and missing her.*]
Daughter, you've such a pestilent hussy there
I can't live with her longer, without sin.

[27] As given at the Comedie francaise, the action is as follows: While Orgon says, "You must approve of my design," Dorine is making signs to Mariane to resist his orders; Orgon turns around suddenly; but Dorine quickly changes her gesture and with the hand which she had lifted calmly arranges her hair and her cap. Orgon goes on, "Think of the husband . . ." and stops before the middle of his sentence to turn and catch the beginning of Dorine's gesture; but he is too quick this time, and Dorine stands looking at his furious countenance with a sweet and gentle expression. He turns and goes on, and the obstinate Dorine again lifts her hand behind his shoulder to urge Mariane to resistance: this time he catches her; but just as he swings his shoulder to give her the promised blow, she stops him by changing the intent of her gesture, and carefully picking from the top of his sleeve a bit of fluff which she holds carefully between her fingers, then blows into the air, and watches intently as it floats away. Orgon is paralysed by her innocence of expression, and compelled to hide his rage.—Regnier, *Le Tartuffe des Comediens.*

I can't discuss things in the state I'm in.
My mind's so flustered by her insolent talk,
To calm myself, I must go take a walk.

SCENE III.

[MARIANE, DORINE.]

DORINE. Say, have you lost the tongue from out your head?
And must I speak your role from A to Zed?
You let them broach a project that's absurd,
And don't oppose it with a single word!
MARIANE. What can I do? My father is the master.
DORINE. Do? Everything, to ward off such disaster.
MARIANE. But what?
DORINE. Tell him one doesn't love by proxy;
Tell him you'll marry for yourself, not him;
Since you're the one for whom the thing is done,
You are the one, not he, the man must please;
If his Tartuffe has charmed him so, why let him
Just marry him himself—no one will hinder.
MARIANE. A father's rights are such, it seems to me,
That I could never dare to say a word.
DORINE. Came, talk it out. Valere has asked your hand:
Now do you love him, pray, or do you not?
MARIANE. Dorine! How can you wrong my love so much,
And ask me such a question? Have I not
A hundred times laid bare my heart to you?
Do you know how ardently I love him?
DORINE. How do I know if heart and words agree,
And if in honest truth you really love him?
MARIANE. Dorine, you wrong me greatly if you doubt it;
I've shown my inmost feelings, all too plainly.
DORINE. So then, you love him?
MARIANE. Yes, devotedly.
DORINE. And he returns your love, apparently?
MARIANE. I think so.
DORINE. And you both alike are eager
To be well married to each other?
MARIANE. Surely.
DORINE. Then what's your plan about this other match?
MARIANE. To kill myself, if it is forced upon me.
DORINE. Good! That's a remedy I hadn't thought of.
Just die, and everything will be all right.
This medicine is marvellous, indeed!

It drives me mad to hear folk talk such nonsense.
MARIANE. Oh dear, Dorine you get in such a temper!
You have no sympathy for people's troubles.
DORINE. I have no sympathy when folk talk nonsense,
And flatten out as you do, at a pinch.
MARIANE. But what can you expect?—if one is timid?—
DORINE. But what is love worth, if it has no courage?
MARIANE. Am I not constant in my love for him?
Is't not his place to win me from my father?
DORINE. But if your father is a crazy fool,
And quite bewitched with his Tartuffe? And breaks
His bounden word? Is that your lover's fault?
MARIANE. But shall I publicly refuse and scorn
This match, and make it plain that I'm in love?
Shall I cast off for him, whate'er he be,
Womanly modesty and filial duty?
You ask me to display my love in public . . . ?
DORINE. No, no, I ask you nothing. You shall be
Mister Tartuffe's; why, now I think of it,
I should be wrong to turn you from this marriage.
What cause can I have to oppose your wishes?
So fine a match! An excellent good match!
Mister Tartuffe! Oh ho! No mean proposal!
Mister Tartuffe, sure, take it all in all,
Is not a man to sneeze at—oh, by no means!
'Tis no small luck to be his happy spouse.
The whole world joins to sing his praise already;
He's noble—in his parish; handsome too;
Red ears and high complexion—oh, my lud!
You'll be too happy, sure, with him for husband.
MARIANE. Oh dear! . . .
DORINE. What joy and pride will fill your heart
To be the bride of such a handsome fellow!
MARIANE. Oh, stop, I beg you; try to find some way
To help break off the match. I quite give in,
I'm ready to do anything you say.
DORINE. No, no, a daughter must obey her father,
Though he should want to make her wed a monkey.
Besides, your fate is fine. What could be better!
You'll take the stage-coach to his little village,
And find it full of uncles and of cousins,
Whose conversation will delight you. Then
You'll be presented in their best society.
You'll even go to call, by way of welcome,
On Mrs. Bailiff, Mrs. Tax-Collector,

Who'll patronise you with a folding-stool.
There, once a year, at carnival, you'll have
Perhaps—a ball; with orchestra—two bag-pipes;
And sometimes a trained ape, and Punch and Judy;
Though if your husband . . .

MARIANE. Oh, you'll kill me. Please
Contrive to help me out with your advice.

DORINE. I thank you kindly.

MARIANE. Oh! Dorine, I beg you . . .

DORINE. To serve you right, this marriage must go through.

MARIANE. Dear girl!

DORINE. No.

MARIANE. If I say I love Valere . . .

DORINE. No, no. Tartuffe's your man, and you shall taste him.

MARIANE. You know I've always trusted you; now help me . . .

DORINE. No, you shall be, my faith! Tartuffified.

MARIANE. Well, then, since you've no pity for my fate
Let me take counsel only of despair;
It will advise and help and give me courage;
There's one sure cure, I know, for all my troubles.

[*she starts to go.*]

DORINE. There, there! Come back. I can't be angry long.
I must take pity on you, after all.

MARIANE. Oh, don't you see, Dorine, if I must bear
This martyrdom, I certainly shall die.

DORINE. Now don't you fret. We'll surely find some way.
To hinder this . . . But here's Valere, your lover.

SCENE IV.

[VALERE, MARIANE, DORINE.]

VALERE. Madam, a piece of news—quite new to me—
Has just come out, and very fine it is.

MARIANE. What piece of news?

VALERE. Your marriage with Tartuffe.

MARIANE. 'Tis true my father has this plan in mind.

VALERE. Your father, madam . . .

MARIANE. Yes, he's changed his plans,
And did but now propose it to me.

VALERE. What!
Seriously?

MARIANE. Yes, he was serious,

And openly insisted on the match.
VALERE. And what's your resolution in the matter,
Madam?
MARIANE. I don't know.
VALERE. That's a pretty answer.
You don't know?
MARIANE. No.
VALERE. No?
MARIANE. What do you advise?
VALERE. I? My advice is, marry him, by all means.
MARIANE. That's your advice?
VALERE. Yes.
MARIANE. Do you mean it?
VALERE. Surely.
A splendid choice, and worthy of your acceptance.
MARIANE. Oh, very well, sir! I shall take your counsel.
VALERE. You'll find no trouble taking it, I warrant.
MARIANE. No more than you did giving it, be sure.
VALERE. I gave it, truly, to oblige you, madam.
MARIANE. And I shall take it to oblige you, sir.
DORINE. [*withdrawing to the back of the stage.*]
Let's see what this affair will come to.
VALERE. So,
That is your love? And it was all deceit
When you . . .
MARIANE. I beg you, say no more of that.
You told me, squarely, sir, I should accept
The husband that is offered me; and I
Will tell you squarely that I mean to do so,
Since you have given me this good advice.
VALERE. Don't shield yourself with talk of my advice.
You had your mind made up, that's evident;
And now you're snatching at a trifling pretext
To justify the breaking of your word.
MARIANE. Exactly so.
VALERE. Of course it is; your heart
Has never known true love for me.
MARIANE. Alas!
You're free to think so, if you please.
VALERE. Yes, yes,
I'm free to think so; and my outraged love
May yet forestall you in your perfidy,
And offer elsewhere both my heart and hand.
MARIANE. No doubt of it; the love your high deserts
May win . . .

VALERE. Good Lord, have done with my deserts!
I know I have but few, and you have proved it.
But I may find more kindness in another;
I know of someone, who'll not be ashamed
To take your leavings, and make up my loss.
MARIANE. The loss is not so great; you'll easily
Console yourself completely for this change.
VALERE. I'll try my best, that you may well believe.
When we're forgotten by a woman's heart,
Our pride is challenged; we, too, must forget;
Or if we cannot, must at least pretend to.
No other way can man such baseness prove,
As be a lover scorned, and still in love.
MARIANE. In faith, a high and noble sentiment.
VALERE. Yes; and it's one that all men must approve.
What! Would you have me keep my love alive,
And see you fly into another's arms
Before my very eyes; and never offer
To someone else the heart that you had scorned?
MARIANE. Oh, no, indeed! For my part, I could wish
That it were done already.
VALERE. What! You wish it?
MARIANE. Yes.
VALERE. This is insult heaped on injury;
I'll go at once and do as you desire.

[*he takes a step or two as if to go away.*]

MARIANE. Oh, very well then.
VALERE. [*turning back.*] But remember this.
'Twas you that drove me to this desperate pass.
MARIANE. Of course.
VALERE. [*turning back again.*]
And in the plan that I have formed
I only follow your example.
MARIANE. Yes.
VALERE. [*at the door.*] Enough; you shall be punctually obeyed.
MARIANE. So much the better.
VALERE. [*coming back again.*] This is once for all.
MARIANE. So be it, then.
VALERE. [*he goes toward the door, but just as he reaches it, turns around.*] Eh?
MARIANE. What?
VALERE. You didn't call me?
MARIANE. I? You are dreaming.

VALERE. Very well, I'm gone.
    Madam, farewell.

[*he walks slowly away.*]

MARIANE. Farewell, sir.
DORINE. I must say
    You've lost your senses and both gone clean daft!
    I've let you fight it out to the end o' the chapter
    To see how far the thing could go. Oho, there,
    Mister Valere!

[*she goes and seizes him by the arm, to stop him. He makes a great show of resistance.*]

VALERE. What do you want, Dorine?
DORINE. Come here.
VALERE. No, no, I'm quite beside myself.
    Don't hinder me from doing as she wishes.
DORINE. Stop!
VALERE. No. You see, I'm fixed, resolved, determined.
DORINE. So!
MARIANE. [*aside.*] Since my presence pains him, makes him go,
    I'd better go myself, and leave him free.
DORINE. [*leaving* VALERE, *and running after* MARIANE.]
    Now t'other! Where are you going?
MARIANE. Let me be.
DORINE. Come back.
MARIANE. No, no, it isn't any use.
VALERE. [*aside.*] 'Tis clear the sight of me is torture to her;
    No doubt, t'were better I should free her from it.
DORINE. [*leaving* MARIANE *and running after* VALERE.]
    Same thing again! Deuce take you both, I say.
    Now stop your fooling; come here, you; and you.

[*she pulls first one, then the other, toward the middle of the stage.*]

VALERE. [*to* DORINE.] What's your idea?
MARIANE. [*to* DORINE.] What can you mean to do?
DORINE. Set you to rights, and pull you out o' the scrape.

[*to* VALERE.]

Are you quite mad, to quarrel with her now?

VALERE. Didn't you hear the things she said to me?
DORINE. [*to* MARIANE.] Are you quite mad, to get in such a passion?
MARIANE. Didn't you see the way he treated me?
DORINE. Fools, both of you.

[*to* VALERE.]

She thinks of nothing else
But to keep faith with you, I vouch for it.

[*to* MARIANE.]

And he loves none but you, and longs for nothing
But just to marry you, I stake my life on't.

MARIANE. [*to* VALERE.] Why did you give me such advice then, pray?
VALERE. [*to* MARIANE.] Why ask for my advice on such a matter?
DORINE. You both are daft, I tell you. Here, your hands.

[*to* VALERE.]

Come, yours.

VALERE. [*giving* DORINE *his hand.*] What for?
DORINE. [*to* MARIANE.] Now, yours.
MARIANE. [*giving* DORINE *her hand.*] But what's the use?
DORINE. Oh, quick now, come along. There, both of you—
You love each other better than you think.

[VALERE *and* MARIANE *hold each other's hands some time without looking at each other.*]

VALERE. [*at last turning toward* MARIANE.] Come, don't be so ungracious now about it;
Look at a man as if you didn't hate him.

[MARIANE *looks sideways toward* VALERE, *with just a bit of a smile.*]

DORINE. My faith and troth, what fools these lovers be!
VALERE. [*to* MARIANE.] But come now, have I not a just complaint?
And truly, are you not a wicked creature
To take delight in saying what would pain me?

MARIANE. And are you not yourself the most ungrateful . . . ?
DORINE. Leave this discussion till another time;
Now, think how you'll stave off this plaguey marriage.
MARIANE. Then tell us how to go about it.
DORINE. Well,
We'll try all sorts of ways.

[*to* MARIANE.]

Your father's daft;

[*to* VALERE.]

This plan is nonsense.

[*to* MARIANE.]

You had better humour
His notions by a semblance of consent,
So that in case of danger, you can still
Find means to block the marriage by delay.
If you gain time, the rest is easy, trust me.
One day you'll fool them with a sudden illness,
Causing delay; another day, ill omens:
You've met a funeral, or broke a mirror,
Or dreamed of muddy water. Best of all,
They cannot marry you to anyone
Without your saying yes. But now, methinks,
They mustn't find you chattering together.

[*to* VALERE.]

You, go at once and set your friends at work
To make him keep his word to you; while we
Will bring the brother's influence to bear,
And get the step-mother on our side, too.
Good-bye.
VALERE. [*to* MARIANE.] Whatever efforts we may make,
My greatest hope, be sure, must rest on you.
MARIANE. [*to* VALERE.] I cannot answer for my father's whims;
But no one save Valere shall ever have me.
VALERE. You thrill me through with joy! Whatever comes . . .
DORINE. Oho! These lovers! Never done with prattling!
Now go.
VALERE. [*starting to go, and coming back again.*] One last word . . .

DORINE. What a gabble and pother!
Be off! By this door, you. And you, by t'other.

[*she pushes them off, by the shoulders, in opposite directions.*]

ACT III.

SCENE I.

[DAMIS, DORINE.]

DAMIS. May lightning strike me dead this very instant,
May I be everywhere proclaimed a scoundrel,
If any reverence or power shall stop me,
And if I don't do straightway something desperate!
DORINE. I beg you, moderate this towering passion;
Your father did but merely mention it.
Not all things that are talked of turn to facts;
The road is long, sometimes, from plans to acts.
DAMIS. No, I must end this paltry fellow's plots,
And he shall hear from me a truth or two.
DORINE. So ho! Go slow now. Just you leave the fellow—
Your father too—in your step-mother's hands.
She has some influence with this Tartuffe,
He makes a point of heeding all she says,
And I suspect that he is fond of her.
Would God 'twere true!—'Twould be the height of humour
Now, she has sent for him, in your behalf,
To sound him on this marriage, to find out
What his ideas are, and to show him plainly
What troubles he may cause, if he persists
In giving countenance to this design.
His man says, he's at prayers, I mustn't see him,
But likewise says, he'll presently be down.
So off with you, and let me wait for him.
DAMIS. I may be present at this interview.
DORINE. No, no! They must be left alone.
DAMIS. I won't
So much as speak to him.
DORINE. Go on! We know you
And your high tantrums. Just the way to spoil things!
Be off.
DAMIS. No, I must see—I'll keep my temper.
DORINE. Out on you, what a plague! He's coming. Hide!

[DAMIS *goes and hides in the closet at the back of the stage.*]

SCENE II.

[TARTUFFE, DORINE.]

TARTUFFE. [*speaking to his valet, off the stage, as soon as he sees* DORINE *is there.*]
Lawrence, put up my hair-cloth shirt and scourge,
And pray that Heaven may shed its light upon you.
If any come to see me, say I'm gone
To share my alms among the prisoners.
DORINE. [*aside.*] What affectation and what showing off!
TARTUFFE. What do you want with me?
DORINE. To tell you . . .
TARTUFFE. [*taking a handkerchief from his pocket.*] Ah!
Before you speak, pray take this handkerchief.
DORINE. What?
TARTUFFE. Cover up that bosom, which I can't
Endure to look on. Things like that offend
Our souls, and fill our minds with sinful thoughts.
DORINE. Are you so tender to temptation, then,
And has the flesh such power upon your senses?
I don't know how you get in such a heat;
For my part, I am not so prone to lust,
And I could see you stripped from head to foot,
And all your hide not tempt me in the least.
TARTUFFE. Show in your speech some little modesty,
Or I must instantly take leave of you.
DORINE. No, no, I'll leave you to yourself; I've only
One thing to say: Madam will soon be down,
And begs the favour of a word with you.
TARTUFFE. Ah! Willingly.
DORINE. [*aside.*] How gentle all at once!
My faith, I still believe I've hit upon it.
TARTUFFE. Will she come soon?
DORINE. I think I hear her now.
Yes, here she is herself; I'll leave you with her.

Scene III.

[ELMIRE, TARTUFFE.]

TARTUFFE. May Heaven's overflowing kindness ever
Give you good health of body and of soul,
And bless your days according to the wishes
And prayers of its most humble votary!
ELMIRE. I'm very grateful for your pious wishes.
But let's sit down, so we may talk at ease.
TARTUFFE. [*after sitting down.*]
And how are you recovered from your illness?
ELMIRE. [*sitting down also.*]
Quite well; the fever soon let go its hold.
TARTUFFE. My prayers, I fear, have not sufficient merit
To have drawn down this favour from on high;
But each entreaty that I made to Heaven
Had for its object your recovery.
ELMIRE. You're too solicitous on my behalf.
TARTUFFE. We could not cherish your dear health too much;
I would have given mine, to help restore it.
ELMIRE. That's pushing Christian charity too far;
I owe you many thanks for so much kindness.
TARTUFFE. I do far less for you than you deserve.
ELMIRE. There is a matter that I wished to speak of
In private; I am glad there's no one here
To listen.
TARTUFFE. Madam, I am overjoyed.
'Tis sweet to find myself alone with you.
This is an opportunity I've asked
Of Heaven, many a time; till now, in vain.
ELMIRE. All that I wish, is just a word from you,
Quite frank and open, hiding nothing from me.

[DAMIS, *without their seeing him, opens the closet door halfway.*]

TARTUFFE. I too could wish, as Heaven's especial favour,
To lay my soul quite open to your eyes,
And swear to you, the trouble that I made
About those visits which your charms attract,
Does not result from any hatred toward you,
But rather from a passionate devotion,
And purest motives . . .
ELMIRE. That is how I take it,

I think 'tis my salvation that concerns you.
TARTUFFE. [*pressing her finger tips.*] Madam, 'tis so; and such is my devotion . . .
ELMIRE. Ouch! but you squeeze too hard.
TARTUFFE. Excess of zeal.
In no way could I ever mean to hurt you,
And I'd as soon . . .

[*he puts his hand on her knee.*]

ELMIRE. What's your hand doing there?
TARTUFFE. Feeling your gown; the stuff is very soft.
ELMIRE. Let be, I beg you; I am very ticklish.

[*she moves her chair away, and* TARTUFFE *brings his nearer.*]

TARTUFFE. [*handling the lace yoke of* ELMIRE'*s dress.*]
Dear me how wonderful in workmanship
This lace is! They do marvels, nowadays;
Things of all kinds were never better made.
ELMIRE. Yes, very true. But let us come to business.
They say my husband means to break his word.
And marry Mariane to you. Is't so?
TARTUFFE. He did hint some such thing; but truly, madam,
That's not the happiness I'm yearning after;
I see elsewhere the sweet compelling charms
Of such a joy as fills my every wish.
ELMIRE. You mean you cannot love terrestrial things.
TARTUFFE. The heart within my bosom is not stone.
ELMIRE. I well believe your sighs all tend to Heaven,
And nothing here below can stay your thoughts.
TARTUFFE. Love for the beauty of eternal things
Cannot destroy our love for earthly beauty;
Our mortal senses well may be entranced
By perfect works that Heaven has fashioned here.
Its charms reflected shine in such as you,
And in yourself, its rarest miracles;
It has displayed such marvels in your face,
That eyes are dazed, and hearts are rapt away;
I could not look on you, the perfect creature,
Without admiring Nature's great Creator,
And feeling all my heart inflamed with love
For you, His fairest image of Himself.
At first I trembled lest this secret love
Might be the Evil Spirit's artful snare;

I even schooled my heart to flee your beauty,
Thinking it was a bar to my salvation.
But soon, enlightened, O all lovely one,
I saw how this my passion may be blameless,
How I may make it fit with modesty,
And thus completely yield my heart to it.
'Tis I must own, a great presumption in me
To dare make you the offer of my heart;
My love hopes all things from your perfect goodness,
And nothing from my own poor weak endeavour.
You are my hope, my stay, my peace of heart;
On you depends my torment or my bliss;
And by your doom of judgment, I shall be
Blest, if you will; or damned, by your decree.

ELMIRE. Your declaration's turned most gallantly;
But truly, it is just a bit surprising.
You should have better armed your heart, methinks,
And taken thought somewhat on such a matter.
A pious man like you, known everywhere . . .

TARTUFFE. Though pious, I am none the less a man;
And when a man beholds your heavenly charms,
The heart surrenders, and can think no more.
I know such words seem strange, coming from me;
But, madam, I'm no angel, after all;
If you condemn my frankly made avowal
You only have your charming self to blame.
Soon as I saw your more than human beauty,
You were thenceforth the sovereign of my soul;
Sweetness ineffable was in your eyes,
That took by storm my still resisting heart,
And conquered everything, fasts, prayers, and tears,
And turned my worship wholly to yourself.
My looks, my sighs, have spoke a thousand times;
Now, to express it all, my voice must speak.
If but you will look down with gracious favour
Upon the sorrows of your worthless slave,
If in your goodness you will give me comfort
And condescend unto my nothingness,
I'll ever pay you, O sweet miracle,
An unexampled worship and devotion.
Then too, with me your honour runs no risk;
With me you need not fear a public scandal.
These court gallants, that women are so fond of,
Are boastful of their acts, and vain in speech;
They always brag in public of their progress;

Soon as a favour's granted, they'll divulge it;
Their tattling tongues, if you but trust to them,
Will foul the altar where their hearts have worshipped.
But men like me are so discreet in love,
That you may trust their lasting secrecy.
The care we take to guard our own good name
May fully guarantee the one we love;
So you may find, with hearts like ours sincere,
Love without scandal, pleasure without fear.
ELMIRE. I've heard you through—your speech is clear, at least.
But don't you fear that I may take a fancy
To tell my husband of your gallant passion,
And that a prompt report of this affair
May somewhat change the friendship which he bears you?
TARTUFFE. I know that you're too good and generous,
That you will pardon my temerity,
Excuse, upon the score of human frailty,
The violence of passion that offends you,
And not forget, when you consult your mirror,
That I'm not blind, and man is made of flesh.
ELMIRE. Some women might do otherwise, perhaps,
But I am willing to employ discretion,
And not repeat the matter to my husband;
But in return, I'll ask one thing of you:
That you urge forward, frankly and sincerely,
The marriage of Valere to Mariane;
That you give up the unjust influence
By which you hope to win another's rights;
And . . .

SCENE IV.

[ELMIRE, DAMIS, TARTUFFE.]

DAMIS. [*coming out of the closet-room where he had been hiding.*]
No, I say! This thing must be made public.
I was just there, and overheard it all;
And Heaven's goodness must have brought me there
On purpose to confound this scoundrel's pride
And grant me means to take a signal vengeance
On his hypocrisy and arrogance,
And undeceive my father, showing up
The rascal caught at making love to you.
ELMIRE. No, no; it is enough if he reforms,
Endeavouring to deserve the favour shown him.

And since I've promised, do not you belie me.
'Tis not my way to make a public scandal;
An honest wife will scorn to heed such follies,
And never fret her husband's ears with them.
DAMIS. You've reasons of your own for acting thus;
And I have mine for doing otherwise.
To spare him now would be a mockery;
His bigot's pride has triumphed all too long
Over my righteous anger, and has caused
Far too much trouble in our family.
The rascal all too long has ruled my father,
And crossed my sister's love, and mine as well.
The traitor now must be unmasked before him:
And Providence has given me means to do it.
To Heaven I owe the opportunity,
And if I did not use it now I have it,
I should deserve to lose it once for all.
ELMIRE. Damis . . .
DAMIS. No, by your leave; I'll not be counselled.
I'm overjoyed. You needn't try to tell me
I must give up the pleasure of revenge.
I'll make an end of this affair at once;
And, to content me, here's my father now.

SCENE V.

[ORGON, ELMIRE, DAMIS, TARTUFFE.]

DAMIS. Father, we've news to welcome your arrival,
That's altogether novel, and surprising.
You are well paid for your caressing care,
And this fine gentleman rewards your love
Most handsomely, with zeal that seeks no less
Than your dishonour, as has now been proven.
I've just surprised him making to your wife
The shameful offer of a guilty love.
She, somewhat over gentle and discreet,
Insisted that the thing should be concealed;
But I will not condone such shamelessness,
Nor so far wrong you as to keep it secret.
ELMIRE. Yes, I believe a wife should never trouble
Her husband's peace of mind with such vain gossip;
A woman's honour does not hang on telling;
It is enough if she defend herself;
Or so I think; Damis, you'd not have spoken,

If you would but have heeded my advice.

SCENE VI.

[ORGON, DAMIS, TARTUFFE.]

ORGON. Just Heaven! Can what I hear be credited?
TARTUFFE. Yes, brother, I am wicked, I am guilty,
A miserable sinner, steeped in evil,
The greatest criminal that ever lived.
Each moment of my life is stained with soilures;
And all is but a mass of crime and filth;
Heaven, for my punishment, I see it plainly,
Would mortify me now. Whatever wrong
They find to charge me with, I'll not deny it
But guard against the pride of self-defence.
Believe their stories, arm your wrath against me,
And drive me like a villain from your house;
I cannot have so great a share of shame
But what I have deserved a greater still.
ORGON. [*to his son.*] You miscreant, can you dare, with such a falsehood,
To try to stain the whiteness of his virtue?
DAMIS. What! The feigned meekness of this hypocrite
Makes you discredit . . .
ORGON. Silence, cursed plague!
TARTUFFE. Ah! Let him speak; you chide him wrongfully;
You'd do far better to believe his tales.
Why favour me so much in such a matter?
How can you know of what I'm capable?
And should you trust my outward semblance, brother,
Or judge therefrom that I'm the better man?
No, no; you let appearances deceive you;
I'm anything but what I'm thought to be,
Alas! and though all men believe me godly,
The simple truth is, I'm a worthless creature.

[*to* DAMIS.]

Yes, my dear son, say on, and call me traitor,
Abandoned scoundrel, thief, and murderer;
Heap on me names yet more detestable,
And I shall not gainsay you; I've deserved them;
I'll bear this ignominy on my knees,
To expiate in shame the crimes I've done.

ORGON. [*to* TARTUFFE.] Ah, brother, 'tis too much!

[*to his son.*]

You'll not relent,
You blackguard?
DAMIS. What! His talk can so deceive you . . .
ORGON. Silence, you scoundrel!

[*to* TARTUFFE.]

Brother, rise, I beg you.

[*to his son.*]

Infamous villain!
DAMIS. Can he . . .
ORGON. Silence!
DAMIS. What . . .
ORGON. Another word, I'll break your every bone.
TARTUFFE. Brother, in God's name, don't be angry with him!
I'd rather bear myself the bitterest torture
Than have him get a scratch on my account.
ORGON. [*to his son.*] Ungrateful monster!
TARTUFFE. Stop. Upon my knees
I beg you pardon him . . .
ORGON. [*throwing himself on his knees too, and embracing* TARTUFFE.]
Alas! How can you?

[*to his son.*]

Villain! Behold his goodness!
DAMIS. So . . .
ORGON. Be still.
DAMIS. What! I . . .
ORGON. Be still, I say. I know your motives
For this attack. You hate him, all of you;
Wife, children, servants, all let loose upon him,
You have recourse to every shameful trick
To drive this godly man out of my house;
The more you strive to rid yourselves of him,
The more I'll strive to make him stay with me;
I'll have him straightway married to my daughter,
Just to confound the pride of all of you.

DAMIS. What! Will you force her to accept his hand?
ORGON. Yes, and this very evening, to enrage you,
Young rascal! Ah! I'll brave you all, and show you
That I'm the master, and must be obeyed.
Now, down upon your knees this instant, rogue,
And take back what you said, and ask his pardon.
DAMIS. Who? I? Ask pardon of that cheating scoundrel . . . ?
ORGON. Do you resist, you beggar, and insult him?
A cudgel, here! a cudgel!

[*to* TARTUFFE.]

Don't restrain me.

[*to his son.*]

Off with you! Leave my house this instant, sirrah,
And never dare set foot in it again.
DAMIS. Yes, I will leave your house, but . . .
ORGON. Leave it quickly.
You reprobate, I disinherit you,
And give you, too, my curse into the bargain.

SCENE VII.

[ORGON, TARTUFFE.]

ORGON. What! So insult a saintly man of God!
TARTUFFE. Heaven, forgive him all the pain he gives me![28]

[*to* ORGON.]

Could you but know with what distress I see
Them try to vilify me to my brother!

---

[28] Some modern editions have adopted the reading, preserved by tradition as that of the earliest stage version:

Heaven, forgive him even as I forgive him!

Voltaire gives still another reading:

Heaven, forgive me even as I forgive him!

Whichever was the original version, it appears in none of the early editions, and Moliere probably felt forced to change it on account of its too close resemblance to the Biblical phrase.

ORGON. Ah!
TARTUFFE. The mere thought of such ingratitude
Makes my soul suffer torture, bitterly . . .
My horror at it . . . Ah! my heart's so full
I cannot speak . . . I think I'll die of it.
ORGON. [*in tears, running to the door through which he drove away his son.*]
Scoundrel! I wish I'd never let you go,
But slain you on the spot with my own hand.

[*to* TARTUFFE.]

Brother, compose yourself, and don't be angry.
TARTUFFE. Nay, brother, let us end these painful quarrels.
I see what troublous times I bring upon you,
And think 'tis needful that I leave this house.
ORGON. What! You can't mean it?
TARTUFFE. Yes, they hate me here,
And try, I find, to make you doubt my faith.
ORGON. What of it? Do you find I listen to them?
TARTUFFE. No doubt they won't stop there. These same reports
You now reject, may some day win a hearing.
ORGON. No, brother, never.
TARTUFFE. Ah! my friend, a woman
May easily mislead her husband's mind.
ORGON. No, no.
TARTUFFE. So let me quickly go away
And thus remove all cause for such attacks.
ORGON. No, you shall stay; my life depends upon it.
TARTUFFE. Then I must mortify myself. And yet,
If you should wish . . .
ORGON. No, never!
TARTUFFE. Very well, then;
No more of that. But I shall rule my conduct
To fit the case. Honour is delicate,
And friendship binds me to forestall suspicion,
Prevent all scandal, and avoid your wife.
ORGON. No, you shall haunt her, just to spite them all.
'Tis my delight to set them in a rage;
You shall be seen together at all hours
And what is more, the better to defy them,
I'll have no other heir but you; and straightway
I'll go and make a deed of gift to you,
Drawn in due form, of all my property.
A good true friend, my son-in-law to be,

Is more to me than son, and wife, and kindred.
You will accept my offer, will you not?
TARTUFFE. Heaven's will be done in everything!
ORGON. Poor man!
We'll go make haste to draw the deed aright,
And then let envy burst itself with spite!

ACT IV.

SCENE I.

[CLEANTE, TARTUFFE.]

CLEANTE. Yes, it's become the talk of all the town,
And make a stir that's scarcely to your credit;
And I have met you, sir, most opportunely,
To tell you in a word my frank opinion.
Not to sift out this scandal to the bottom,
Suppose the worst for us—suppose Damis
Acted the traitor, and accused you falsely;
Should not a Christian pardon this offence,
And stifle in his heart all wish for vengeance?
Should you permit that, for your petty quarrel,
A son be driven from his father's house?
I tell you yet again, and tell you frankly,
Everyone, high or low, is scandalised;
If you'll take my advice, you'll make it up,
And not push matters to extremities.
Make sacrifice to God of your resentment;
Restore the son to favour with his father.
TARTUFFE. Alas! So far as I'm concerned, how gladly
Would I do so! I bear him no ill will;
I pardon all, lay nothing to his charge,
And wish with all my heart that I might serve him;
But Heaven's interests cannot allow it;
If he returns, then I must leave the house.
After his conduct, quite unparalleled,
All intercourse between us would bring scandal;
God knows what everyone's first thought would be!
They would attribute it to merest scheming
On my part—say that conscious of my guilt
I feigned a Christian love for my accuser,
But feared him in my heart, and hoped to win him
And underhandedly secure his silence.
CLEANTE. You try to put us off with specious phrases;

But all your arguments are too far-fetched.
Why take upon yourself the cause of Heaven?
Does Heaven need our help to punish sinners?
Leave to itself the care of its own vengeance,
And keep in mind the pardon it commands us;
Besides, think somewhat less of men's opinions,
When you are following the will of Heaven.
Shall petty fear of what the world may think
Prevent the doing of a noble deed?
No!—let us always do as Heaven commands,
And not perplex our brains with further questions.

TARTUFFE. Already I have told you I forgive him;
And that is doing, sir, as Heaven commands.
But after this day's scandal and affront
Heaven does not order me to live with him.

CLEANTE. And does it order you to lend your ear
To what mere whim suggested to his father,
And to accept gift of his estates,
On which, in justice, you can make no claim?

TARTUFFE. No one who knows me, sir, can have the thought
That I am acting from a selfish motive.
The goods of this world have no charms for me;
I am not dazzled by their treacherous glamour;
And if I bring myself to take the gift
Which he insists on giving me, I do so,
To tell the truth, only because I fear
This whole estate may fall into bad hands,
And those to whom it comes may use it ill
And not employ it, as is my design,
For Heaven's glory and my neighbours' good.

CLEANTE. Eh, sir, give up these conscientious scruples
That well may cause a rightful heir's complaints.
Don't take so much upon yourself, but let him
Possess what's his, at his own risk and peril;
Consider, it were better he misused it,
Than you should be accused of robbing him.
I am astounded that unblushingly
You could allow such offers to be made!
Tell me—has true religion any maxim
That teaches us to rob the lawful heir?
If Heaven has made it quite impossible
Damis and you should live together here,
Were it not better you should quietly
And honourably withdraw, than let the son
Be driven out for your sake, dead against

All reason? 'Twould be giving, sir, believe me,
Such an example of your probity . . .
TARTUFFE. Sir, it is half-past three; certain devotions
Recall me to my closet; you'll forgive me
For leaving you so soon.
CLEANTE. [*alone.*] Ah!

SCENE II.

[ELMIRE, MARIANE, CLEANTE, DORINE.]

DORINE. [*to* CLEANTE.] Sir, we beg you
To help us all you can in her behalf;
She's suffering almost more than heart can bear;
This match her father means to make to-night
Drives her each moment to despair. He's coming.
Let us unite our efforts now, we beg you,
And try by strength or skill to change his purpose.

SCENE III.

[ORGON, ELMIRE, MARIANE, CLEANTE, DORINE.]

ORGON. So ho! I'm glad to find you all together.

[*to* MARIANE.]

Here is the contract that shall make you happy,
My dear. You know already what it means.
MARIANE. [*on her knees before* ORGON.] Father, I beg you, in the name of Heaven
That knows my grief, and by whate'er can move you,
Relax a little your paternal rights,
And free my love from this obedience!
Oh, do not make me, by your harsh command,
Complain to Heaven you ever were my father;
Do not make wretched this poor life you gave me.
If, crossing that fond hope which I had formed,
You'll not permit me to belong to one
Whom I have dared to love, at least, I beg you
Upon my knees, oh, save me from the torment
Of being possessed by one whom I abhor!
And do not drive me to some desperate act
By exercising all your rights upon me.
ORGON. [*a little touched.*] Come, come, my heart, be firm! no human

weakness!

MARIANE. I am not jealous of your love for him;
Display it freely; give him your estate,
And if that's not enough, add all of mine;
I willingly agree, and give it up,
If only you'll not give him me, your daughter;
Oh, rather let a convent's rigid rule
Wear out the wretched days that Heaven allots me.

ORGON. These girls are ninnies!—always turning nuns
When fathers thwart their silly love-affairs.
Get on your feet! The more you hate to have him,
The more 'twill help you earn your soul's salvation.
So, mortify your senses by this marriage,
And don't vex me about it any more.

DORINE. But what . . . ?

ORGON. You hold your tongue, before your betters.
Don't dare to say a single word, I tell you.

CLEANTE. If you will let me answer, and advise . . .

ORGON. Brother, I value your advice most highly;
'Tis well thought out; no better can be had;
But you'll allow me—not to follow it.

ELMIRE. [*to her husband.*] I can't find words to cope with such a case;
Your blindness makes me quite astounded at you.
You are bewitched with him, to disbelieve
The things we tell you happened here to-day.

ORGON. I am your humble servant, and can see
Things, when they're plain as noses on folks' faces,
I know you're partial to my rascal son,
And didn't dare to disavow the trick
He tried to play on this poor man; besides,
You were too calm, to be believed; if that
Had happened, you'd have been far more disturbed.

ELMIRE. And must our honour always rush to arms
At the mere mention of illicit love?
Or can we answer no attack upon it
Except with blazing eyes and lips of scorn?
For my part, I just laugh away such nonsense;
I've no desire to make a loud to-do.
Our virtue should, I think, be gentle-natured;
Nor can I quite approve those savage prudes
Whose honour arms itself with teeth and claws
To tear men's eyes out at the slightest word.
Heaven preserve me from that kind of honour!
I like my virtue not to be a vixen,
And I believe a quiet cold rebuff

No less effective to repulse a lover.
ORGON. I know . . . and you can't throw me off the scent.
ELMIRE. Once more, I am astounded at your weakness;
I wonder what your unbelief would answer,
If I should let you see we've told the truth?
ORGON. See it?
ELMIRE. Yes.
ORGON. Nonsense.
ELMIRE. Come! If I should find
A way to make you see it clear as day?
ORGON. All rubbish.
ELMIRE. What a man! But answer me.
I'm not proposing now that you believe us;
But let's suppose that here, from proper hiding,
You should be made to see and hear all plainly;
What would you say then, to your man of virtue?
ORGON. Why, then, I'd say . . . say nothing. It can't be.
ELMIRE. Your error has endured too long already,
And quite too long you've branded me a liar.
I must at once, for my own satisfaction,
Make you a witness of the things we've told you.
ORGON. Amen! I take you at your word. We'll see
What tricks you have, and how you'll keep your promise.
ELMIRE. [*to* DORINE.] Send him to me.
DORINE. [*to* ELMIRE.] The man's a crafty codger,
Perhaps you'll find it difficult to catch him.
ELMIRE. [*to* DORINE.] Oh no! A lover's never hard to cheat,
And self-conceit leads straight to self-deceit.
Bid him come down to me.

[*to* CLEANTE *and* MARIANE.]

And you, withdraw.

SCENE IV.

[ELMIRE, ORGON.]

ELMIRE. Bring up this table, and get under it.
ORGON. What?
ELMIRE. One essential is to hide you well.
ORGON. Why under there?
ELMIRE. Oh, dear! Do as I say;
I know what I'm about, as you shall see.
Get under, now, I tell you; and once there

Be careful no one either sees or hears you.
ORGON. I'm going a long way to humour you,
I must say; but I'll see you through your scheme.
ELMIRE. And then you'll have, I think, no more to say.

[*to her husband, who is now under the table.*]

But mind, I'm going to meddle with strange matters;
Prepare yourself to be in no wise shocked.
Whatever I may say must pass, because
'Tis only to convince you, as I promised.
By wheedling speeches, since I'm forced to do it,
I'll make this hypocrite put off his mask,
Flatter the longings of his shameless passion,
And give free play to all his impudence.
But, since 'tis for your sake, to prove to you
His guilt, that I shall feign to share his love,
I can leave off as soon as you're convinced,
And things shall go no farther than you choose.
So, when you think they've gone quite far enough,
It is for you to stop his mad pursuit,
To spare your wife, and not expose me farther
Than you shall need, yourself, to undeceive you.
It is your own affair, and you must end it
When . . . Here he comes. Keep still, don't show yourself.

Scene V.

[TARTUFFE, ELMIRE; ORGON (*under the table.*)]

TARTUFFE. They told me that you wished to see me here.
ELMIRE. Yes. I have secrets for your ear alone.
But shut the door first, and look everywhere
For fear of spies.

[TARTUFFE *goes and closes the door, and comes back.*]

We surely can't afford
Another scene like that we had just now;
Was ever anyone so caught before!
Damis did frighten me most terribly
On your account; you saw I did my best
To baffle his design, and calm his anger.
But I was so confused, I never thought
To contradict his story; still, thank Heaven,

Things turned out all the better, as it happened,
And now we're on an even safer footing.
The high esteem you're held in, laid the storm;
My husband can have no suspicion of you,
And even insists, to spite the scandal-mongers,
That we shall be together constantly;
So that is how, without the risk of blame,
I can be here locked up with you alone,
And can reveal to you my heart, perhaps
Only too ready to allow your passion.

TARTUFFE. Your words are somewhat hard to understand,
Madam; just now you used a different style.

ELMIRE. If that refusal has offended you,
How little do you know a woman's heart!
How ill you guess what it would have you know,
When it presents so feeble a defence!
Always, at first, our modesty resists
The tender feelings you inspire us with.
Whatever cause we find to justify
The love that masters us, we still must feel
Some little shame in owning it; and strive
To make as though we would not, when we would.
But from the very way we go about it
We let a lover know our heart surrenders,
The while our lips, for honour's sake, oppose
Our heart's desire, and in refusing promise.
I'm telling you my secret all too freely
And with too little heed to modesty.
But—now that I've made bold to speak—pray tell me.
Should I have tried to keep Damis from speaking,
Should I have heard the offer of your heart
So quietly, and suffered all your pleading,
And taken it just as I did—remember—
If such a declaration had not pleased me,
And, when I tried my utmost to persuade you
Not to accept the marriage that was talked of,
What should my earnestness have hinted to you
If not the interest that you've inspired,
And my chagrin, should such a match compel me
To share a heart I want all to myself?

TARTUFFE. 'Tis, past a doubt, the height of happiness,
To hear such words from lips we dote upon;
Their honeyed sweetness pours through all my senses
Long draughts of suavity ineffable.
My heart employs its utmost zeal to please you,

And counts your love its one beatitude;
And yet that heart must beg that you allow it
To doubt a little its felicity.
I well might think these words an honest trick
To make me break off this approaching marriage;
And if I may express myself quite plainly,
I cannot trust these too enchanting words
Until the granting of some little favour
I sigh for, shall assure me of their truth
And build within my soul, on firm foundations,
A lasting faith in your sweet charity.

ELMIRE. [*coughing to draw her husband's attention.*]
What! Must you go so fast?—and all at once
Exhaust the whole love of a woman's heart?
She does herself the violence to make
This dear confession of her love, and you
Are not yet satisfied, and will not be
Without the granting of her utmost favours?

TARTUFFE. The less a blessing is deserved, the less
We dare to hope for it; and words alone
Can ill assuage our love's desires. A fate
Too full of happiness, seems doubtful still;
We must enjoy it ere we can believe it.
And I, who know how little I deserve
Your goodness, doubt the fortunes of my daring;
So I shall trust to nothing, madam, till
You have convinced my love by something real.

ELMIRE. Ah! How your love enacts the tyrant's role,
And throws my mind into a strange confusion!
With what fierce sway it rules a conquered heart,
And violently will have its wishes granted!
What! Is there no escape from your pursuit?
No respite even?—not a breathing space?
Nay, is it decent to be so exacting,
And so abuse by urgency the weakness
You may discover in a woman's heart?

TARTUFFE. But if my worship wins your gracious favour,
Then why refuse me some sure proof thereof?

ELMIRE. But how can I consent to what you wish,
Without offending Heaven you talk so much of?

TARTUFFE. If Heaven is all that stands now in my way,
I'll easily remove that little hindrance;
Your heart need not hold back for such a trifle.

ELMIRE. But they affright us so with Heaven's commands!

TARTUFFE. I can dispel these foolish fears, dear madam;

I know the art of pacifying scruples
Heaven forbids, 'tis true, some satisfactions;
But we find means to make things right with Heaven.

['*tis a scoundrel speaking*.][29]

There is a science, madam, that instructs us
How to enlarge the limits of our conscience
According to our various occasions,
And rectify the evil of the deed
According to our purity of motive.
I'll duly teach you all these secrets, madam;
You only need to let yourself be guided.
Content my wishes, have no fear at all;
I answer for't, and take the sin upon me.

[ELMIRE *coughs still louder*.]

Your cough is very bad.
ELMIRE. Yes, I'm in torture.
TARTUFFE. Would you accept this bit of licorice?
ELMIRE. The case is obstinate, I find; and all
The licorice in the world will do no good.
TARTUFFE. 'Tis very trying.
ELMIRE. More than words can say.
TARTUFFE. In any case, your scruple's easily
Removed. With me you're sure of secrecy,
And there's no harm unless a thing is known.
The public scandal is what brings offence,
And secret sinning is not sin at all.
ELMIRE. [*after coughing again*.] So then, I see I must resolve to yield;
I must consent to grant you everything,
And cannot hope to give full satisfaction
Or win full confidence, at lesser cost.
No doubt 'tis very hard to come to this;
'Tis quite against my will I go so far;
But since I must be forced to it, since nothing
That can be said suffices for belief,
Since more convincing proof is still demanded,
I must make up my mind to humour people.
If my consent give reason for offence,
So much the worse for him who forced me to it;
The fault can surely not be counted mine.

---

[29] Moliere's note, in the original edition.

TARTUFFE. It need not, madam; and the thing itself . . .
ELMIRE. Open the door, I pray you, and just see
Whether my husband's not there, in the hall.
TARTUFFE. Why take such care for him? Between ourselves,
He is a man to lead round by the nose.
He's capable of glorying in our meetings;
I've fooled him so, he'd see all, and deny it.
ELMIRE. No matter; go, I beg you, look about,
And carefully examine every corner.

SCENE VI.

[ORGON, ELMIRE.]

ORGON. [*crawling out from under the table.*] That is, I own, a man . . . abominable!
I can't get over it; the whole thing floors me.
ELMIRE. What? You come out so soon? You cannot mean it!
Get back under the table; 'tis not time yet;
Wait till the end, to see, and make quite certain,
And don't believe a thing on mere conjecture.
ORGON. Nothing more wicked e'er came out of Hell.
ELMIRE. Dear me! Don't go and credit things too lightly.
No, let yourself be thoroughly convinced;
Don't yield too soon, for fear you'll be mistaken.

[*as* TARTUFFE *enters, she makes her husband stand behind her.*]

SCENE VII.

[TARTUFFE, ELMIRE, ORGON.]

TARTUFFE. [*not seeing* ORGON.] All things conspire toward my satisfaction,
Madam, I've searched the whole apartment through.
There's no one here; and now my ravished soul . . .
ORGON. [*stopping him.*] Softly! You are too eager in your amours;
You needn't be so passionate. Ah ha!
My holy man! You want to put it on me!
How is your soul abandoned to temptation!
Marry my daughter, eh?—and want my wife, too?
I doubted long enough if this was earnest,
Expecting all the time the tone would change;
But now the proof's been carried far enough;
I'm satisfied, and ask no more, for my part.

ELMIRE. [*to* TARTUFFE.] 'Twas quite against my character to play
This part; but I was forced to treat you so.
TARTUFFE. What? You believe . . . ?
ORGON. Come, now, no protestations.
Get out from here, and make no fuss about it.
TARTUFFE. But my intent . . .
ORGON. That talk is out of season.
You leave my house this instant.
TARTUFFE. You're the one
To leave it, you who play the master here!
This house belongs to me, I'll have you know,
And show you plainly it's no use to turn
To these low tricks, to pick a quarrel with me,
And that you can't insult me at your pleasure,
For I have wherewith to confound your lies,
Avenge offended Heaven, and compel
Those to repent who talk to me of leaving.

SCENE VIII.

[ELMIRE, ORGON.]

ELMIRE. What sort of speech is this? What can it mean?
ORGON. My faith, I'm dazed. This is no laughing matter.
ELMIRE. What?
ORGON. From his words I see my great mistake;
The deed of gift is one thing troubles me.
ELMIRE. The deed of gift . . .
ORGON. Yes, that is past recall.
But I've another thing to make me anxious.
ELMIRE. What's that?
ORGON. You shall know all. Let's see at once
Whether a certain box is still upstairs.

ACT V.

SCENE I.

[ORGON, CLEANTE.]

CLEANTE. Whither away so fast?
ORGON. How should I know?
CLEANTE. Methinks we should begin by taking counsel
To see what can be done to meet the case.
ORGON. I'm all worked up about that wretched box.

More than all else it drives me to despair.
CLEANTE. That box must hide some mighty mystery?
ORGON. Argas, my friend who is in trouble, brought it
Himself, most secretly, and left it with me.
He chose me, in his exile, for this trust;
And on these documents, from what he said,
I judge his life and property depend.
CLEANTE. How could you trust them to another's hands?
ORGON. By reason of a conscientious scruple.
I went straight to my traitor, to confide
In him; his sophistry made me believe
That I must give the box to him to keep,
So that, in case of search, I might deny
My having it at all, and still, by favour
Of this evasion, keep my conscience clear
Even in taking oath against the truth.
CLEANTE. Your case is bad, so far as I can see;
This deed of gift, this trusting of the secret
To him, were both—to state my frank opinion—
Steps that you took too lightly; he can lead you
To any length, with these for hostages;
And since he holds you at such disadvantage,
You'd be still more imprudent, to provoke him;
So you must go some gentler way about.
ORGON. What! Can a soul so base, a heart so false,
Hide neath the semblance of such touching fervour?
I took him in, a vagabond, a beggar! . . .
'Tis too much! No more pious folk for me!
I shall abhor them utterly forever,
And henceforth treat them worse than any devil.
CLEANTE. So! There you go again, quite off the handle!
In nothing do you keep an even temper.
You never know what reason is, but always
Jump first to one extreme, and then the other.
You see your error, and you recognise
That you've been cozened by a feigned zeal;
But to make up for't, in the name of reason,
Why should you plunge into a worse mistake,
And find no difference in character
Between a worthless scamp, and all good people?
What! Just because a rascal boldly duped you
With pompous show of false austerity,
Must you needs have it everybody's like him,
And no one's truly pious nowadays?
Leave such conclusions to mere infidels;

Distinguish virtue from its counterfeit,
Don't give esteem too quickly, at a venture,
But try to keep, in this, the golden mean.
If you can help it, don't uphold imposture;
But do not rail at true devoutness, either;
And if you must fall into one extreme,
Then rather err again the other way.

SCENE II.

[DAMIS, ORGON, CLEANTE.]

DAMIS. What! father, can the scoundrel threaten you,
Forget the many benefits received,
And in his base abominable pride
Make of your very favours arms against you?
ORGON. Too true, my son. It tortures me to think on't.
DAMIS. Let me alone, I'll chop his ears off for him.
We must deal roundly with his insolence;
'Tis I must free you from him at a blow;
'Tis I, to set things right, must strike him down.
CLEANTE. Spoke like a true young man. Now just calm down,
And moderate your towering tantrums, will you?
We live in such an age, with such a king,
That violence can not advance our cause.

SCENE III.

[MADAME PERNELLE, ORGON, ELMIRE, CLEANTE, MARIANE, DAMIS, DORINE.]

MADAME PERNELLE. What's this? I hear of fearful mysteries!
ORGON. Strange things indeed, for my own eyes to witness;
You see how I'm requited for my kindness,
I zealously receive a wretched beggar,
I lodge him, entertain him like my brother,
Load him with benefactions every day,
Give him my daughter, give him all my fortune:
And he meanwhile, the villain, rascal, wretch,
Tries with black treason to suborn my wife,
And not content with such a foul design,
He dares to menace me with my own favours,
And would make use of those advantages
Which my too foolish kindness armed him with,
To ruin me, to take my fortune from me,

And leave me in the state I saved him from.

DORINE. Poor man!

MADAME PERNELLE. My son, I cannot possibly
Believe he could intend so black a deed.

ORGON. What?

MADAME PERNELLE. Worthy men are still the sport of envy.

ORGON. Mother, what do you mean by such a speech?

MADAME PERNELLE. There are strange goings-on about your house,
And everybody knows your people hate him.

ORGON. What's that to do with what I tell you now?

MADAME PERNELLE. I always said, my son, when you were little:
That virtue here below is hated ever;
The envious may die, but envy never.

ORGON. What's that fine speech to do with present facts?

MADAME PERNELLE. Be sure, they've forged a hundred silly lies . . .

ORGON. I've told you once, I saw it all myself.

MADAME PERNELLE. For slanderers abound in calumnies . . .

ORGON. Mother, you'd make me damn my soul. I tell you
I saw with my own eyes his shamelessness.

MADAME PERNELLE. Their tongues for spitting venom never lack,
There's nothing here below they'll not attack.

ORGON. Your speech has not a single grain of sense.
I saw it, harkee, saw it, with these eyes
I saw—d'ye know what saw means?—must I say it
A hundred times, and din it in your ears?

MADAME PERNELLE. My dear, appearances are oft deceiving,
And seeing shouldn't always be believing.

ORGON. I'll go mad.

MADAME PERNELLE. False suspicions may delude,
And good to evil oft is misconstrued.

ORGON. Must I construe as Christian charity
The wish to kiss my wife!

MADAME PERNELLE. You must, at least,
Have just foundation for accusing people,
And wait until you see a thing for sure.

ORGON. The devil! How could I see any surer?
Should I have waited till, before my eyes,
He . . . No, you'll make me say things quite improper.

MADAME PERNELLE. In short, 'tis known too pure a zeal inflames him;
And so, I cannot possibly conceive
That he should try to do what's charged against him.

ORGON. If you were not my mother, I should say

Such things! . . . I know not what, I'm so enraged!
DORINE. [*to* ORGON.] Fortune has paid you fair, to be so doubted;
You flouted our report, now yours is flouted.
CLEANTE. We're wasting time here in the merest trifling,
Which we should rather use in taking measures
To guard ourselves against the scoundrel's threats.
DAMIS. You think his impudence could go far?
ELMIRE. For one, I can't believe it possible;
Why, his ingratitude would be too patent.
CLEANTE. Don't trust to that; he'll find abundant warrant
To give good colour to his acts against you;
And for less cause than this, a strong cabal
Can make one's life a labyrinth of troubles.
I tell you once again: armed as he is
You never should have pushed him quite so far.
ORGON. True; yet what could I do? The rascal's pride
Made me lose all control of my resentment.
CLEANTE. I wish with all my heart that some pretence
Of peace could be patched up between you two
ELMIRE. If I had known what weapons he was armed with,
I never should have raised such an alarm,
And my . . .
ORGON. [*to* DORINE, *seeing* MR. LOYAL *come in.*] Who's coming now? Go quick, find out.
I'm in a fine state to receive a visit!

SCENE IV.

[ORGON, MADAME PERNELLE, ELMIRE, MARIANE, CLEANTE, DAMIS, DORINE, MR. LOYAL.]

MR. LOYAL. [*to* DORINE, *at the back of the stage.*]
Good day, good sister. Pray you, let me see
The master of the house.
DORINE. He's occupied;
I think he can see nobody at present.
MR. LOYAL. I'm not by way of being unwelcome here.
My coming can, I think, nowise displease him;
My errand will be found to his advantage.
DORINE. Your name, then?
MR. LOYAL. Tell him simply that his friend
Mr. Tartuffe has sent me, for his goods . . .
DORINE. [*to* ORGON.] It is a man who comes, with civil manners,
Sent by Tartuffe, he says, upon an errand
That you'll be pleased with.

CLEANTE. [*to* ORGON.] Surely you must see him,
And find out who he is, and what he wants.
ORGON. [*to* CLEANTE.] Perhaps he's come to make it up between us:
How shall I treat him?
CLEANTE. You must not get angry;
And if he talks of reconciliation
Accept it.
MR. LOYAL. [*to* ORGON.] Sir, good-day. And Heaven send
Harm to your enemies, favour to you.
ORGON. [*aside to* CLEANTE.] This mild beginning suits with my conjectures
And promises some compromise already.
MR. LOYAL. All of your house has long been dear to me;
I had the honour, sir, to serve your father.
ORGON. Sir, I am much ashamed, and ask your pardon
For not recalling now your face or name.
MR. LOYAL. My name is Loyal. I'm from Normandy.
My office is court-bailiff, in despite
Of envy; and for forty years, thank Heaven,
It's been my fortune to perform that office
With honour. So I've come, sir, by your leave
To render service of a certain writ . . .
ORGON. What, you are here to . . .
MR. LOYAL. Pray, sir, don't be angry.
'Tis nothing, sir, but just a little summons:—
Order to vacate, you and yours, this house,
Move out your furniture, make room for others,
And that without delay or putting off,
As needs must be . . .
ORGON. I? Leave this house?
MR. LOYAL. Yes, please, sir
The house is now, as you well know, of course,
Mr. Tartuffe's. And he, beyond dispute,
Of all your goods is henceforth lord and master
By virtue of a contract here attached,
Drawn in due form, and unassailable.
DAMIS. [*to* MR. LOYAL.] Your insolence is monstrous, and astounding!
MR. LOYAL. [*to* DAMIS.] I have no business, sir, that touches you;

[*pointing to* ORGON.]

This is the gentleman. He's fair and courteous,
And knows too well a gentleman's behaviour
To wish in any wise to question justice.

ORGON. But . . .
MR. LOYAL. Sir, I know you would not for a million
Wish to rebel; like a good citizen
You'll let me put in force the court's decree.
DAMIS. Your long black gown may well, before you know it,
Mister Court-bailiff, get a thorough beating.
MR. LOYAL. [*to* ORGON.] Sir, make your son be silent or withdraw.
I should be loath to have to set things down,
And see your names inscribed in my report.
DORINE. [*aside*.] This Mr. Loyal's looks are most disloyal.
MR. LOYAL. I have much feeling for respectable
And honest folk like you, sir, and consented
To serve these papers, only to oblige you,
And thus prevent the choice of any other
Who, less possessed of zeal for you than I am
Might order matters in less gentle fashion.
ORGON. And how could one do worse than order people
Out of their house?
MR. LOYAL. Why, we allow you time;
And even will suspend until to-morrow
The execution of the order, sir.
I'll merely, without scandal, quietly,
Come here and spend the night, with half a score
Of officers; and just for form's sake, please,
You'll bring your keys to me, before retiring.
I will take care not to disturb your rest,
And see there's no unseemly conduct here.
But by to-morrow, and at early morning,
You must make haste to move your least belongings;
My men will help you—I have chosen strong ones
To serve you, sir, in clearing out the house.
No one could act more generously, I fancy,
And, since I'm treating you with great indulgence,
I beg you'll do as well by me, and see
I'm not disturbed in my discharge of duty.
ORGON. I'd give this very minute, and not grudge it,
The hundred best gold louis I have left,
If I could just indulge myself, and land
My fist, for one good square one, on his snout.
CLEANTE. [*aside to* ORGON.] Careful!—don't make things worse.
DAMIS. Such insolence!
I hardly can restrain myself. My hands
Are itching to be at him.
DORINE. By my faith,
With such a fine broad back, good Mr. Loyal,

A little beating would become you well.
MR. LOYAL. My girl, such infamous words are actionable.
And warrants can be issued against women.
CLEANTE. [*to* MR. LOYAL.] Enough of this discussion, sir; have done.
Give us the paper, and then leave us, pray.
MR. LOYAL. Then *au revoir*. Heaven keep you from disaster!
ORGON. May Heaven confound you both, you and your master!

SCENE V.

[ORGON, MADAME PERNELLE, ELMIRE, CLEANTE, MARIANE, DAMIS, DORINE.]

ORGON. Well, mother, am I right or am I not?
This writ may help you now to judge the matter.
Or don't you see his treason even yet?
MADAME PERNELLE. I'm all amazed, befuddled, and beflustered!
DORINE. [*to* ORGON.] You are quite wrong, you have no right to blame him;
This action only proves his good intentions.
Love for his neighbour makes his virtue perfect;
And knowing money is a root of evil,
In Christian charity, he'd take away
Whatever things may hinder your salvation.
ORGON. Be still. You always need to have that told you.
CLEANTE. [*to* ORGON.] Come, let us see what course you are to follow.
ELMIRE. Go and expose his bold ingratitude.
Such action must invalidate the contract;
His perfidy must now appear too black
To bring him the success that he expects.

SCENE VI.

[VALERE, ORGON, MADAME PERNELLE, ELMIRE, CLEANTE, MARIANE, DAMIS, DORINE.]

VALERE. 'Tis with regret, sir, that I bring bad news;
But urgent danger forces me to do so.
A close and intimate friend of mine, who knows
The interest I take in what concerns you,
Has gone so far, for my sake, as to break
The secrecy that's due to state affairs,
And sent me word but now, that leaves you only

The one expedient of sudden flight.
The villain who so long imposed upon you,
Found means, an hour ago, to see the prince,
And to accuse you (among other things)
By putting in his hands the private strong-box
Of a state-criminal, whose guilty secret,
You, failing in your duty as a subject,
(He says) have kept. I know no more of it
Save that a warrant's drawn against you, sir,
And for the greater surety, that same rascal
Comes with the officer who must arrest you.

CLEANTE. His rights are armed; and this is how the scoundrel
Seeks to secure the property he claims.

ORGON. Man is a wicked animal, I'll own it!

VALERE. The least delay may still be fatal, sir.
I have my carriage, and a thousand louis,
Provided for your journey, at the door.
Let's lose no time; the bolt is swift to strike,
And such as only flight can save you from.
I'll be your guide to seek a place of safety,
And stay with you until you reach it, sir.

ORGON. How much I owe to your obliging care!
Another time must serve to thank you fitly;
And I pray Heaven to grant me so much favour
That I may some day recompense your service.
Good-bye; see to it, all of you . . .

CLEANTE. Come hurry;
We'll see to everything that's needful, brother.

Scene VII.

[TARTUFFE, AN OFFICER, MADAME PERNELLE, ORGON, ELMIRE, CLEANTE, MARIANE, VALERE, DAMIS, DORINE.]

TARTUFFE. [*stopping* ORGON.] Softly, sir, softly; do not run so fast;
You haven't far to go to find your lodging;
By order of the prince, we here arrest you.

ORGON. Traitor! You saved this worst stroke for the last;
This crowns your perfidies, and ruins me.

TARTUFFE. I shall not be embittered by your insults,
For Heaven has taught me to endure all things.

CLEANTE. Your moderation, I must own, is great.

DAMIS. How shamelessly the wretch makes bold with Heaven!

TARTUFFE. Your ravings cannot move me; all my thought

Is but to do my duty.

MARIANE. You must claim
Great glory from this honourable act.

TARTUFFE. The act cannot be aught but honourable,
Coming from that high power which sends me here.

ORGON. Ungrateful wretch, do you forget 'twas I
That rescued you from utter misery?

TARTUFFE. I've not forgot some help you may have given;
But my first duty now is toward my prince.
The higher power of that most sacred claim
Must stifle in my heart all gratitude;
And to such puissant ties I'd sacrifice
My friend, my wife, my kindred, and myself.

ELMIRE. The hypocrite!

DORINE. How well he knows the trick
Of cloaking him with what we most revere!

CLEANTE. But if the motive that you make parade of
Is perfect as you say, why should it wait
To show itself, until the day he caught you
Soliciting his wife? How happens it
You have not thought to go inform against him
Until his honour forces him to drive you
Out of his house? And though I need not mention
That he'd just given you his whole estate,
Still, if you meant to treat him now as guilty,
How could you then consent to take his gift?

TARTUFFE. [*to the* OFFICER.] Pray, sir, deliver me from all this clamour;
Be good enough to carry out your order.

THE OFFICER. Yes, I've too long delayed its execution;
'Tis very fitting you should urge me to it;
So therefore, you must follow me at once
To prison, where you'll find your lodging ready.

TARTUFFE. Who? I, sir?

THE OFFICER. You.

TARTUFFE. By why to prison?

THE OFFICER. You
Are not the one to whom I owe account.
You, sir [*to* ORGON.], recover from your hot alarm.
Our prince is not a friend to double dealing,
His eyes can read men's inmost hearts, and all
The art of hypocrites cannot deceive him.
His sharp discernment sees things clear and true;
His mind cannot too easily be swayed,
For reason always holds the balance even.

He honours and exalts true piety,
But knows the false, and views it with disgust.
This fellow was by no means apt to fool him,
Far subtler snares have failed against his wisdom,
And his quick insight pierced immediately
The hidden baseness of this tortuous heart.
Accusing you, the knave betrayed himself,
And by true recompense of Heaven's justice
He stood revealed before our monarch's eyes
A scoundrel known before by other names,
Whose horrid crimes, detailed at length, might fill
A long-drawn history of many volumes.
Our monarch—to resolve you in a word—
Detesting his ingratitude and baseness,
Added this horror to his other crimes,
And sent me hither under his direction
To see his insolence out-top itself,
And force him then to give you satisfaction.
Your papers, which the traitor says are his,
I am to take from him, and give you back;
The deed of gift transferring your estate
Our monarch's sovereign will makes null and void;
And for the secret personal offence
Your friend involved you in, he pardons you:
Thus he rewards your recent zeal, displayed
In helping to maintain his rights, and shows
How well his heart, when it is least expected,
Knows how to recompense a noble deed,
And will not let true merit miss its due,
Remembering always rather good than evil.

DORINE. Now Heaven be praised!

MADAME PERNELLE. At last I breathe again.

ELMIRE. A happy outcome!

MARIANE. Who'd have dared to hope it?

ORGON. [*to* TARTUFFE, *who is being led by the officer.*] There traitor! Now you're . . .

SCENE VIII.

[MADAME PERNELLE, ORGON, ELMIRE, MARIANE, CLEANTE, VALERE, DAMIS, DORINE.]

CLEANTE. Brother, hold!—and don't
Descend to such indignities, I beg you.
Leave the poor wretch to his unhappy fate,

And let remorse oppress him, but not you.
Hope rather that his heart may now return
To virtue, hate his vice, reform his ways,
And win the pardon of our glorious prince;
While you must straightway go, and on your knees
Repay with thanks his noble generous kindness.

ORGON. Well said! We'll go, and at his feet kneel down,
With joy to thank him for his goodness shown;
And this first duty done, with honours due,
We'll then attend upon another, too.
With wedded happiness reward Valere,
And crown a lover noble and sincere.

[*curtain.*]

The Misanthrope

[Le Misanthrope ou l'Atrabilaire amoureux]

Translated by HENRI VAN LAUN

DRAMATIS PERSONAE

ALCESTE, *in love with Célimène.*
PHILINTE, *his friend.*
ORONTE, *in love with Célimène.*
CÉLIMÈNE, *beloved by Alceste.*
ELIANTE, *her cousin.*
ARSINOÉ, *Célimène's friend.*
ACASTE, *marquises.*
CLITANDRE, *marquises.*
BASQUE, *servant to Célimène.*
DUBOIS, *servant to Alceste.*
An Officer of the Maréchaussée.

Scene.—At Paris, in CÉLIMÈNE'S *House*

ACT I.

SCENE I.

[PHILINTE, ALCESTE.]

PHILINTE. What is the matter? What ails you?
ALCESTE. [*seated.*] Leave me, I pray.
PHILINTE. But, once more, tell me what strange whim—
ALCESTE. Leave me, I tell you, and get out of my sight.
PHILINTE. But you might at least listen to people, without getting angry.
ALCESTE. I choose to get angry, and I do not choose to listen.
PHILINTE. I do not understand you in these abrupt moods, and although we are friends, I am the first—
ALCESTE. [*rising quickly.*] I, your friend? Lay not that flattering unction to your soul. I have until now professed to be so; but after what I have just seen of you, I tell you candidly that I am such no longer; I have no wish to occupy a place in a corrupt heart.
PHILINTE. I am then very much to be blamed from your point of view, Alceste?
ALCESTE. To be blamed? You ought to die from very shame; there is

no excuse for such behaviour, and every man of honour must be disgusted at it. I see you almost stifle a man with caresses, show him the most ardent affection, and overwhelm him with protestations, offers, and vows of friendship. Your ebullitions of tenderness know no bounds; and when I ask you who that man is, you can scarcely tell me his name; your feelings for him, the moment you have turned your back, suddenly cool; you speak of him most indifferently to me. Zounds! I call it unworthy, base, and infamous, so far to lower one's self as to act contrary to one's own feelings, and if, by some mischance, I had done such a thing, I should hang myself at once out of sheer vexation.

PHILINTE. I do not see that it is a hanging matter at all; and I beg of you not to think it amiss if I ask you to show me some mercy, for I shall not hung myself, if it be all the same to you.

ALCESTE. That is a sorry joke.

PHILINTE. But, seriously, what would you have people do?

ALCESTE. I would have people be sincere, and that, like men of honour, no word be spoken that comes not from the heart.

PHILINTE. When a man comes and embraces you warmly, you must pay him back in his own coin, respond as best you can to his show of feeling, and return offer for offer, and vow for vow.

ALCESTE. Not so. I cannot bear so base a method which your fashionable people generally affect; there is nothing I detest so much as the contortions of these great time-and-lip servers, these affable dispensers of meaningless embraces, these obliging utterers of empty words, who view every one in civilities, and treat the man of worth and the fop alike. What good does it do if a man heaps endearments on you, vows that he is your friend, that he believes in you, is full of zeal for you, esteems and loves you, and lauds you to the skies, when he rushes to do the same to the first rapscallion he meets? No, no, no heart with the least self-respect cares for esteem so prostituted; he will hardly relish it, even when openly expressed, when he finds that he shares it with the whole universe. Preference must be based on esteem, and to esteem every one is to esteem no one. Since you abandon yourself to the vices of the times, zounds! you are not the man for me. I decline this over-complaisant kindness, which uses no discrimination. I like to be distinguished; and, to cut the matter short, the friend of all mankind is no friend of mine.

PHILINTE. But when we are of the world, we must confirm to the outward civilities which custom demands.

ALCESTE. I deny it. We ought to punish pitilessly that shameful pretence of friendly intercourse. I like a man to be a man, and to show on all occasions the bottom of his heart in his discourse. Let that be the thing to speak, and never let our feelings be hidden beneath vain compliments.

PHILINTE. There are many cases in which plain speaking would become ridiculous, and could hardly be tolerated. And, with all due allowance for your unbending honesty, it is as well to conceal your feelings sometimes. Would it be right or decent to tell thousands of people what we think of them? And when we meet with some one whom we hate or who displeases us, must we tell him so openly?

ALCESTE. Yes.

PHILINTE. What! Would you tell old Emilia, that it ill becomes her to set up for a beauty at her age, and that the paint she uses disgusts everyone?

ALCESTE. Undoubtedly.

PHILINTE. Or Dorilas, that he is a bore, and that there is no one at court who is not sick of hearing him boast of his courage, and the lustre of his house?

ALCESTE. Decidedly so.

PHILINTE. You are jesting.

ALCESTE. I am not jesting at all; and I would not spare any one in that respect. It offends my eyes too much; and whether at Court or in town, I behold nothing but what provokes my spleen. I become quite melancholy and deeply grieved to see men behave to each other as they do. Everywhere I find nothing but base flattery, injustice, self-interest, deceit, roguery. I cannot bear it any longer; I am furious; and my intention is to break with all mankind.

PHILINTE. This philosophical spleen is somewhat too savage. I cannot but laugh to see you in these gloomy fits, and fancy that I perceive in us two, brought up together, the two brothers described in *The School for Husbands*, who—

ALCESTE. Good Heavens! drop your insipid comparisons.

PHILINTE. Nay, seriously, leave off these vagaries. The world will not alter for all your meddling. And as plain speaking has such charms for you, I shall tell you frankly that this complaint of yours is as good as a play, wherever you go, and that all those invectives against the manners of the age, make you a laughing stock to many people.

ALCESTE. So much the better Zounds! so much the better. That is just what I want. It is a very good sign, and I rejoice at it. All men are so odious to me, that I should be sorry to appear rational in their eyes.

PHILINTE. But do you wish harm to all mankind?

ALCESTE. Yes I have conceived a terrible hatred for them.

PHILINTE. Shall all poor mortals, without exception, be included in this aversion? There are some, even in the age in which we live—

ALCESTE. No, they are all alike; and I hate all men: some, because they are wicked and mischievous; others because they lend themselves to the wicked, and have not that healthy contempt with which vice ought to inspire all virtuous minds. You can see how unjustly and excessively complacent people are to that bare-faced scoundrel with whom I am at law. You may plainly perceive the traitor through his mask; he is well known every-where in his true colors; his rolling eyes and his honeyed tones impose only on those who do not know him. People are aware that this low-bred fellow, who deserves to be pilloried, has, by the dirtiest jobs, made his way in the world; and that the splendid position he has acquired makes merit repine and virtue blush. Yet whatever dishonourable epithets may be launched against him everywhere, nobody defends his wretched honour. Call him a rogue, an infamous wretch, a confounded scoundrel if you like, all the world will say "yea," and no one contradicts you. But for all that, his bowing and scraping are welcome everywhere; he is received, smiled upon, and wriggles himself into all kinds of society; and, if any appointment is to be secured by intriguing, he will carry the day over a man of the greatest worth. Zounds! these are mortal stabs to me, to see vice parleyed with; and sometimes times I feel suddenly inclined to fly into a wilderness far from the approach of men.

PHILINTE. Great Heaven? let us torment ourselves a little less about the vices of our age, and be a little more lenient to human nature. Let us not scrutinize it with the utmost severity, but look with some indulgence at its failings. In society, we need virtue to be more pliable. If we are too wise, we may be equally to blame. Good sense avoids all extremes, and requires us to be soberly rational. This unbending and virtuous stiffness of ancient times shocks too much the ordinary customs of our own; it requires too great perfection from us mortals; we must yield to the times without being too stubborn; it is the height of folly to busy ourselves in correcting the world. I, as well as yourself, notice a hundred things every day which might be better managed, differently enacted; but whatever I may discover at any moment, people do not see me in a rage like you. I take men quietly just as they are; I accustom my mind to bear with what they do; and I believe that at Court, as well as in the city, my phlegm is as philosophical as your bile.

ALCESTE. But this phlegm, good sir, you who reason so well, could it not be disturbed by anything? And if perchance a friend should betray you; if he forms a subtle plot to get hold of what is yours; if people should try to spread evil reports about you, would you tamely submit to all this without flying into a rage?

PHILINTE. Ay, I look upon all these faults of which you complain as vices inseparably connected with human nature; in short, my mind is no more shocked at seeing a man a rogue, unjust, or selfish, than at seeing vultures, eager for prey, mischievous apes, or fury-lashed wolves.

ALCESTE. What! I should see myself deceived, torn to pieces, robbed, without being—Zounds! I shall say no more about it; all this reasoning is beside the point!

PHILINTE. Upon my word, you would do well to keep silence. Rail a little less at your opponent, and attend a little more to your suit.

ALCESTE. That I shall not do; that is settled long ago.

PHILINTE. But whom then do you expect to solicit for you?

ALCESTE. Whom? Reason, my just right, equity.

PHILINTE. Shall you not pay a visit to any of the judges?

ALCESTE. No. Is my cause unjust or dubious?

PHILINTE. I am agreed on that; but you know what harm intrigues do, and—

ALCESTE. No. I am resolved not to stir a step. I am either right or wrong.

PHILINTE. Do not trust to that.

ALCESTE. I shall not budge an inch.

PHILINTE. Your opponent is powerful, and by his underhand work, may induce—

ALCESTE. It does not matter.

PHILINTE. You will make a mistake.

ALCESTE. Be it so. I wish to see the end of it.

PHILINTE. But—

ALCESTE. I shall have the satisfaction of losing my suit.

PHILINTE. But after all—

ALCESTE. I shall see by this trial whether men have sufficient impudence, are wicked, villainous, and perverse enough to do me this injustice in the face of the whole world.

PHILINTE. What a strange fellow!

ALCESTE. I could wish, were it to cost me ever so much, that, for the fun of the thing, I lost my case.

PHILINTE. But people will really laugh at you, Alceste, if they hear you go on in this fashion.

ALCESTE. So much the worse for those who will.

PHILINTE. But this rectitude, which you exact so carefully in every case, this absolute integrity in which you intrench yourself, do you perceive it in the lady you love? As for me, I am astonished that, appearing to be at war with the whole human race, you yet, notwithstanding everything that can render it odious to you, have found aught to charm your eyes. And what surprises me still more, is the strange choice your heart has made. The sincere Eliante has a liking for you, the prude Arsinoé looks with favour upon you, yet your heart does not respond to their passion; whilst you wear the chains of Célimène, who sports with you, and whose coquettish humour and malicious wit seems to accord so well with the manner of the times. How comes it that, hating these things as mortally as you do, you endure so much of them in that lady? Are they no longer faults in so sweet a charmer? Do not you perceive them, or if you do, do you excuse them?

ALCESTE. Not so. The love I feel for this young window does not make me blind to her faults, and, notwithstanding the great passion with which she has inspired me, I am the first to see, as well as to condemn, them. But for all this, do what I will, I confess my weakness, she has the art of pleasing me. In vain I see her faults; I may even blame them; in spite of all, she makes me love her. Her charms conquer everything, and, no doubt, my sincere love will purify her heart from the vices of our times.

PHILINTE. If you accomplish this, it will be no small task, Do you believe yourself beloved by her?

ALCESTE. Yes, certainly! I should not love her at all, did I not think so.

PHILINTE. But if her love for you is so apparent, how comes it that your rivals cause you so much uneasiness?

ALCESTE. It is because a heart, deeply smitten, claims all to itself; I come here only with the intention of telling her what, on this subject, my feelings dictate.

PHILINTE. Had I but to choose, her cousin Eliante would have all my love. Her heart, which values yours, is stable and sincere; and this more compatible choice would have suited you better.

ALCESTE. It is true; my good sense tells me so every day; but good sense does not always rule love.

PHILINTE. Well, I fear much for your affections; and the hope which you cherish may perhaps—

SCENE II.

[ORONTE, ALCESTE, PHILINTE.]

ORONTE. [*to* ALCESTE.] I have been informed yonder, that Eliante and Célimène have gone out to make some purchases. But as I heard that you were here, I came to tell you, most sincerely, that I have conceived the greatest regard for you, and that, for a long time, this regard has inspired me with the most ardent wish to be reckoned among your friends. Yes; I like to do homage to merit; and I am most anxious that a bond of friendship should unite us. I suppose that a zealous friend, and of my standing, is not altogether to be rejected. [*all this time* ALCESTE *has been musing, and seems not to be aware that* ORONTE *is addressing him. He looks up only when* ORONTE *says to him.*]—It is to you, if you please, that this speech is addressed.

ALCESTE. To me, sir?

ORONTE. To you. Is it in any way offensive to you?

ALCESTE. Not in the least. But my surprise is very great; and I did not expect that honour.

ORONTE. The regard in which I hold you ought not to astonish you, and you can claim it from the whole world.

ALCESTE. Sir—

ORONTE. Our whole kingdom contains nothing above the dazzling merit which people discover in you.

ALCESTE. Sir—

ORONTE. Yes; for my part, I prefer you to the most important in it.

ALCESTE. Sir—

ORONTE. May Heaven strike me dead, if I lie! And, to convince you, on this very spot, of my feelings, allow me, sir, to embrace you with all my heart, and to solicit a place in your friendship. your hand, if you please. Will you promise me your friendship?

ALCESTE. Sir—

ORONTE. What! you refuse me?

ALCESTE. Sir, you do me too much honour; but friendship is a sacred thing, and to lavish it on every occasion is surely to profane it. Judgment and choice should preside at such a compact; we ought to know more of each other before engaging ourselves; and it may happen that our dispositions are such that we may both of us repent of our bargain.

ORONTE. Upon my word! that is wisely said; and I esteem you all the more for it. Let us therefore leave it to time to form such a pleasing bond; but, meanwhile I am entirely at your disposal. If you have any business at Court, every one knows how well I stand with the King; I have his private ear; and, upon my word, he treats me in everything with the utmost intimacy. In short, I am yours in every emergency; and, as you are a man of brilliant parts, and to inaugurate our charming amity, I come to read you a sonnet which I made a little while ago, and to find out whether it be good enough for publicity.

ALCESTE. I am not fit, sir, to decide such a matter. You will therefore excuse me.

ORONTE. Why so?

ALCESTE. I have the failing of being a little more sincere in those things than is necessary.

ORONTE. The very thing I ask; and I should have reason to complain, if, in laying myself open to you that you might give me your frank opinion, you should deceive me, and disguise anything from me.

ALCESTE. If that be the case, sir, I am perfectly willing.

ORONTE. Sonnet—It is a sonnet—Hope—It is to a lady who flattered my passion with some hope. Hope—They are not long, pompous verses, but mild, tender and melting little lines. [*at every one of these interruptions he looks at* ALCESTE.]

ALCESTE. We shall see.

ORONTE. Hope—I do not know whether the style will strike you as sufficiently clear and easy and whether you will approve of my choice of words.

ALCESTE. We shall soon see, sir.

ORONTE. Besides, you must know that I was only a quarter of an hour in composing it.

ALCESTE. Let us hear, sir; the time signifies nothing.

ORONTE. [*reads.*] Hope, it is true, oft gives relief,
Rocks for a while our tedious pain,
But what a poor advantage, Phillis,
When nought remains, and all is gone!

PHILINTE. I am already charmed with this little bit.

ALCESTE. [*softly to* PHILINTE.] What! do you mean to tell me that you like this stuff?

ORONTE. You once showed some complaisance,
But less would have sufficed,
You should not take that trouble
To give me nought but hope.

PHILINTE. In what pretty terms these thoughts are put!

ALCESTE. How now! you vile flatterer, you praise this rubbish!

ORONTE. If I must wait eternally,
My passion, driven to extremes,
Will fly to death.
Your tender cares cannot prevent this,
Fair Phillis, aye we're in despair,
When we must hope for ever.

PHILINTE. The conclusion is pretty, amorous, admirable.

ALCESTE. [*softly, and aside to* PHILINTE.] A plague on the conclusion! I wish you had concluded to break your nose, you poisoner to the devil!

PHILINTE. I never heard verses more skilfully turned.

ALCESTE. [*softly, and aside.*] Zounds!—

ORONTE. [*to* PHILINTE.] You flatter me; and you are under the impression perhaps—

PHILINTE. No, I am not flattering at all.

ALCESTE. [*softly, and aside.*] What else are you doing, you wretch?

ORONTE. [*to* ALCESTE.] But for you, you know our agreement. Speak to me, I pray, in all sincerity.

ALCESTE. These matters, Sir, are always more or less delicate, and every one is fond of being praised for his wit. But I was saying one day to a certain person, who shall be nameless, when he showed me some of his verses, that a gentleman ought at all times to exercise a great control over that itch for writing which sometimes attacks us, and should keep a tight rein over the strong propensity which one has to display such amusements; and that, in the frequent anxiety to show their productions, people are frequently exposed to act a very foolish part.

ORONTE. Do you wish to convey to me by this that I am wrong in desiring—

ALCESTE. I do not say that exactly. But I told him that writing without warmth becomes a bore; that there needs no other weakness to disgrace a man; that, even if people, on the other hand, had a hundred good qualities, we view them from their worst sides.

ORONTE. Do you find anything to object to in my sonnet?

ALCESTE. I do not say that. But, to keep him from writing, I set before his eyes how, in our days, that desire had spoiled a great many very worthy people.

ORONTE. Do I write badly? Am I like them in any way?

ALCESTE. I do not say that. But, in short, I said to him, What pressing need is there for you to rhyme, and what the deuce drives you into print? If we can pardon the sending into the world of a badly-written book, it will only be in those unfortunate men who write for their livelihood. Believe me, resist your temptations, keep these effusions from the public, and do not, how much so-ever you may be asked, forfeit the reputation which you enjoy at Court of being a man of sense and a gentleman, to take, from the hands of a greedy printer, that of a ridiculous and wretched author. That is what I tried to make him understand.

ORONTE. This is all well and good, and I seem to understand you. But I should like to know what there is in my sonnet to—

ALCESTE. Candidly, you had better put it in your closet. You have been following bad models, and your expressions are not at all natural. Pray what is it—Rocks for a while our tedious pain? And what, When nought remains, and all is gone? What, You should not take that trouble to give me nought but hope? And what, Phillis, aye we're in despair when we must hope for ever? This figurative style, that people are so vain of, is beside all good taste and truth; it is only a play upon words, sheet affectation, and it is not thus that nature speaks. The wretched taste of the age is what I dislike in this. Our forefathers, unpolished as they were, had a much better one; and I value all that is admired now-a-days far less than an old song which I am going to repeat to you:

"Had our great monarch granted me
His Paris large and fair;
And I straightway must quit for aye
The love of my true dear;
Then would I say, King Hal, I pray,
Take back your Paris fair,
I love much mo my dear, I trow,
I love much mo my dear."

This versification is not rich, and the style is antiquated; but do you not see that it is far better than all those trumpery trifles against which good sense revolts, and that in this, passion speaks from the heart?

"Had our great monarch granted me
His Paris large and fair;
And I straightway must quit for aye
The love of my true dear;
Then would I say, King Hal, I pray,
Take back your Paris fair,
I love much mo my dear, I trow,
I love much mo my dear."

This is what a really loving heart would say. [*to* PHILINTE, *who is laughing*.] Yes, master wag, in spite of all your wit, I care more for this than for all the florid pomp and the tinsel which everybody is admiring now-a-days.

ORONTE. And I, I maintain that my verses are very good.

ALCESTE. Doubtless you have your reasons for thinking them so; but you will allow me to have mine, which, with your permission, will remain independent.

ORONTE. It is enough for me that others prize them.

ALCESTE. That is because they know how to dissemble, which I do not.

ORONTE. Do you really believe that you have such a great share of wit?

ALCESTE. If I praised your verses, I should have more.

ORONTE. I shall do very well without your approbation.

ALCESTE. You will have to do without it, if it be all the same.

ORONTE. I should like much to see you compose some on the same subject, just to have a sample of your style.

ALCESTE. I might, perchance, make some as bad; but I should take good care not to show them to any one.

ORONTE. You are mighty positive; and this great sufficiency—

ALCESTE. Pray, seek some one else to flatter you, and not me.

ORONTE. But, my little Sir, drop this haughty tone.

ALCESTE. In truth, my big Sir, I shall do as I like.

PHILINTE. [*coming between them.*] Stop, gentlemen! that is carrying the matter too far. Cease, I pray.

ORONTE. Ah! I am wrong, I confess; and I leave the field to you. I am your servant, Sir, most heartily.

ALCESTE. And I, Sir, am your most humble servant.

SCENE III.

[PHILINTE, ALCESTE.]

PHILINTE. Well! you see. By being too sincere, you have got a nice affair on your hands; I saw that Oronte, in order to be flattered—

ALCESTE. Do not talk to me.

PHILINTE. But—

ALCESTE. No more society for me.

PHILINTE. Is it too much—

ALCESTE. Leave me alone.

PHILINTE. If I—

ALCESTE. Not another word.

PHILINTE. But what—

ALCESTE. I will hear no more.

PHILINTE. But—

ALCESTE. Again?

PHILINTE. People insult—

ALCESTE. Ah! zounds! this is too much. Do not dog my steps.

PHILINTE. You are making fun of me; I shall not leave you.

ACT II.

SCENE I.

[ALCESTE, CÉLIMÈNE.]

ALCESTE. Will you have me speak candidly to you, madam? Well, then, I am very much dissatisfied with your behaviour. I am very angry when I think of it; and I perceive that we shall have to break with each other. Yes; I should only deceive you were I to speak otherwise. Sooner or later a rupture is unavoidable; and if I were to promise the contrary a thousand times, I should not be able to bear this any longer.

CÉLIMÈNE. Oh, I see! it is to quarrel with me, that you wished to conduct me home?

ALCESTE. I do not quarrel. But your disposition, madam, is too ready to give any first comer an entrance into your heart. Too many admirers beset you; and my temper cannot put up with that.

CÉLIMÈNE. Am I to blame for having too many admirers? Can I prevent people from thinking me amiable? and am I to take a stick to drive them away, when they endeavour by tender means to visit me?

ALCESTE. No, madam, there is no need for a stick, but only a heart less yielding and less melting at their love-tales. I am aware that your good looks accompany you, go where you will; but your reception retains those whom your eyes attract; and that gentleness, accorded to those who surrender their arms, finishes on their hearts the sway which your charms began. The too agreeable expectation which you offer them increases their assiduities towards you; and your complacency, a little less extended, would drive away the great crowd of so many admirers. But, tell me, at least, madam, by what good fortune Clitandre has the happiness of pleasing you so mightily? Upon what basis of merit and sublime virtue do you ground the honour of your regard for him? Is it by the long nail on his little finger that he has acquired the esteem which you display for him? Are you, like all the rest of the fashionable world, fascinated by the dazzling merit of his fair wig? Do his great rolls make you love him? Do his many ribbons charm you? Is it by the attraction of his great German breeches that he has conquered your heart, whilst at the same time he pretended to be your slave? Or have his manner of smiling, and his falsetto voice, found out the secret of moving your feelings?

CÉLIMÈNE. How unjustly you take umbrage at him! Do not you know why I countenance him; and that he has promised to interest all his friends in my lawsuit?

ALCESTE. Lose your lawsuit, madam, with patience, and do not countenance a rival whom I detest.

CÉLIMÈNE. But you are getting jealous of the whole world.

ALCESTE. It is because the whole world is so kindly received by you.

CÉLIMÈNE. That is the very thing to calm your frightened mind, because my goodwill is diffused over all: you would have more reason to be offended if you saw me entirely occupied with one.

ALCESTE. But as for me, whom you accuse of too much jealousy, what have I more than any of them, madam, pray?

CÉLIMÈNE. The happiness of knowing that you are beloved.

ALCESTE. And what grounds has my love-sick heart for believing it?

CÉLIMÈNE. I think that, as I have taken the trouble to tell you so, such an avowal ought to satisfy you.

ALCESTE. But who will assure me that you may not, at the same time, say as much to everybody else perhaps?

CÉLIMÈNE. Certainly, for a lover, this is a pretty amorous speech, and you make me out a very nice lady. Well! to remove such a suspicion, I retract this moment everything I have said; and no one but yourself shall for the future impose upon you. Will that satisfy you?

ALCESTE. Zounds! why do I love you so! Ah! if ever I get heart-whole out of your hands, I shall bless Heaven for this rare good fortune. I make no secret of it; I do all that is possible to tear this unfortunate attachment from my heart; but hitherto my greatest efforts have been of no avail; and it is for my sins that I love you thus.

CÉLIMÈNE. It is very true that your affection for me is unequalled.

ALCESTE. As for that, I can challenge the whole world. My love for you cannot be conceived; and never, madam, has any man loved as I do.

CÉLIMÈNE. Your method, however, is entirely new, for you love people only to quarrel with them; it is in peevish expression alone that your feelings vent themselves; no one ever saw such a grumbling swain.

ALCESTE. But it lies with you alone to dissipate this ill-humour. For mercy's sake let us make an end of all these bickerings; deal openly with each other, and try to put a stop—

Scene II.

[CÉLIMÈNE, ALCESTE, BASQUE.]

CÉLIMÈNE. What is the matter?

BASQUE. Acaste is below.

CÉLIMÈNE. Very well! bid him come up.

Scene III.

[CÉLIMÈNE, ALECESTE.]

ALCESTE. What! can one never have a little private conversation with you? You are always ready to receive company; and you cannot, for a single instant, make up your mind to be "not at home."

CÉLIMÈNE. Do you wish me to quarrel with Acaste?

ALCESTE. You have such regard for people, which I by no means like.

CÉLIMÈNE. He is a man never to forgive me, if he knew that his presence could annoy me.

ALCESTE. And what is that to you, to inconvenience yourself so—

CÉLIMÈNE. But, good Heaven! the amity of such as he is of importance; they are a kind of people who, I do not know how, have acquired the right to be heard at Court. They take their part in every conversation; they can do you no good, but they may do you harm; and, whatever support one may find elsewhere, it will never do to be on bad terms with these very noisy gentry.

ALCESTE. In short, whatever people may say or do, you always find reasons to bear with every one; and your very careful judgment—

Scene IV.

[ALCESTE, CÉLIMÈNE, BASQUE.]

BASQUE. Clitandre is here too, madam.

ALCESTE. Exactly so. [*wishes to go.*]

CÉLIMÈNE. Where are you running to?

ALCESTE. I am going.

CÉLIMÈNE. Stay.

ALCESTE. For what?

CÉLIMÈNE. Stay.

ALCESTE. I cannot.

CÉLIMÈNE. I wish it.

ALCESTE. I will not. These conversations only weary me; and it is too bad of you to wish me to endure them.

CÉLIMÈNE. I wish it, I wish it.

ALCESTE. No, it is impossible.

CÉLIMÈNE. Very well, then; go, begone; you can do as you like.

Scene V.

[ELIANTE, PHILINTE, ACASTE, CLITANDRE, ALCESTE, CÉLIMÈNE, BASQUE.]

ELIANTE. [*to* CÉLIMÈNE.] Here are the two marquises coming up with us. Has anyone told you?

CÉLIMÈNE. Yes. [*to* BASQUE.] Place chairs for everyone.

[BASQUE *places chairs, and goes out.*]

[*to* ALCESTE.] You are not gone?

ALCESTE. No; but I am determined, madam, to have you make up your mind either for them or for me.

CÉLIMÈNE. Hold your tongue.

ALCESTE. This very day you shall explain yourself.

CÉLIMÈNE. You are losing your senses.

ALCESTE. Not at all. You shall declare yourself.

CÉLIMÈNE. Indeed!

ALCESTE. You must take your stand.

CÉLIMÈNE. You are jesting, I believe.

ALCESTE. Not so. But you must choose. I have been too patient.

CLITANDRE. Egad! I have just come from the Louvre, where Cléonte, at the levee, made himself very ridiculous. Has he not some friend who could charitably enlighten him upon his manners?

CÉLIMÈNE. Truth to say, he compromises himself very much in society; everywhere he carries himself with an air that is noticed at first sight, and when after a short absence you meet him again, he is still more absurd than ever.

ACASTE. Egad! Talk of absurd people, just now, one of the most tedious ones was annoying me. That reasoner, Damon, kept me, if you please, for a full hour in the broiling sun, away from my Sedan chair.

CÉLIMÈNE. He is a strange talker, and one who always finds the means of telling you nothing with a great flow of words. There is no sense at all in his tittle-tattle, and all that we hear is but noise.

ELIANTE. [*to* PHILINTE.] This beginning is not bad; and the conversation takes a sufficiently agreeable turn against our neighbours.

CLITANDRE. Timante, too, Madam, is another original.

CÉLIMÈNE. He is a complete mystery from top to toe, who throws upon you, in passing, a bewildered glance, and who, without having anything to do, is always busy. Whatever he utters is accompanied with grimaces; he quite oppresses people by his ceremonies. To interrupt a conversation, he has always a secret to whisper to you, and that secret turns out to be nothing. Of the merest molehill he makes a mountain, and whispers everything in your ear, even to a "good-day."

ACASTE. And Geralde, Madam?

CÉLIMÈNE. That tiresome story-teller! He never comes down from his nobleman's pedestal; he continually mixes with the best society, and never quotes any one of minor rank than a Duke, Prince, or Princess. Rank is his hobby, and his conversation is of nothing but horses, carriages, and dogs. He thee's and thou's persons of the highest standing, and the word Sir is quite obsolete with him.

CLITANDRE. It is said that he is on the best of terms with Bélise.

CÉLIMÈNE. Poor silly woman, and the dreariest company! When she comes to visit me, I suffer from martyrdom; one has to rack one's brain perpetually to find out what to say to her; and the impossibility of her expressing her thoughts allows the conversation to drop every minute. In vain you try to overcome her stupid silence by the assistance of the most commonplace topics; even the fine weather, the rain, the heat and the cold are subjects, which, with her, are soon exhausted. Yet for all that, her calls, unbearable enough, are prolonged to an insufferable length; and you may consult the clock, or yawn twenty times, but she stirs no more than a log of wood.

ACASTE. What think you of Adraste?

CÉLIMÈNE. Oh! What excessive pride! He is a man positively puffed out with conceit. His self-importance is never satisfied with the Court, against which he inveighs daily; and whenever an office, a place, or a living is bestowed on another, he is sure to think himself unjustly treated.

CLITANDRE. But young Cléon, whom the most respectable people go to see, what say you of him?

CÉLIMÈNE. That it is to his cook he owes his distinction, and to his table that people pay visits.

ELIANTE. He takes pains to provide the most dainty dishes.

CÉLIMÈNE. True; but I should be very glad if he would not dish up himself. His foolish person is a very bad dish, which, to my thinking, spoils every entertainment which he gives.

PHILINTE. His uncle Damis is very much esteemed; what say you to him, Madam?

CÉLIMÈNE. He is one of my friends.

PHILINTE. I think him a perfect gentleman, and sensible enough.

CÉLIMÈNE. True; but he pretends to too much wit, which annoys me. he is always upon stilts, and, in all his conversations, one sees him labouring to say smart things. Since he took it into his head to be clever, he is so difficult to please that nothing suits his taste. he must needs find mistakes in everything that one writes, and thinks that to bestow praise does not become a wit, that to find fault shows learning, that only fools admire and laugh, and that, by not approving of anything in the works of our time, he is superior to all other people. Even in conversations he finds something to cavil at, the subjects are too trivial for his condescension; and, with arms crossed on his breast, he looks down from the height of his intellect with pity on what everyone says.

ACASTE. Drat it! his very picture.

CLITANDRE. [*to* CÉLIMÈNE.] You have an admirable knack of portraying people to the life.

ALCESTE. Capital, go on, my fine courtly friends. You spare no one, and everyone will have his turn. Nevertheless, let but any one of those persons appear, and we shall see you rush to meet him, offer him your hand, and, with a flattering kiss, give weight to your protestations of being his servant.

CLITANDRE. Why this to us? If what is said offends you, the reproach must be addressed to this lady.

ALCESTE. No, gadzooks! it concerns you; for your assenting smiles draw from her wit all these slanderous remarks. Her satirical vein is incessantly recruited by the culpable incense of your flattery; and her mind would find fewer charms in raillery, if she discovered that no one applauded her. Thus it is that to flatterers we ought everywhere to impute the vices which are sown among mankind.

PHILINTE. But why do you take so great an interest in those people, for you would condemn the very things that are blamed in them?

CÉLIMÈNE. And is not this gentleman bound to contradict? Would you have him subscribe to the general opinion; and must he not everywhere display the spirit of contradiction with which Heaven has endowed him? Other people's sentiments can never please him. He always supports a contrary idea, and he would think himself too much of the common herd, were he observed to be of any one's opinion but his own. The honour of gainsaying has so many charms for him, that he very often takes up the cudgels against himself; he combats his own sentiments as soon as he hears them from other folks' lips.

ALCESTE. In short, madam, the laughters are on your side; and you may launch your satire against me.

PHILINTE. But it is very true, too, that you always take up arms against everything that is said; and, that your avowed spleen cannot bear people to be praised or blamed.

ALCESTE. 'Sdeath! spleen against mankind is always seasonable, because they are never in the right, and I see that, in all their dealings, they either praise impertinently, or censure rashly.

CÉLIMÈNE. But—

ALCESTE. No, Madam, no, though I were to die for it, you have pastimes which I cannot tolerate; and people are very wrong to nourish in your heart this great attachment to the very faults which they blame in you.

CLITANDRE. As for myself, I do not know; but I openly acknowledge that hitherto I have thought this lady faultless.

ACASTE. I see that she is endowed with charms and attractions; but the faults which she has have not struck me.

ALCESTE. So much the more have they struck me; and far from appearing blind, she knows that I take care to reproach her with them. The more we love any one, the less we ought to flatter her. True love shows itself by overlooking nothing; and, were I a lady, I would banish all those mean-spirited lovers who submit to all my sentiments, and whose mild complacencies every moment offer up incense to my vagaries.

CÉLIMÈNE. In short, if hearts were ruled by you we ought, to love well, to relinquish all tenderness, and make it the highest aim of perfect attachment to rail heartily at the persons we love.

ELIANTE. Love, generally speaking, is little apt to put up with these decrees, and lovers are always observed to extol their choice. Their passion never sees aught to blame in it, and in the beloved all things become loveable. They think their faults perfections, and invent sweet terms to call them by. The pale one vies with the jessamine in fairness; another, dark enough to frighten people, becomes an adorable brunette; the lean one has a good shape and is lithe; the stout one has a portly and majestic bearing; the slattern, who has few charms, passes under the name of a careless beauty; the giantess seems a very goddess in their sight; the dwarf is an epitome of all the wonders of Heaven; the proud one has a soul worthy of diadem; the artful brims with wit; the silly one is very good-natured; the chatterbox is good-tempered; and the silent one modest and reticent. Thus a passionate swain loves even the very faults of those of whom he is enamoured.

ALCESTE. And I maintain that—

CÉLIMÈNE. Let us drop the subject, and take a turn or two in the gallery. What! are you going, gentlemen?

CLITANDRE and ACASTE. No, no, Madam.

ALCESTE. The fear of their departure troubles you very much. Go when you like, gentlemen; but I tell you beforehand that I shall not leave until you leave.

ACASTE. Unless it inconveniences this lady, I have nothing to call me elsewhere the whole day.

CLITANDRE. I, provided I am present when the King retires, I have no other matter to call me away.

CÉLIMÈNE. [*to* ALCESTE.] You only joke, I fancy.

ALCESTE. Not at all. We shall soon see whether it is me of whom you wish to get rid.

Scene VI.

[ALCESTE, CÉLIMÈNE, ELIANTE, ACASTE, PHILINTE, CLITANDRE, BASQUE.]

BASQUE. [*to* ALCESTE.] There is a man down stairs, sir, who wishes to speak to you on business which cannot be postponed.

ALCESTE. Tell him that I have no such urgent business.

BASQUE. He wears a jacket with large plaited skirts embroidered with gold.

CÉLIMÈNE. [*to* ALCESTE.] Go and see who it is, or else let him come in.

SCENE VII.

[ALCESTE, CÉLIMÈNE, ELIANTE, ACASTE, PHILINTE, CLITANDRE, A GUARD OF THE MARÉCHAUSSÉE.]

ALCESTE. [*going to meet the guard.*] What may be your pleasure? Come in, sir.

GUARD. I would have a few words privately with you, sir.

ALCESTE. You may speak aloud, sir, so as to let me know.

GUARD. The Marshals of France, whose commands I bear, hereby summon you to appear before them immediately, sir.

ALCESTE. Whom? Me, sir?

GUARD. Yourself.

ALCESTE. And for what?

PHILINTE. [*to* ALCESTE.] It is this ridiculous affair between you and Oronte.

CÉLIMÈNE. [*to* PHILINTE.] What do you mean?

PHILINTE. Oronte and he have been insulting each other just now about some trifling verses which he did not like; and the Marshals wish to nip the affair in the bud.

ALCESTE. Well, I shall never basely submit.

PHILINTE. But you must obey the summons: come, get ready.

ALCESTE. How will they settle this between us? Will the edict of these gentlemen oblige me to approve of the verses which are the cause of our quarrel? I will not retract what I have said; I think them abominable.

PHILINTE. But with a little milder tone—

ALCESTE. I will not abate one jot; the verses are execrable.

PHILINTE. You ought to show a more accommodating spirit. Come along.

ALCESTE. I shall go, but nothing shall induce me to retract.

PHILINTE. Go and show yourself.

ALCESTE. Unless an express order from the King himself commands me to approve of the verses which cause all this trouble, I shall ever maintain, egad, that they are bad, and that a fellow deserves hanging for making them. [*to* CLITANDRE *and* ACASTE *who are laughing.*] Hang it! gentlemen, I did not think I was so amusing.

CÉLIMÈNE. Go quickly whither you are wanted.

ALCESTE. I am going, Madam; but shall come back here to finish our discussion.

ACT III.

SCENE I.

[CLITANDRE, ACASTE.]

CLITANDRE. My dear marquis, you appear mightily pleased with yourself; everything amuses you, and nothing discomposes you. But really and truly, think you, without flattering yourself, that you have good reasons for appearing so joyful?

ACASTE. Egad, I do not find, on looking at myself, any matter to be sorrowful about. I am wealthy, I am young, and am descended from a family which, with some appearance of truth, may be called noble; and I think that, by the rank which my lineage confers upon me, there are very few offices to which I might not aspire. As for courage, which we ought especially to value, it is well known—this without vanity—that I do not lack it; and people have seen me carry on an affair of honour in a manner sufficiently vigorous and brisk. As for wit, I have some, no doubt; and as for good taste, to judge and reason upon everything without study; at "first nights," of which I am very fond, to take my place as a critic upon the stage, to give my opinion as a judge, to applaud, and point out the best passages by repeated bravoes, I am sufficiently adroit; I carry myself well, and am good-looking, have particularly fine teeth, and a good figure. I believe, without flattering myself, that, as for dressing in good taste, very few will dispute the palm with me. I find myself treated with every possible consideration, very much beloved by the fair sex; and I stand very well with the King. With all that, I think, dear marquis, that one might be satisfied with oneself anywhere.

CLITANDRE. True But, finding so many easy conquests elsewhere, why come you here to utter fruitless sighs?

ACASTE. I? Zounds! I have neither the wish nor the disposition to put up with the indifference of any woman. I leave it to awkward and ordinary people to burn constantly for cruel fair maidens, to languish at their feet, and to bear with their severities, to invoke the aid of sighs and tears, and to endeavour, by long and persistent assiduities, to obtain what is denied to their little merit. But men of my stamp, marquis, are not made to love on trust, and be at all the expenses themselves. Be the merit of the fair ever so great, I think, thank Heaven, that we have our value as well as they; that it is not reasonable to enthrall a heart like mine without its costing them anything; and that, to weigh everything in a just scale, the advances should be, at least, reciprocal.

CLITANDRE. Then you think that you are right enough here, marquis?

ACASTE. I have some reason, marquis to think so.

CLITANDRE. Believe me, divest yourself of this great mistake: you flatter yourself, dear friend, and are altogether self-deceived.

ACASTE. It is true. I flatter myself, and am, in fact, altogether, self-deceived.

CLITANDRE. But what causes you to judge your happiness to be complete?

ACASTE. I flatter myself.

CLITANDRE. Upon what do you ground your belief?

ACASTE. I am altogether self-deceived.

CLITANDRE. Have you any sure proofs?

ACASTE. I am mistaken, I tell you.

CLITANDRE. Has Célimène made you any secret avowal of her inclinations?

ACASTE. No, I am very badly treated by her.

CLITANDRE. Answer me, I pray.

ACASTE. I meet with nothing but rebuffs.

CLITANDRE. A truce to your raillery; and tell me that hope she has held out to you.

ACASTE. I am the rejected, and you are the lucky one. She has a great aversion to me, and one of these days I shall have to hang myself.

CLITANDRE. Nonsense. Shall we two, marquis, to adjust our love affairs, make a compact together? Whenever one of us shall be able to show a certain proof of having the greater share in Célimène's heart, the other shall leave the field free to the supposed conqueror, and by that means rid him of an obstinate rival.

ACASTE. Egad! you please me with these words, and I agree to that from the bottom of my heart. But, hush.

Scene II.

[CÉLIMÈNE, ACASTE, CLITANDRE.]

CÉLIMÈNE. What! here still?

CLITANDRE. Love, madam, detains us.

CÉLIMÈNE. I hear a carriage below. Do you know whose it is?

CLITANDRE. No.

Scene III.

[CÉLIMÈNE, ACASTE, CLITANDRE, BASQUE.]

BASQUE. Arsinoé, Madam, is coming up to see you.
CÉLIMÈNE. What does the woman want with me?
BASQUE. Eliante is down stairs talking to her.
CÉLIMÈNE. What is she thinking about, and what brings her here?
ACASTE. She has everywhere the reputation of being a consummate prude, and her fervent zeal—
CÉLIMÈNE. Psha, downright humbug. In her inmost soul she is as worldly as any; and her every nerve is strained to hook some one, without being successful, however. She can only look with envious eyes on the accepted lovers of others; and in her wretched condition, forsaken by all, she is for ever railing against the blindness of the age. She endeavours to hide the dreadful isolation of her home under a false cloak of prudishness; and to save the credit of her feeble charms, she brands as criminal the power which they lack. Yet a swain would not come at all amiss to the lady; and she has even a tender hankering after Alceste. Every attention that he pays me, she looks upon as a theft committed by me, and as an insult to her attractions; and her jealous spite, which she can hardly hide, breaks out against me at every opportunity, and in an underhand manner. In short, I never saw anything, to my fancy, so stupid. She is impertinent to the last degree—

Scene IV.

[ARSINOÉ, CÉLIMÈNE, CLITANDRE, ACASTE.]

CÉLIMÈNE. Ah! what happy chance brings you here, Madam? I was really getting uneasy about you.
ARSINOÉ. I have come to give you some advice as a matter of duty.
CÉLIMÈNE. How very glad I am to see you! [*exeunt* CLITANDRE *and* ACASTE, *laughing.*]

Scene V.

[ARSINOÉ, CÉLIMÈNE.]

ARSINOÉ. They could not have left at a more convenient opportunity.
CÉLIMÈNE. Shall we sit down?
ARSINOÉ. It is not necessary. Friendship, Madam, must especially show itself in matters which may be of consequence to us; and as

there are none of greater importance than honour and decorum, I come to prove to you, by an advice which closely touches your reputation, the friendship which I feel for you. Yesterday I was with some people of rare virtue, where the conversation turned upon you; and there, your conduct, which is causing some stir, was unfortunately, Madam, far from being commended. That crowd of people, whose visits you permit, your gallantry and the noise it makes, were criticised rather more freely and more severely than I could have wished. You can easily imagine whose part I took. I did all I could to defend you. I exonerated you, and vouched for the purity of your heart, and the honesty of your intentions. But you know there are things in life, which one cannot well defend, although one may have the greatest wish to do so; and I was at last obliged to confess that the way in which you lived did you some harm; that, in the eyes of the world, it had a doubtful look; that there was no story so ill-natured as not to be everywhere told about it; and that, if you liked, your behaviour might give less cause for censure. Not that I believe that decency is in any way outraged. Heaven forbid that I should harbour such a thought! But the world is so ready to give credit to the faintest shadow of a crime, and it is not enough to live blameless one's self. Madam, I believe you to be too sensible not to take in good part this useful counsel, and not to ascribe it only to the inner promptings of an affection that feels an interest in your welfare.

CÉLIMÈNE. Madam, I have a great many thanks to return you. Such counsel lays me under an obligation; and, far from taking it amiss, I intend this very moment to repay the favour, by giving you an advice, which also touches your reputation closely; and as I see you prove yourself my friend by acquainting me with the stories that are current of me, I shall follow so nice an example, by informing you what is said of you. In a house the other day, where I paid a visit, I met some people of exemplary merit, who, while talking of the proper duties of a well spent life, turned the topic of the conversation upon you, Madam. There your prudishness and your too fervent zeal were not at all cited as a good example. This affectation of a grave demeanour, your eternal conversations on wisdom and honor, your mincings and mouthings at the slightest shadows of indecency, which an innocent though ambiguous word may convey, that lofty esteem in which you hold yourself, and those pitying glances which you cast upon all, your frequent lectures and your acrid censures on things which are pure and harmless; all this, if I may speak frankly to you, Madam, was blamed unanimously. What is the good, said they, of this modest mien and this prudent exterior, which is belied by all the rest? She says her prayers with the utmost exactness; but she beats her servants and pays them no wages. She displays great fervour in every place of devotion; but she paints and wishes to appear handsome. She covers the nudities in her pictures; but loves the reality. As for me, I undertook your defence against everyone, and positively assured them that it was nothing but scandal; but the general opinion went against me, as they came to the conclusion that you would do well to concern yourself less about the actions of others, and take a little more pains with your own; that one ought to look a long time at one's self before thinking of condemning other people; that when we wish to correct others, we ought to add the weight of a blameless life; and that even then, it would be better to leave it to those whom Heaven has ordained for the task. Madam, I also believe you to be too sensible not to take in good part this useful counsel, and not to ascribe it only to the inner promptings of an affection that feels an interest in your welfare.

ARSINOÉ. To whatever we may be exposed when we reprove, I did not expect this retort, Madam, and, by its very sting, I see how my sincere advice has hurt your feelings.

CÉLIMÈNE. On the contrary, Madam; and, if we were reasonable, these mutual counsels would become customary. If honestly made use of, it would to a great extent destroy the excellent opinion people have of themselves. It depends entirely on you whether we shall continue this trustworthy practice with equal zeal, and whether we shall take great care to tell each other, between ourselves, what we hear, you of me, I of you.

ARSINOÉ. Ah! Madam, I can hear nothing said of you. It is in me that people find so much to reprove.

CÉLIMÈNE. Madam, it is easy, I believe, to blame or praise everything; and everyone may be right, according to their age and taste. There is a time for gallantry, there is one also for prudishness. One may out of policy take to it, when youthful attractions have faded away. It sometimes serves to hide vexatious ravages of time. I do not say that I shall not follow your example, one of these days. Those things come with old age; but twenty, as everyone well knows, is not an age to play the prude.

ARSINOÉ. You certainly pride yourself upon a very small advantage, and you boast terribly of your age. Whatever difference there may be between your years and mine, there is no occasion to make such a tremendous fuss about it; and I am at a loss to know, Madam, why you should get so angry, and what makes you goad me in this manner.

CÉLIMÈNE. And I, Madam, am at an equal loss to know why one hears you inveigh so bitterly against me everywhere. Must I always suffer for your vexations? Can I help it, if people refuse to pay you any attentions? If men will fall in love with me, and will persist in offering me each day those attentions of which your heart would wish to see me deprived, I cannot alter it, and it is not my fault. I leave you the field free, and do not prevent you from having charms to attract people.

ARSINOÉ. Alas! and do you think that I would trouble myself about this crowd of lovers of which you are so vain, and that it is not very easy to judge at what price they may be attracted now-a-days? Do you wish to make it be believed, that, judging by what is going on, your merit alone attracts this crowd; that their affection for you is strictly honest, and that it is for nothing but your virtue that they all pay you their court? People are not blinded by those empty pretences; the world is not duped in that way; and I see many ladies who are capable of inspiring a tender feeling, yet who do not succeed in attracting a crowd of beaux; and from that fact we may draw our conclusion that those conquests are not altogether made without some great advances; that no one cares to sigh for us, for our handsome looks only; and that the attentions bestowed on us are generally dearly bought. Do not therefore pull yourself up with vain-glory about the trifling advantages of a poor victory; and moderate slightly the pride on your good looks, instead of looking down upon people on account of them. If I were at all envious about your conquests, I dare say, that I might manage like other people; be under no restraint, and thus show plainly that one may have lovers, when one wishes for them.

CÉLIMÈNE. Do have some then, Madam, and let us see you try it; endeavour to please by this extraordinary secret; and without—

ARSINOÉ. Let us break off this conversation, madam, it might excite too much both your temper and mine; and I would have already taken my leave, had I not been obliged to wait for my carriage.

CÉLIMÈNE. Please stay as long as you like, and do not hurry yourself on that account, madam. But instead of wearying you any longer with my presence, I am going to give you some more pleasant company. This gentleman, who comes very opportunely, will better supply my place in entertaining you.

Scene VI.

[ALCESTE, CÉLIMÈNE, ARSINOÉ.]

CÉLIMÈNE. Alceste, I have to write a few lines, which I cannot well delay. Please to stay with this lady; she will all the more easily excuse my rudeness.

Scene VII.

[ALCESTE, ARSINOÉ.]

ARSINOÉ. You see, I am left here to entertain you, until my coach comes round. She could have devised no more charming treat for me, than such a conversation. Indeed, people of exceptional merit attract the esteem and love of every one; and yours has undoubtedly some secret charm, which makes me feel interested in all your doings. I could wish that the Court, with a real regard to your merits would do more justice to your deserts. You have reason to complain; and it vexes me to see that day by day nothing is done for you.

ALCESTE. For me, Madam? And by what right could I pretend to anything? What service have I rendered to the State? Pray, what have I done, so brilliant in itself, to complain of the Court doing nothing for me?

ARSINOÉ. Not everyone whom the State delights to honour, has rendered signal services; there must be an opportunity as well as the power; and the abilities which you allow us to perceive, ought—

ALCESTE. For Heaven's sake, let us have no more of my abilities, I pray. What would you have the Court to do? It would have enough to do, and have its hands full, to discover the merits of people.

ARSINOÉ. Sterling merit discovers itself. A great deal is made of yours in certain places; and let me tell you that, not later than yesterday, you were highly spoken of in two distinguished circles, by people of very great standing.

ALCESTE. As for that, Madam, everyone is praised now-a-days, and very little discrimination is shown in our times. Everything is equally endowed with great merit, so that it is no longer an honour to be lauded. Praises abound, they throw them at one's head, and even my valet is put in the gazette.

ARSINOÉ. As for me, I could wish that, to bring yourself into greater notice, some place at Court might tempt you. If you will only give me a hint that you seriously think about it, a great many engines might be set in motion to serve you; and I know some people whom I could employ for you, and who would manage the matter smoothly enough.

ALCESTE. And what should I do when I got there, Madam? My disposition rather prompts me to keep away from it. Heaven, when ushering me into the world, did not give me a mind suited for the atmosphere of a Court. I have not the qualifications necessary for success, nor for making my fortune there. To be open and candid is my chief talent; I possess not the art of deceiving people in conversation; and he who has not the gift of concealing his thoughts, ought not to stay long in those places. When not at Court, one has not, doubtless, that standing, and the advantage of those honourable titles which it bestows now-a-days; but, on the other hand, one has not the vexation of playing the silly fool. One has not to bear a thousand galling rebuffs; one is not, as it were, forced to praise the verses of mister so-and-so, to laud Madam such and such, and to put up with the whims of some ingenious marquis.

ARSINOÉ. Since you wish it, let us drop the subject of the Court: but I cannot help grieving for your amours; and, to tell you my opinions candidly on that head, I could heartily wish your affections better bestowed. You certainly deserve a much happier fate, and she who has fascinated you is unworthy of you.

ALCESTE. But in saying so, Madam, remember, I pray, that this lady is your friend.

ARSINOÉ. True. But really my conscience revolts at the thought of suffering any longer the wrong that is done to you. The position in which I see you afflicts my very soul, and I caution you that your affections are betrayed.

ALCESTE. This is certainly showing me a deal of good feeling, Madam, and such information is very welcome to a lover.

ARSINOÉ. Yes, for all Célimène is my friend, I do not hesitate to call her unworthy of possessing the heart of a man of honour; and hers only pretends to respond to yours.

ALCESTE. That is very possible, Madam, one cannot look into the heart; but your charitable feelings might well have refrained from awakening such a suspicion as mine.

ARSINOÉ. Nothing is easier than to say no more about it, if you do not wish to be undeceived.

ALCESTE. Just so. But whatever may be openly said on this subject is not half so annoying as hints thrown out; and I for one would prefer to be plainly told that only which could be clearly proved.

ARSINOÉ. Very well! and that is sufficient; I can fully enlighten you upon this subject. I will have you believe nothing but what your own eyes see. Only have the kindness to escort me as far as my house; and I will give you undeniable proof of the faithlessness of your fair one's heart; and if, after that, you can find charms in anyone else, we will perhaps find you some consolation.

Act IV.

Scene I.

[ELIANTE, PHILINTE.]

PHILINTE. No, never have I seen so obstinate a mind, nor a reconciliation more difficult to effect. In vain was Alceste tried on all sides; he would still maintain his opinion; and never, I believe, has a more curious dispute engaged the attention of those gentlemen. "No, gentlemen," exclaimed he, "I will not retract, and I shall agree with you on every point, except on this one. At what is Oronte offended? and with what does he reproach me? Does it reflect upon his honour that he cannot write well? What is my opinion to him, which he has altogether wrongly construed? One may be a perfect gentleman, and write bad verses; those things have nothing to do with honour. I take him to be a gallant man in every way; a man of standing, of merit, and courage, anything you like, but he is a wretched author. I shall praise, if you wish, his mode of living, his lavishness, his skill in riding, in fencing, in dancing; but as to praising his verses, I am his humble servant; and if one has not the gift of composing better, one ought to leave off rhyming altogether, unless condemned to it on forfeit of one's life." In short, all the modification they could with difficulty obtain from him, was to say, in what he thought a much gentler tone—"I am sorry, Sir, to be so difficult to please; and out of regard to you, I could wish, with all my heart, to have found your sonnet a little better." And they compelled them to settle this dispute quickly with an embrace.

ELIANTE. He is very eccentric in his doings; but I must confess that I think a great deal of him; and the candour upon which he prides himself has something noble and heroic in it. It is a rare virtue now-a-days, and I, for one, should not be sorry to meet with it everywhere.

PHILINTE. As for me, the more I see of him, the more I am amazed at that passion to which his whole heart is given up. I cannot conceive how, with a disposition like his, he has taken it into his head to love at all; and still less can I understand how your cousin happens to be the person to whom his feelings are inclined.

ELIANTE. That shows that love is not always produced by compatibility of temper; and in this case, all the pretty theories of gentle sympathies are belied.

PHILINTE. But do you think him beloved in return, to judge from what we see?

ELIANTE. That is a point not easily decided. How can we judge whether it be true she loves? Her own heart is not so very sure of what it feels. It sometimes loves, without being quite aware of it, and at other times thinks it does, without the least grounds.

PHILINTE. I think that our friend will have more trouble with this cousin of yours than he imagines; and to tell you the truth, if he were of my mind, he would bestow his affections elsewhere; and by a better choice, we should see him, Madam, profit by the kind feelings which your heart evinces for him.

ELIANTE. As for me, I do not mince matters, and I think that in such cases we ought to act with sincerity. I do not run counter to his tender feelings; on the contrary, I feel interested in them; and, if it depended only on me, I would unite him to the object of his love. But if, as it may happen in love affairs, his affections should receive a check, and if Célimène should respond to the love of any one else, I could easily be prevailed upon to listen to his addresses, and I should have no repugnance whatever to them on account of their rebuff elsewhere.

PHILINTE. Nor do I, from my side, oppose myself, Madam, to the tender feelings which you entertain for him; and he himself, if he wished, could inform you what I have taken care to say to him on that score. But if, by the union of those two, you should be prevented from accepting his attentions, all mine would endeavour to gain that great favour which your kind feelings offer to him; only too happy, Madam, to have them transferred to myself, if his heart could not respond to yours.

ELIANTE. You are in the humour to jest, Philinte.

PHILINTE. Not so, Madam, I am speaking my inmost feelings. I only wait the opportune moment to offer myself openly, and am wishing most anxiously to hurry its advent.

Scene II.

[ALCESTE, ELIANTE, PHILINTE.]

ALCESTE. Ah, Madam! obtain me justice, for an offence which triumphs over all my constancy.

ELIANTE. What ails you? What disturbs you?

ALCESTE. This much ails me, that it is death to me to think of it; and the upheaving of all creation would less overwhelm me than this accident. It is all over with me—My love—I cannot speak.

ELIANTE. Just endeavour to be composed.

ALCESTE. Oh, just Heaven; can the odious vices of the basest minds be joined to such beauty?

ELIANTE. But, once more, what can have—

ALCESTE. Alas! All is ruined! I am! I am betrayed! I am stricken to death! Célimène—would you credit it! Célimène deceives me and is faithless.

ELIANTE. Have you just grounds for believing so?

PHILINTE. Perhaps it is a suspicion, rashly conceived; and your jealous temper often harbours fancies—

ALCESTE. Ah! 'Sdeath, please to mind your own business, Sir. [*to* ELIANTE.] Her treachery is but too certain, for I have in my pocket a letter in her own handwriting. Yes, Madam, a letter, intended for Oronte, has placed before my eyes my disgrace and her shame; Oronte, whose addresses I believed she avoided, and whom, of all my rivals, I feared the least.

PHILINTE. A letter may deceive by appearances, and is sometimes not so culpable as may be thought.

ALCESTE. Once more, sir, leave me alone, if you please, and trouble yourself only about your own concerns.

ELIANTE. You should moderate your passion; and the insult—

ALCESTE. You must be left to do that, Madam; it is to you that my heart has recourse to-day to free itself from this goading pain. Avenge me on an ungrateful and perfidious relative who basely deceives such constant tenderness. Avenge me for an act that ought to fill you with horror.

ELIANTE. I avenge you? How?

ALCESTE. By accepting my heart. Take it, Madam, instead of the false one; it is in this way that I can avenge myself upon her; and I shall punish her by the sincere attachment, and the profound love, the respectful cares, the eager devotions, the ceaseless attentions which this heart will henceforth offer up at your shrine.

ELIANTE. I certainly sympathize with you in your sufferings, and do not despise your proffered heart; but the wrong done may not be so great as you think, and you might wish to forego this desire for revenge. When the injury proceeds from a beloved object, we form many designs which we never execute; we may find as powerful a reason as we like to break off the connection, the guilty charmer is soon again innocent; all the harm we wish her quickly vanishes, and we know what a lover's anger means.

ALCESTE. No, no, Madam, no. The offence is too cruel; there will be no relenting, and I have done with her. Nothing shall change the resolution I have taken, and I should hate myself for ever loving her again. Here she comes. My anger increases at her approach. I shall taunt her with her black guilt, completely put her to the blush, and, after that, bring you a heart wholly freed from her deceitful attractions.

Scene III.

[CÉLIMÈNE, ALCESTE.]

ALCESTE. [*aside.*] Grant, Heaven, that I may control my temper.

CÉLIMÈNE. [*aside.*] Ah! [*to* ALCESTE.] What is all this trouble that I see you in, and what means those long-drawn sighs, and those black looks which you cast at me?

ALCESTE. That all the wickedness of a heart that is capable is not to be compared to your perfidy; that neither fate, hell, nor Heaven in its wrath, ever produced anything so wicked as you are.

CÉLIMÈNE. These are certainly pretty compliments, which I admire very much.

ALCESTE. Do not jest. This is no time for laughing. Blush rather, you have cause to do so; and I have undeniable proofs of your treachery. This is what the agitations of my mind prognosticated; it was not without cause that my love took alarm; by these frequent suspicions, which were hateful to you, I was trying to discover the misfortune which my eyes have beheld; and in spite of all your care and your skill in dissembling, my star foretold me what I had to fear. But do not imagine that I will bear unavenged this slight of being insulted. I know that we have no command over our inclinations, that love will everywhere spring up spontaneously, that there is no entering a heart by force, and that every soul is free to name its conqueror: I should thus have no reason to complain if you had spoken to me without dissembling, and rejected my advances from the very beginning; my heart would then have been justified in blaming fortune alone. But to see my love encouraged by a deceitful avowal on your part, is an action so treacherous and perfidious, that it cannot meet with too great a punishment; and I can allow my resentment to do anything. Yes, yes; after such an outrage, fear everything; I am no longer myself, I am mad with rage. My senses, struck by the deadly blow with which you kill me, are no longer governed by reason; I give way to the outbursts of a just wrath, and am no longer responsible for what I may do.

CÉLIMÈNE. Whence comes, I pray, such a passion? Speak! Have you lost your senses?

ALCESTE. Yes, yes, I lost them when, to my misfortune, I beheld you, and thus took the poison which kills me, and when I thought to meet with some sincerity in those treacherous charms that bewitched me.

CÉLIMÈNE. Of what treachery have you to complain?

ALCESTE. Ah! how double-faced she is! how well she knows how to dissemble! But I am fully prepared with the means of driving her to extremities. Cast your eyes here and recognize your writing. This picked-up note is sufficient to confound you, and such proof cannot easily be refuted.

CÉLIMÈNE. And this is the cause of your perturbation of spirits?

ALCESTE. You do not blush on beholding this writing!

CÉLIMÈNE. And why should I blush?

ALCESTE. What! You add boldness to craft! Will you disown this note because it bears no name?

CÉLIMÈNE. Why should I disown it, since I wrote it.

ALCESTE. And you can look at it without becoming confused at the crime of which its style accuses you!

CÉLIMÈNE. You are, in truth, a very eccentric man.

ALCESTE. What! you thus out-brave this convincing proof! And the contents so full of tenderness for Oronte, need have nothing in them to outrage me, or to shame you?

CÉLIMÈNE. Oronte! Who told you that this letter is for him?

ALCESTE. The people who put it into my hands this day. But I will even suppose that is for some one else. Has my heart any less cause to complain of yours? Will you, in fact, be less guilty toward me?

CÉLIMÈNE. But if it is a woman to whom this letter is addressed, how can it hurt you, or what is there culpable in it?

ALCESTE. Hem! The prevarication is ingenious, and the excuse excellent. I must own that I did not expect this turn; and nothing but that was wanting to convince me. Do you dare to have recourse to such palpable tricks? Do you think people entirely destitute of common sense? Come, let us see a little by what subterfuge, with what air, you will support so palpable a falsehood; and how you can apply to a woman every word of this note which evinces so much tenderness! Reconcile, if you can, to hide your deceit, what I am about to read.—

CÉLIMÈNE. It does not suit me to do so. I think it ridiculous that you should take so much upon yourself, and tell me to my face what you have the daring to say to me!

ALCESTE. No, no, without flying into a rage, take a little trouble to explain these terms.

CÉLIMÈNE. No, I shall do nothing of the kind, and it matters very little to me what you think upon the subject.

ALCESTE. I pray you, show me, and I shall be satisfied, if this letter can be explained as meant for a woman.

CÉLIMÈNE. Not at all. It is for Oronte; and I will have you believe it. I accept all his attentions gladly; I admire what he says, I like him, and I shall agree to whatever you please. Do as you like, and act as you think proper; let nothing hinder you and do not harass me any longer.

ALCESTE. [*aside.*] Heavens! can anything more cruel be conceived, and was ever heart treated like mine? What! I am justly angry with her, I come to complain, and I am quarreled with instead! My grief and my suspicions are excited to the utmost, I am allowed to believe everything, she boasts of everything; and yet, my heart is still sufficiently mean not to be able to break the bonds that hold it fast, and not to arm itself with a generous contempt for the ungrateful object of which it is too much enamoured. [*to Célimène.*] Perfidious woman, you know well how to take advantage of my great weakness, and to employ for your own purpose that excessive, astonishing, and fatal love which your treacherous looks have inspired! Defend yourself at least from this crime that overwhelms me, and stop pretending to be guilty. Show me, if you can, that this letter is innocent; my affection will even consent to assist you. At any rate, endeavour to appear faithful, and I shall strive to believe you such.

CÉLIMÈNE. Bah, you are mad with your jealous frenzies, and do not deserve the love which I have for you. I should much like to know what could compel me to stoop for you to the baseness of dissembling; and why, if my heart were disposed towards another, I should not say so candidly. What! does the kind assurance of my sentiments towards you not defend me sufficiently against all your suspicions? Ought they to possess any weight at all with such a guarantee? Is it not insulting me even to listen to them? And since it is with the utmost difficulty that we can resolve to confess our love, since the strict honour of our sex, hostile to our passion, strongly opposes such a confession, ought a lover who sees such an obstacle overcome for his sake, doubt with impunity our avowal? And is he not greatly to blame in not assuring himself of the truth of that which is never said but after a severe struggle with oneself? Begone, such suspicions deserve my anger, and you are not worthy of being cared for. I am silly, and am vexed at my own simplicity in still preserving the least kindness for you. I ought to place my affections elsewhere, and give you a just cause for complaint.

ALCESTE. Ah! you traitress! mine is a strange infatuation for you; those tender expressions are, no doubt, meant only to deceive me. But it matters little, I must submit to my fate; my very soul is wrapt up in you; I will see to the bitter end how your heart will act towards me, and whether it will be black enough to deceive me.

CÉLIMÈNE. No, you do not love me as you ought to love.

ALCESTE. Indeed! Nothing is to be compared to my exceeding love; and, in its eagerness to show itself to the whole world, it goes even so far as to form wishes against you. Yes, I could wish that no one thought you handsome, that you were reduced to a miserable existence; that Heaven, at your birth, had bestowed upon you nothing; that you had no rank, no nobility, no wealth, so that I might openly proffer my heart, and thus make amends to you for the injustice of such a lot; and that, this very day, I might have the joy and the glory of seeing you owe everything to my love.

CÉLIMÈNE. This is wishing me well in a strange way! Heaven grant that you may never have occasion—But here comes Monsieur Dubois curiously decked out.

SCENE IV.

[CÉLIMÈNE, ALCESTE, DUBOIS.]

ALCESTE. What means this strange attire, and that frightened look? What ails you?

DUBOIS. Sir—

ALCESTE. Well?

DUBOIS. The most mysterious event.

ALCESTE. What is it?

DUBOIS. Our affairs are turning out badly, Sir.

ALCESTE. What?

DUBOIS. Shall I speak out?

ALCESTE. Yes, do, and quickly.

DUBOIS. Is there no one there?

ALCESTE. Curse your trifling! Will you speak?

DUBOIS. Sir, we must beat a retreat.

ALCESTE. What do you mean?

DUBOIS. We must steal away from this quietly.

ALCESTE. And why?

DUBOIS. I tell you that we must leave this place.

ALCESTE. The reason?

DUBOIS. You must go, Sir, without staying to take leave.

ALCESTE. But what is the meaning of this strain?

DUBOIS. The meaning is, Sir, that you must make yourself scarce.

ALCESTE. I shall knock you on the head to a certainty, booby, if you do not explain yourself more clearly.

DUBOIS. A fellow, Sir, with a black dress, and as black a look, got as far as the kitchen to leave a paper with us, scribbled over in such a fashion that old Nick himself could not have read it. It is about your law-suit, I make no doubt; but the very devil, I believe, could not make head nor tail of it.

ALCESTE. Well! what then? What has the paper to do with the going away of which you speak, you scoundrel?

DUBOIS. I must tell you, Sir, that, about an hour afterwards, a gentleman who often calls, came to ask for you quite eagerly, and not finding you at home, quietly told me, knowing how attached I am to you, to let you know—Stop a moment, what the deuce is his name?

ALCESTE. Never mind his name, you scoundrel, and tell me what he told you.

DUBOIS. He is one of your friends, in short, that is sufficient. He told me that for your very life you must get away from this, and that you are threatened with arrest.

ALCESTE. But how! has he not specified anything?

DUBOIS. No He asked me for ink and paper, and has sent you a line from which you can, I think, fathom the mystery!

ALCESTE. Hand it over then.

CÉLIMÈNE. What can all this mean?

ALCESTE. I do not know; but I am anxious to be informed. Have you almost done, devil take you?

DUBOIS. [*after having fumbled for some time for the note.*] After all, Sir, I have left it on your table.

ALCESTE. I do not know what keeps me from—

CÉLIMÈNE. Do not put yourself in a passion, but go and unravel this perplexing business.

ALCESTE. It seems that fate, whatever I may do has sworn to prevent my having a conversation with you. But, to get the better of her, allow me to see you again, Madam, before the end of the day.

Act V.

Scene I.

[ALCESTE, PHILINTE.]

ALCESTE. I tell you, my mind is made up about it.

PHILINTE. But, whatever this blow may be, does it compel you—

ALCESTE. You may talk and argue till doomsday if you like, nothing can avert me from what I have said. The age we live in is too perverse, and I am determined to withdraw altogether from intercourse with the world. What! when honour, probity, decency, and the laws, are all against my adversary; when the equity of my claim is everywhere cried up; when my mind is at rest as to the justice of my cause, I meanwhile see myself betrayed by its issue! What! I have got justice on my side, and I lose my case! A wretch, whose scandalous history is well known, comes off triumphant by the blackest falsehood! All good faith yields to his treachery! He finds the means of being in the right, whilst cutting my throat! The weight of his dissimulation, so full of cunning, overthrows the right and turns the scales of justice! He obtains even a decree of court to crown his villainy. And, not content with the wrong he is doing me, there is abroad in society an abominable book, of which the very reading is to be condemned, a book that deserves the utmost severity, and of which the scoundrel has the impudence to proclaim me the author. Upon this, Oronte is observed to mutter, and tries wickedly to support the imposture! He, who holds an honourable position at Court, to whom I have done nothing except having been sincere and candid, who came to ask me in spite of myself of my opinion of some of his verses; and because I treat him honestly, and will not betray either him or truth, he assists in overwhelming me with a trumped-up crime. Behold him now my greatest enemy! And I shall never obtain his sincere forgiveness, because I did not think that his sonnet was good! 'Sdeath! to think that mankind is made thus! The thirst for fame induces them to do such things! This is the good faith, the virtuous zeal, the justice and the honour to be found amongst them! Let us begone; it is too much to endure the vexations they are devising; let us get out of this wood, this cut-throat hole; and since men behave towards each other like real wolves, wretches, you shall never see me again as long as I live.

PHILINTE. I think you are acting somewhat hastily; and the harm done is not so great as you would make it out. Whatever your adversary dares to impute to you has not had the effect of causing you to be arrested. We see his false reports defeating themselves, and this action is likely to hurt him much more than you.

ALCESTE. Him? he does not mind the scandal of such tricks as these. He has a license to be an errant knave; and this event, far from damaging his position, will obtain him a still better standing to-morrow.

PHILINTE. In short, it is certain that little notice has been taken of the report which his malice spread against you; from that side you have already nothing to fear; and as for your law-suit, of which you certainly have reason to complain, it is easy for you to bring the trial on afresh, and against this decision—

ALCESTE. No, I shall leave it as it is. Whatever cruel wrong this verdict may inflict, I shall take particular care not to have it set aside. We see too plainly how right is maltreated in it, and I wish to go down to posterity as a signal proof, as a notorious testimony of the wickedness of the men of our age. It may indeed cost me twenty thousand francs, but at the cost of twenty thousand francs I shall have the right of railing against the iniquity of human nature, and of nourishing an undying hatred of it.

PHILINTE. But after all—

ALCESTE. But after all, your pains are thrown away. What can you, sir, say upon this head? Would you have the assurance to wish, to my face, to excuse the villainy of all that is happening?

PHILINTE. No, I agree with you in all that you say. Everything goes by intrigue, and by pure influence. It is only trickery which carries the day in our time, and men ought to act differently. But is their want of equity a reason for wishing to withdraw from their society? All human failings give us, in life, the means of exercising our philosophy. It is the best employment for virtue; and if probity reigned everywhere, if all hearts were candid, just, and tractable, most of our virtues would be useless to us, inasmuch as their functions are to bear, without annoyance, the injustice of others in our good cause; and just in the same way as a heart full of virtue—

ALCESTE. I know that you are a most fluent speaker, sir; that you always abound in fine arguments; but you are wasting your time, and all your fine speeches. Reason tells me to retire for my own good. I cannot command my tongue sufficiently; I cannot answer for what I might say, and should very probably get myself into a hundred scrapes. Allow me, without any more words, to wait for Célimène. She must consent to the plan that brings me here. I shall see whether her heart has any love for me; and this very hour will prove it to me.

PHILINTE. Let us go upstairs to Eliante, and wait her coming.

ALCESTE. No, my mind is too harassed. You go and see her, and leave me in this little dark corner with my black care.

PHILINTE. That is strange company to leave you in; I will induce Eliante to come down.

Scene II.

[CÉLIMÈNE, ORONTE, ALCESTE.]

ORONTE. Yes, Madam, it remains for you to consider whether, by ties so dear, you will make me wholly yours, I must be absolutely certain of your affection: a lover dislikes to be held in suspense upon such a subject. If the ardour of my affection has been able to move your feelings, you ought not to hesitate to let me see it; and the proof, after all, which I ask of you, is not to allow Alceste to wait upon you any longer; to sacrifice him to my love, and, in short, to banish him from your house this very day.

CÉLIMÈNE. But why are you so incensed against him; you, whom I have so often heard speak of his merits?

ORONTE. There is no need, Madam, of these explanations; the question is, what are your feelings? Please to choose between the one or the other; my resolution depends entirely upon yours.

ALCESTE. [*coming out of his corner.*] Yes, this gentleman is right, Madam, you must make a choice; and his request agrees perfectly with mine. I am equally eager, and the same anxiety brings me here. My love requires a sure proof. Things cannot go on any longer in this way, and the moment has arrived for explaining your feelings.

ORONTE. I have no wish, Sir, in any way to disturb, by an untimely affection, your good fortune.

ALCESTE. And I have no wish, Sir, jealous or not jealous, to share aught in her heart with you.

ORONTE. If she prefers your affection to mine—

ALCESTE. If she has the slightest inclination towards you—

ORONTE. I swear henceforth not to pretend to it again.

ALCESTE. I peremptorily swear never to see her again.

ORONTE. Madam, it remains with you now to speak openly.

ALCESTE. Madam, you can explain yourself fearlessly.

ORONTE. You have simply to tell us where your feelings are engaged.

ALCESTE. You may simply finish the matter, by choosing between us two.

ORONTE. What! you seem to be at a loss to make such a choice.

ALCESTE. What! your heart still wavers, and appears uncertain!

CÉLIMÈNE. Good Heavens, how out of place is this persistence, and how very unreasonable you both show yourselves! It is not that I do not know whom to prefer, nor is it my heart that wavers. It is not at all in doubt between you two; and nothing could be more quickly accomplished than the choice of my affections. But to tell the truth, I feel too confused to pronounce such an avowal before you; I think that disobliging words ought not to be spoken in people's presence; that a heart can give sufficient proof of its attachment without going so far as to break with everyone; and gentler intimations suffice to inform a lover of the ill success of his suit.

ORONTE. No, no, I do not fear a frank avowal; for my part I consent to it.

ALCESTE. And I demand it; it is just its very publicity that I claim, and I do not wish you to spare my feelings in the least. Your great study has always been to keep friends with everyone; but no more trifling, no more uncertainty. You must explain yourself clearly, or I shall take your refusal as a verdict; I shall know, for my part, how to interpret your silence, and shall consider it as a confirmation of the worst.

ORONTE. I owe you many thanks, sir, for this wrath, and I say in every respect as you do.

CÉLIMÈNE. How you weary me with such a whim! Is there any justice in what you ask? And have I not told you what motive prevents me? I will be judged by Eliante, who is just coming.

SCENE III.

[ELIANTE, PHILINTE, CÉLIMÈNE, ORONTE, ALCESTE.]

CÉLIMÈNE. Good cousin, I am being persecuted here by people who have concerted to do so. They both demand, with the same warmth, that I should declare whom my heart has chosen, and that, by a decision which I must give before their very faces, I should forbid one of them to tease me any more with his attentions. Say, has ever such a thing been done?

ÉLIANTE. Pray, do not consult me upon such a matter. You may perhaps address yourself to a wrong person, for I am decidedly for people who speak their mind.

ORONTE. Madam, it is useless for you to decline.

ALCESTE. All your evasions here will be badly supported.

ORONTE. You must speak, you must, and no longer waver.

ALCESTE. You need do no more than remain silent.

ORONTE. I desire but one word to end our discussions.

ALCESTE. To me your silence will convey as much as speech.

SCENE IV.

[ARSINOÉ, CÉLIMÈNE, ELIANTE, ALCESTE, PHILINTE, ACASTE, CLITANDRE, ORONTE.]

ACASTE. [*to* CÉLIMÈNE.] We have both come, by your leave, Madam, to clear up a certain little matter with you.

CLITANDRE. [*to* ORONTE *and* ALCESTE.] Your presence happens fortunately, gentlemen; for this affair concerns you also.

ARSINOÉ. [*to* CÉLIMÈNE.] No doubt you are surprised at seeing me here, Madam; but these gentlemen are the cause of my intrusion. They both came to see me, and complained of a proceeding which I could not have credited. I have too high an opinion of your kindness of heart ever to believe you capable of such a crime; my eyes even have refused to give credence to their strongest proofs, and in my friendship, forgetting trivial disagreements, I have been induced to accompany them here, to hear you refute this slander.

ACASTE. Yes, Madam, let us see, with composure, how you will manage to bear this out. This letter has been written by you, to Clitandre.

CLITANDRE. And this tender epistle you have addressed to Acaste.

ACASTE. [*to* ORONTE *and* ALCESTE.] This writing is not altogether unknown to you, gentlemen, and I have no doubt that her kindness has before now made you familiar with her hand. But this is well worth the trouble of reading.

"You are a strange man to condemn my liveliness of spirits, and to reproach me that I am never so merry as when I am not with you. Nothing could be more unjust; and if you do not come very soon to ask my pardon for this offence, I shall never forgive you as long as I live. Our great hulking booby of a Viscount." He ought to have been here. "Our great hulking booby of a Viscount, with whom you begin your complaints, is a man who would not at all suit me; and ever since I watched him for full three-quarters of an hour spitting in a well to make circles in the water, I never could have a good opinion of him. As for the little Marquis..." that is myself, ladies and gentlemen, be it said without the slightest vanity,... "as for the little Marquis, who held my hand yesterday for a long while, I think that there is nothing so diminutive as his whole person, and his sole merit consists in his cloak and sword. As to the man with the green shoulder knot." [*to* ALCESTE.] It is your turn now, Sir. "As to the man with the green shoulder knot, he amuses me sometimes with his bluntness and his splenetic behaviour; but there are hundreds of times when I think him the greatest bore in the world. Respecting the man with the big waistcoat..." [*to* ORONTE.] This is your share. "Respecting the man with the big waistcoat, who has thought fit to set up as a wit, and wishes to be an author in spite of everyone, I cannot even take the trouble to listen to what he says; and his prose bores me just as much as his poetry. Take it for granted that I do not always enjoy myself so much as you think; and that I wish for you, more than I care to say, amongst all the entertainments to which I am dragged; and that the presence of those we love is an excellent relish to our pleasures."

CLITANDRE. Now for myself.

"Your Clitandre, whom you mention to me, and who has always such a quantity of soft expressions at his command, is the last man for whom I could feel any affection. He must be crazed in persuading himself that I love him; and you are so too in believing that I do not love you. You had better change your fancies for his, and come and see me as often as you can, to help me in bearing the annoyance of being pestered by him." This shows the model of a lovely character, Madam; and I need not tell you what to call it. It is enough. We shall, both of us, show this admirable sketch of your heart everywhere and to everybody.

ACASTE. I might also say something, and the subject is tempting; but I deem you beneath my anger; and I will show you that little marquises can find worthier hearts than yours to console themselves.

SCENE V.

[CÉLIMÈNE, ELIANTE, ARSINOÉ, ALCESTE, ORONTE, PHILINTE.]

ORONTE. What! Am I to be pulled to pieces in this fashion, after all that you have written to me? And does your heart, with all its semblance of love, plight its faith to all mankind by turns! Bah, I have been too great a dupe, but I shall be so no longer. You have done me a service, in showing yourself in your true colours to me. I am the richer by a heart which you thus restore to me, and find my revenge in your loss. [*to* ALCESTE.] Sir, I shall no longer be an obstacle to your flame, and you may settle matters with this lady as soon as you please.

SCENE VI.

[CÉLIMÈNE, ELIANTE, ARSINOÉ, ALCESTE, PHILINTE.]

ARSINOÉ. [*to* CÉLIMÈNE.] This is certainly one of the basest actions which I have ever seen; I can no longer be silent, and feel quite upset. Has any one ever seen the like of it? I do not concern myself much in the affairs of other people, but this gentleman, [*pointing to* ALCESTE.] who has staked the whole of his happiness on you, an honourable and deserving man like this, and who worshipped you to madness, ought he to have been—

ALCESTE. Leave me, I pray you, madam, to manage my own affairs; and do not trouble yourself unnecessarily. In vain do I see you espouse my quarrel. I am unable to repay you for this great zeal; and if ever I intended to avenge myself by choosing some one else it would not be you whom I would select.

ARSINOÉ. And do you imagine, sir, that I ever harboured such a thought, and that I am so very anxious to secure you? You must be very vain, indeed, to flatter yourself with such an idea. Célimène's leavings are a commodity, of which no one needs be so very much enamoured. Pray, undeceive yourself, and do not carry matters with so high a hand. People like me are not for such as you. You will do much better to remain dangling after her skirts, and I long to see so beautiful a match.

SCENE VII.

[CÉLIMÈNE, ELIANTE, ALCESTE, PHILINTE.]

ALCESTE. [*to* CÉLIMÈNE.] Well! I have held my tongue, notwithstanding all I have seen, and I have let everyone have his say before me. Have I controlled myself long enough? and will you now allow me—

CÉLIMÈNE. Yes, you may say what you like; you are justified when you complain, and you may reproach me with anything you please. I confess that I am in the wrong; and overwhelmed by confusion I do not seek by any idle excuse to palliate my fault. The anger of the others I have despised; but I admit my guilt towards you. No doubt, your resentment is just; I know how culpable I must appear to you, that everything speaks of my treachery to you, and that, in short, you have cause to hate me. Do so, I consent to it.

ALCESTE. But can I do so, you traitress? Can I thus get the better of all my tenderness for you? And although I wish to hate you with all my soul, shall I find a heart quite ready to obey me. [*to* ELIANTE *and* PHILINTE.] You see what an unworthy passion can do, and I call you both as witnesses of my infatuation. Nor, truth to say, is this all, and you will see me carry it out to the bitter end, to show you that it is wrong to call us wise, and that in all hearts there remains still something of the man. [*to* CÉLIMÈNE.] Yes, perfidious creature, I am willing to forget your crimes. I can find, in my own heart, an excuse for all your doings, and hide them under the name of a weakness into which the vices of the age betrayed your youth, provided your heart will second the design which I have formed of avoiding all human creatures, and that you are determined to follow me without delay into the solitude in which I have made a vow to pass my days. It is by that only, that, in everyone's opinion, you can repair the harm done by your letters, and that, after the scandal which every noble heart must abhor, it may still be possible for me to love you.

CÉLIMÈNE. What! I renounce the world before I grow old, and bury myself in your wilderness!

ALCESTE. If your affection responds to mine what need the rest of the world signify to you? Am I not sufficient for you?

CÉLIMÈNE. Solitude is frightful to a widow of twenty. I do not feel my mind sufficiently grand and strong to resolve to adopt such a plan. If the gift of my hand can satisfy your wishes, I might be induced to tie such bonds; and marriage—

ALCESTE. No. My heart loathes you now, and this refusal alone effects more than all the rest. As you are not disposed, in those sweet ties, to find all in all in me, as I would find all in all in you, begone, I refuse your offer, and this much-felt outrage frees me for ever from your unworthy toils.

SCENE VIII.

[ELIANTE, ALCESTE, PHILINTE.]

ALCESTE. [*to* ELIANTE.] Madam, your beauty is adorned by a hundred virtues; and I never saw anything in you but what was sincere. For a long while I thought very highly of you; but allow me to esteem you thus for ever, and suffer my heart in its various troubles not to offer itself for the honour of your acceptance. I feel too unworthy, and begin to perceive that Heaven did not intend me for the marriage bond; that the homage of only the remainder of a heart unworthy of you, would be below your merit, and that in short—

ELIANTE. You may pursue this thought. I am not at all embarrassed with my hand; and here is your friend, who, without giving me much trouble, might possibly accept it if I asked him.

PHILINTE. Ah! Madam, I ask for nothing better than that honour, and I could sacrifice my life and soul for it.

ALCESTE. May you, to taste true contentment, preserve for ever these feelings towards each other! Deceived on all sides, overwhelmed with injustice, I will fly from an abyss where vice is triumphant, and seek out some small secluded nook on earth, where one may enjoy the freedom of being an honest man.

PHILINTE. Come, Madam, let us leave nothing untried to deter him from the design on which his heart is set.

The Learned Ladies

[*Les Femmes Savantes*]

Translated by CHARLES HERON WALL

A COMEDY IN FIVE ACTS

DRAMATIS PERSONAE

CHRYSALE, *an honest bourgeois.*
PHILAMINTE, *wife to Chrysale.*
ARMANDE & HENRIETTE, *their daughters.*
ARISTE, *brother to Chrysale.*
BÉLISE, *his sister.*
CLITANDRE, *lover to Henriette.*
TRISSOTIN, *a wit.*
VADIUS, *a learned man*
MARTINE, *a kitchen-maid.*
LÉPINE, *servant to Chrysale.*
JULIEN, *servant to Vadius.*
A NOTARY.

ACT I.

SCENE I.

[ARMANDE, HENRIETTE.]

ARMANDE. What! Sister, you will give up the sweet and enchanting title of maiden? You can entertain thoughts of marrying! This vulgar wish can enter your head!

HENRIETTE. Yes, sister.

ARMANDE. Ah! Who can bear that "yes"? Can anyone hear it without feelings of disgust?

HENRIETTE. What is there in marriage which can oblige you, sister, to. . . .

ARMANDE. Ah! Fie!

HENRIETTE. What?

ARMANDE. Fie! I tell you. Can you not conceive what offence the very mention of such a word presents to the imagination, and what a repulsive image it offers to the thoughts? Do you not shudder before it? And can you bring yourself to accept all the consequences which this word implies?

HENRIETTE. When I consider all the consequences which this word implies, I only have offered to my thoughts a husband, children, and a home; and I see nothing in all this to defile the imagination, or to make one shudder.

ARMANDE. O heavens! Can such ties have charms for you?

HENRIETTE. And what at my age can I do better than take a husband who loves me, and whom I love, and through such a tender union secure the delights of an innocent life? If there be conformity of tastes, do you see no attraction in such a bond?

ARMANDE. Ah! heavens! What a groveling disposition! What a poor part you act in the world, to confine yourself to family affairs, and to think of no more soul-stirring pleasures than those offered by an idol of a husband and by brats of children! Leave these base pleasures to the low and vulgar. Raise your thoughts to more exalted objects; endeavour to cultivate a taste for nobler pursuits; and treating sense and matter with contempt, give yourself, as we do, wholly to the cultivation of your mind. You have for an example our mother, who is everywhere honored with the name of learned. Try, as we do, to prove yourself her daughter; aspire to the enlightened intellectuality which is found in our family, and acquire a taste for the rapturous pleasures which the love of study brings to the heart and mind. Instead of being in bondage to the will of a man, marry yourself, sister, to philosophy, for it alone raises you above the rest of mankind, gives sovereign empire to reason, and submits to its laws the animal part, with those groveling desires which lower us to the level of the brute. These are the gentle flames, the sweet ties, which should fill every moment of life. And the cares to which I see so many women given up, appear to me pitiable frivolities.

HENRIETTE. Heaven, whose will is supreme, forms us at our birth to fill different spheres; and it is not every mind which is composed of materials fit to make a philosopher. If your mind is created to soar to those heights which are attained by the speculations of learned men, mine is fitted, sister, to take a meaner flight and to centre its weakness on the petty cares of the world. Let us not interfere with the just decrees of Heaven; but let each of us follow our different instincts. You, borne on the wings of a great and noble genius, will inhabit the lofty regions of philosophy; I, remaining here below, will taste the terrestrial charms of matrimony. Thus, in our several paths, we shall still imitate our mother: you, in her mind and its noble longings; I, in her grosser senses and coarser pleasures; you, in the productions of genius and light, and I, sister, in productions more material.

ARMANDE. When we wish to take a person for a model, it is the nobler side we should imitate; and it is not taking our mother for a model, sister, to cough and spit like her.

HENRIETTE. But you would not have been what you boast yourself to be if our mother had had only her nobler qualities; and well it is for you that her lofty genius did not always devote itself to philosophy. Pray, leave me to those littlenesses to which you owe life, and do not, by wishing me to imitate you, deny some little savant entrance into the world.

ARMANDE. I see that you cannot be cured of the foolish infatuation of taking a husband to yourself. But, pray, let us know whom you intend to marry; I suppose that you do not aim at Clitandre?

HENRIETTE. And why should I not? Does he lack merit? Is it a low choice I have made?

ARMANDE. Certainly not; but it would not be honest to take away the conquest of another; and it is a fact not unknown to the world that Clitandre has publicly sighed for me.

HENRIETTE. Yes; but all those sighs are mere vanities for you; you do not share human weaknesses; your mind has forever renounced matrimony, and philosophy has all your love. Thus, having in your heart no pretensions to Clitandre, what does it matter to you if another has such pretensions?

ARMANDE. The empire which reason holds over the senses does not call upon us to renounce the pleasure of adulation; and we may refuse for a husband a man of merit whom we would willingly see swell the number of our admirers.

HENRIETTE. I have not prevented him from continuing his worship, but have only received the homage of his passion when you had rejected it.

ARMANDE. But do you find entire safety, tell me, in the vows of a rejected lover? Do you think his passion for you so great that all love for me can be dead in his heart?

HENRIETTE. He tells me so, sister, and I trust him.

ARMANDE. Do not, sister, be so ready to trust him; and be sure that, when he says he gives me up and loves you, he really does not mean it, but deceives himself.

HENRIETTE. I cannot say; but if you wish it, it will be easy for us to discover the true state of things. I see him coming, and on this point he will be sure to give us full information.

SCENE II.

[CLITANDRE, ARMANDE, HENRIETTE.]

HENRIETTE. Clitandre, deliver me from a doubt my sister has raised in me. Pray open your heart to us; tell us the truth, and let us know which of us has a claim upon your love.

ARMANDE. No, no; I will not force upon your love the hardship of an explanation. I have too much respect for others, and know how perplexing it is to make an open avowal before witnesses.

CLITANDRE. No; my heart cannot dissemble, and it is no hardship to me to speak openly. Such a step in no way perplexes me, and I acknowledge before all, freely and openly, that the tender chains which bind me, [*pointing to* HENRIETTE.] my homage and my love, are all on this side. Such a confession can cause you no surprise, for you wished things to be thus. I was touched by your attractions, and my tender sighs told you enough of my ardent desires; my heart offered you an immortal love, but you did not think the conquest which your eyes had made noble enough. I have suffered many slights, for you reigned over my heart like a tyrant; but weary at last with so much pain, I looked elsewhere for a conqueror more gentle, and for chains less cruel. [*pointing to* HENRIETTE.] I have met with them here, and my bonds will forever be precious to me. These eyes have looked upon me with compassion, and have dried my tears. They have not despised what you had refused. Such kindness has captivated me, and there is nothing which would now break my chains. Therefore I beseech you, Madam, never to make an attempt to regain a heart which has resolved to die in this gentle bondage.

ARMANDE. Bless me, Sir, who told you that I had such a desire, and, in short, that I cared so much for you? I think it tolerably ridiculous that you should imagine such a thing, and very impertinent in you to declare it to me.

HENRIETTE. Ah! gently, sister. Where is now that moral sense which has so much power over that which is merely animal in us, and which can restrain the madness of anger?

ARMANDE. And you, who speak to me, what moral sense have you when you respond to a love which is offered to you before you have received leave from those who have given you birth? Know that duty subjects you to their laws, and that you may love only in accordance with their choice; for they have a supreme authority over your heart, and it is criminal in you to dispose of it yourself.

HENRIETTE. I thank you for the great kindness you show me in teaching me my duty. My heart intends to follow the line of conduct you have traced; and to show you that I profit by your advice, pray, Clitandre, see that your love is strengthened by the consent of those from whom I have received birth. Acquire thus a right over my wishes, and for me the power of loving you without a crime.

CLITANDRE. I will do so with all diligence. I only waited for this kind permission from you.

ARMANDE. You triumph, sister, and seem to fancy that you thereby give me pain.

HENRIETTE. I, sister? By no means. I know that the laws of reason will always have full power over your senses, and that, through the lessons you derive from wisdom, you are altogether above such weakness. Far from thinking you moved by any vexation, I believe that you will use your influence to help me, will second his demand of my hand, and will by your approbation hasten the happy day of our marriage. I beseech you to do so; and in order to secure this end. . . .

ARMANDE. Your little mind thinks it grand to resort to raillery, and you seem wonderfully proud of a heart which I abandon to you.

HENRIETTE. Abandoned it may be; yet this heart, sister, is not so disliked by you but that, if you could regain it by stooping, you would even condescend to do so.

ARMANDE. I scorn to answer such foolish prating.

HENRIETTE. You do well; and you show us inconceivable moderation.

Scene III.

[CLITANDRE, HENRIETTE.]

HENRIETTE. Your frank confession has rather taken her aback.

CLITANDRE. She deserves such freedom of speech, and all the haughtiness of her proud folly merits my outspokenness! But since you give me leave, I will go to your father, to. . . .

HENRIETTE. The safest thing to do would be to gain my mother over. My father easily consents to everything, but he places little weight on what he himself resolves. He has received from Heaven a certain gentleness which makes him readily submit to the will of his wife. It is she who governs, and who in a dictatorial tone lays down the law whenever she has made up her mind to anything. I wish I could see in you a more pliant spirit towards her and towards my aunt. If you would but fall in with their views, you would secure their favor and their esteem.

CLITANDRE. I am so sincere that I can never bring myself to praise, even in your sister, that side of her character which resembles theirs. Female doctors are not to my taste. I like a woman to have some knowledge of everything; but I cannot admire in her the revolting passion of wishing to be clever for the mere sake of being clever. I prefer that she should, at times, affect ignorance of what she really knows. In short, I like her to hide her knowledge, and to be learned without publishing her learning abroad, quoting the authors, making use of pompous words, and being witty under the least provocation. I greatly respect your mother, but I cannot approve her wild fancies, nor make myself an echo of what she says. I cannot support the praises she bestows upon that literary hero of hers, Mr. Trissotin, who vexes and wearies me to death. I cannot bear to see her have any esteem for such a man, and to see her reckon among men of genius a fool whose writings are everywhere hissed; a pedant whose liberal pen furnishes all the markets with wastepaper.

HENRIETTE. His writings, his speeches, in short, everything in him is unpleasant to me; and I feel towards him as you do. But as he possesses great ascendancy over my mother, you must force yourself to yield somewhat. A lover should make his court where his heart is engaged; he should win the favor of everyone; and in order to have nobody opposed to his love, try to please even the dog of the house.

CLITANDRE. Yes, you are right; but Mr. Trissotin is hateful to me. I cannot consent, in order to win his favor, to dishonor myself by praising his works. It is through them that he was first brought to my notice, and I knew him before I had seen him. I saw in the trash which he writes all that his pedantic person everywhere shows forth; the persistent haughtiness of his presumption, the intrepidity of the good opinion he has of his person, the calm overweening confidence which at all times makes him so satisfied with himself, and with the writings of which he boasts; so that he would not exchange his renown for all the honors of the greatest general.

HENRIETTE. You have good eyes to see all that.

CLITANDRE. I even guessed what he was like; and by means of the verses with which he deluges us, I saw what the poet must be. So well had I pictured to myself all his features and gait that one day, meeting a man in the galleries of the Palace of Justice,[30] I laid a wager that it must be Trissotin—and I won my wager.

HENRIETTE. What a tale!

CLITANDRE. No, I assure you that it is the perfect truth. But I see your aunt coming; allow me, I pray you, to tell her of the longings of my heart, and to gain her kind help with your mother.

SCENE IV.

[BÉLISE, CLITANDRE.]

CLITANDRE. Suffer a lover, Madam, to profit by such a propitious moment to reveal to you his sincere devotion. . . .

BÉLISE. Ah! gently! Beware of opening your heart too freely to me; although I have placed you in the list of my lovers, you must use

---

[30] The resort of the best company in those days.

no interpreter but your eyes, and never explain by another language desires which are an insult to me. Love me; sigh for me; burn for my charms; but let me know nothing of it. I can shut my eyes to your secret flame, as long as you keep yourself to dumb interpreters; but if your mouth meddle in the matter, I must for ever banish you from my sight.

CLITANDRE. Do not be alarmed at the intentions of my heart. Henriette is, Madam, the object of my love, and I come ardently to conjure you to favor the love I have for her.

BÉLISE. Ah! truly now, the subterfuge shows excellent wit. This subtle evasion deserves praise; and in all the romances I have glanced over, I have never met with anything more ingenious.

CLITANDRE. This is no attempt at wit, Madam; it is the avowal of what my heart feels. Heaven has bound me to the beauty of Henriette by the ties of an unchangeable love. Henriette holds me in her lovely chains; and to marry Henriette is the end of all my hopes. You can do much towards it; and what I have come to ask you is that you will condescend to second my addresses.

BÉLISE. I see the end to which your demand would gently head, and I understand whom you mean under that name. The metaphor is clever; and not to depart from it, let me tell you that Henriette rebels against matrimony, and that you must love her without any hope of having your love returned.

CLITANDRE. But, Madam, what is the use of such a perplexing debate? Why will you persist in believing what is not?

BÉLISE. Dear me! Do not trouble yourself so much. Leave off denying what your looks have often made me understand. Let it suffice that I am content with the subterfuge your love has so skillfully adopted, and that under the figure to which respect has limited it, I am willing to suffer its homage; always provided that its transports, guided by honor, offer only pure vows on my altars.

CLITANDRE. But. . . .

BÉLISE. Farewell. This ought really to satisfy you, and I have said more than I wished to say.

CLITANDRE. But your error. . . .

BÉLISE. Leave me. I am blushing now; and my modesty has had much to bear.

CLITANDRE. May I be hanged if I love you; and. . . .[31]

BÉLISE. No, no. I will hear nothing more.

---

[31] Molière ends this line with *sage*, with, apparently, no other motive than to find a rhyme to *davantage*.

SCENE V.

CLITANDRE. [*alone.*] Deuce take the foolish woman with her dreams! Was anything so preposterous ever heard of? I must go and ask the help of a person of more sense.

ACT II.

SCENE I.

ARISTE. [*leaving* CLITANDRE, *and still speaking to him.*] Yes; I will bring you an answer as soon as I can. I will press, insist, do all that should be done. How many things a lover has to say when one would suffice; and how impatient he is for all that he desires! Never. . . .

SCENE II.

[CHRYSALE, ARISTE.]

ARISTE. Good day to you, brother.
CHRYSALE. And to you also, brother.
ARISTE. Do you know what brings me here?
CHRYSALE. No, I do not; but I am ready to hear it, if it pleases you to tell me.
ARISTE. You have known Clitandre for some time now?
CHRYSALE. Certainly; and he often comes to our house.
ARISTE. And what do you think of him?
CHRYSALE. I think him to be a man of honor, wit, courage, and uprightness, and I know very few people who have more merit.
ARISTE. A certain wish of his has brought me here; and I am glad to see the esteem you have for him.
CHRYSALE. I became acquainted with his late father when I was in Rome.
ARISTE. Ah!
CHRYSALE. He was a perfect gentleman.
ARISTE. So it is said.
CHRYSALE. We were only about twenty-eight years of age, and, upon my word, we were, both of us, very gay young fellows.
ARISTE. I believe it.
CHRYSALE. We greatly affected the Roman ladies, and everybody there spoke of our pranks. We made many people jealous, I can tell you.
ARISTE. Excellent; but let us come to what brings me here.

Scene III.

[BÉLISE (*entering softly and listening*), CHRYSALE, ARISTE.]

ARISTE. Clitandre has chosen me to be his interpreter to you; he has fallen in love with Henriette.

CHRYSALE. What! with my daughter?

ARISTE. Yes. Clitandre is delighted with her, and you never saw a lover so smitten!

BÉLISE. [*to* ARISTE.] No, no; you are mistaken. You do not know the story, and the thing is not as you imagine.

ARISTE. How so, sister?

BÉLISE. Clitandre deceives you; it is with another that he is in love.

ARISTE. It is not with Henriette that he is in love? You are joking.

BÉLISE. No; I am telling the perfect truth.

ARISTE. He told me so himself.

BÉLISE. Doubtless.

ARISTE. You see me here, sister, commissioned by him to ask her of her father.

BÉLISE. Yes, I know.

ARISTE. And he besought me, in the name of his love, to hasten the time of an alliance so desired by him.

BÉLISE. Better and better. No more gallant subterfuge could have been employed. But let me tell you that Henriette is an excuse, an ingenious veil, a pretext, brother, to cover another flame, the mystery of which I know; and most willingly will I enlighten you both.

ARISTE. Since you know so much, sister, pray tell us whom he loves.

BÉLISE. You wish to know?

ARISTE. Yes; who is it?

BÉLISE. Me!

ARISTE. You!

BÉLISE. Myself.

ARISTE. Come, I say! sister!

BÉLISE. What do you mean by this "Come, I say"? And what is there so wonderful in what I tell you? I am handsome enough, I should think, to have more than one heart in subjection to my empire; and Dorante, Damis, Cléonte, and Lycidas show well enough the power of my charms.

ARISTE. Do those men love you?

BÉLISE. Yes; with all their might.

ARISTE. They have told you so?

BÉLISE. No one would take such a liberty; they have, up to the present time, respected me so much that they have never spoken to me of their love. But the dumb interpreters have done their office in offering their hearts and lives to me.

ARISTE. I hardly ever see Damis here.

BÉLISE. It is to show me a more respectful submission.

ARISTE. Dorante, with sharp words, abuses you everywhere.

BÉLISE. It is the transport of a jealous passion.

ARISTE. Cléonte and Lycidas are both married.

BÉLISE. It was the despair to which I had reduced their love.

ARISTE. Upon my word, sister, these are mere visions.

CHRYSALE. [*to* BÉLISE.] You had better get rid of these idle fancies.

BÉLISE. Ah! idle fancies! They are idle fancies, you think. I have idle fancies! Really, "idle fancies" is excellent. I greatly rejoice at those idle fancies, brothers, and I did not know that I was addicted to idle fancies.

SCENE IV.

[CHRYSALE, ARISTE.]

CHRYSALE. Our sister is decidedly crazy.

ARISTE. It grows upon her every day. But let us resume the subject that brings me here. Clitandre asks you to give him Henriette in marriage. Tell me what answer we can make to his love.

CHRYSALE. Do you ask it? I consent to it with all my heart; and I consider his alliance a great honor.

ARISTE. You know that he is not wealthy, that . . . .

CHRYSALE. That is a thing of no consequence. He is rich in virtue, and that is better than wealth. Moreover, his father and I were but one mind in two bodies.

ARISTE. Let us speak to your wife, and try to render her favorable to. . . .

CHRYSALE. It is enough. I accept him for my son-in-law.

ARISTE. Yes; but to support your consent, it will not be amiss to have her agree to it also. Let us go. . . .

CHRYSALE. You are joking? There is no need of this. I answer for my wife, and take the business upon myself.

ARISTE. But. . . .

CHRYSALE. Leave it to me, I say, and fear nothing. I will go, and prepare her this moment.

ARISTE. Let it be so. I will go and see Henriette on the subject, and will return to know. . . .

CHRYSALE. It is a settled thing, and I will go without delay and talk to my wife about it.

SCENE V.

[CHRYSALE, MARTINE.]

MARTINE. Just like my luck! Alas! they be true sayings, they be—"Give a dog a bad name and hang him," and—"One doesn't get fat in other folk's service."[32]

CHRYSALE. What is it? What is the matter with you, Martine?

MARTINE. What is the matter?

CHRYSALE. Yes.

MARTINE. The matter is that I am sent away, Sir.

CHRYSALE. Sent away?

MARTINE. Yes; mistress has turned me out.

CHRYSALE. I don't understand; why has she?

MARTINE. I am threatened with a sound beating if I don't go.

CHRYSALE. No; you will stop here. I am quite satisfied with you. My wife is a little hasty at times, and I will not, no. . . .

SCENE VI.

[PHILAMINTE, BÉLISE, CHRYSALE, MARTINE.]

PHILAMINTE. [*seeing* MARTINE.] What! I see you here, you hussy! Quick, leave this place, and never let me set my eyes upon you again.

CHRYSALE. Gently.

PHILAMINTE. No; I will have it so.

CHRYSALE. What?

PHILAMINTE. I insist upon her going.

CHRYSALE. But what has she done wrong, that you wish her in this way to. . . ?

PHILAMINTE. What! you take her part?

CHRYSALE. Certainly not.

PHILAMINTE. You side with her against me?

CHRYSALE. Oh! dear me, no; I only ask what she is guilty of.

PHILAMINTE. Am I one to send her away without just cause?

CHRYSALE. I do not say that; but we must, with servants. . . .

PHILAMINTE. No; she must leave this place, I tell you.

CHRYSALE. Let it be so; who says anything to the contrary?

PHILAMINTE. I will have no opposition to my will.

CHRYSALE. Agreed.

---

[32] Or, more literally, "Service is no inheritance;" but this does not sound familiar enough in English.

PHILAMINTE. And like a reasonable husband, you should take my part against her, and share my anger.

CHRYSALE. So I do. [*turning towards* MARTINE.] Yes; my wife is right in sending you away, baggage that you are; your crime cannot be forgiven.

MARTINE. What is it I have done, then?

CHRYSALE. [*aside.*] Upon my word, I don't know.

PHILAMINTE. She is capable even now of looking upon it as nothing.

CHRYSALE. Has she caused your anger by breaking some looking-glass or some china?

PHILAMINTE. Do you think that I would send her away for that? And do you fancy that I should get angry for so little?

CHRYSALE. [*to* MARTINE.] What is the meaning of this? [*to* PHILAMINTE.] The thing is of great importance, then?

PHILAMINTE. Certainly; did you ever find me unreasonable?

CHRYSALE. Has she, through carelessness, allowed some ewer or silver dish to be stolen from us?

PHILAMINTE. That would be of little moment.

CHRYSALE. [*to* MARTINE.] Oh! oh! I say, Miss! [*to* PHILAMINTE.] What! has she shown herself dishonest?

PHILAMINTE. It is worse than that.

CHRYSALE. Worse than that?

PHILAMINTE. Worse.

CHRYSALE. [*to* MARTINE.] How the deuce! you jade. [*to* PHILAMINTE.] What! has she. . . ?

PHILAMINTE. She has with unparalleled impudence, after thirty lessons, insulted my ear by the improper use of a low and vulgar word condemned in express terms by Vaugelas.[33]

CHRYSALE. Is that. . . ?

PHILAMINTE. What! In spite of our remonstrances to be always sapping the foundation of all knowledge—of grammar which rules even kings, and makes them, with a high hand, obey her laws.

CHRYSALE. I thought her guilty of the greatest crime.

PHILAMINTE. What! You do not think the crime unpardonable?

CHRYSALE. Yes, yes.

PHILAMINTE. I should like to see you excuse her.

CHRYSALE. Heaven forbid!

BÉLISE. It is really pitiful. All constructions are destroyed by her; yet she has a hundred times been told the laws of the language.

MARTINE. All that you preach there is no doubt very fine, but I don't understand your jargon, not I.

PHILAMINTE. Did you ever see such impudence? To call a language founded on reason and polite custom a jargon!

---

[33] The French grammarian, born about 1585; died 1650.

MARTINE. Provided one is understood, one speaks well enough, and all your fine speeches don't do me no good.

PHILAMINTE. You see! Is not that her way of speaking, *don't do me no good*!

BÉLISE. O intractable brains! How is it that, in spite of the trouble we daily take, we cannot teach you to speak with congruity? In putting *not* with *no*, you have spoken redundantly, and it is, as you have been told, a negative too many.

MARTINE. Oh my! I ain't no scholar like you, and I speak straight out as they speaks in our place.

PHILAMINTE. Ah! who can bear it?

BÉLISE. What a horrible solecism!

PHILAMINTE. It is enough to destroy a delicate ear.

BÉLISE. You are, I must acknowledge, very dull of understanding; *they* is in the plural number, and *speaks* is in the singular. Will you thus all your life offend grammar?[34]

MARTINE. Who speaks of offending either gammer or gaffer?

PHILAMINTE. O heavens!

BÉLISE. The word *grammar* is misunderstood by you, and I have told you a hundred times where the word comes from.

MARTINE. Faith, let it come from Chaillot, Auteuil, or l'ontoise,[35] I care precious little.

BÉLISE. What a boorish mind! *Grammar* teaches us the laws of the verb and nominative case, as well as of the adjective and substantive.

MARTINE. Sure, let me tell you, Ma'am, that I don't know those people.

PHILAMINTE. What martyrdom!

BÉLISE. They are names of words, and you ought to notice how they agree with each other.

MARTINE. What does it matter whether they agree or fall out?

PHILAMINTE. [*to* BÉLISE.] Goodness gracious! put an end to such a discussion. [*to* CHRYSALE.] And so you will not send her away?

CHRYSALE. Oh! yes. [*aside.*] I must put up with her caprice, Go, don't provoke her, Martine.

PHILAMINTE. How! you are afraid of offending the hussy! you speak to her in quite an obliging tone.

CHRYSALE. I? Not at all. [*in a rough tone.*] Go, leave this place. [*in a softer tone.*] Go away, my poor girl.

---

[34] *Grammaire* in Molière's time was pronounced as *grand'mère* is now. *Gammer* seems the nearest approach to this in English.

[35] In Molière's time villages close to Paris.

Scene VII.

[PHILAMINTE, CHRYSALE, BÉLISE.]

CHRYSALE. She is gone, and you are satisfied, but I do not approve of sending her away in this fashion. She answers very well for what she has to do, and you turn her out of my house for a trifle.

PHILAMINTE. Do you wish me to keep her forever in my service, for her to torture my ears incessantly, to infringe all the laws of custom and reason, by a barbarous accumulation of errors of speech, and of garbled expressions tacked together with proverbs dragged out of the gutters of all the market-places?

BÉLISE. It is true that one sickens at hearing her talk; she pulls Vaugelas to pieces, and the least defects of her gross intellect are either pleonasm or cacophony.

CHRYSALE. What does it matter if she fails to observe the laws of Vaugelas, provided she does not fail in her cooking? I had much rather that while picking her herbs, she should join wrongly the nouns to the verbs, and repeat a hundred times a coarse or vulgar word, than that she should burn my roast, or put too much salt in my broth. I live on good soup, and not on fine language. Vaugelas does not teach how to make broth; and Malherbe and Balzac, so clever in learned words, might, in cooking, have proved themselves but fools.[36]

PHILAMINTE. How shocking such a coarse speech sounds; and how unworthy of one who calls himself a man, to be always bent on material things, instead of rising towards those which are intellectual. Is that dross, the body, of importance enough to deserve even a passing thought? and ought we not to leave it far behind?

CHRYSALE. Well, my body is myself, and I mean to take care of it; *dross* if you like, but my dross is dear to me.

BÉLISE. The body and the mind, brother, exist together; but if you believe all the learned world, the mind ought to take precedence over the body, and our first care, our most earnest endeavour, must be to feed it with the juices of science.

CHRYSALE. Upon my word, if you talk of feeding your mind, you make use of but poor diet, as everybody knows; and you have no care, no solicitude for. . . .

PHILAMINTE. Ah! *Solicitude* is unpleasant to my ear: it betrays

---

[36] Malherbe, 1555-1628; Balzac, 1594-1654.

strangely its antiquity.[37]

BÉLISE. It is true that it is dreadfully starched and out of fashion.

CHRYSALE. I can bear this no longer. You will have me speak out, then? I will raise the mask, and discharge my spleen. Everyone calls you mad, and I am greatly troubled at. . . .

PHILAMINTE. Ah! what is the meaning of this?

CHRYSALE. [*to* BÉLISE.] I am speaking to you, sister. The least solecism one makes in speaking irritates you; but you make strange ones in conduct. Your everlasting books do not satisfy me, and, except a big Plutarch to put my bands in,[38] you should burn all this useless lumber, and leave learning to the doctors of the town. Take away from the garret that long telescope, which is enough to frighten people, and a hundred other baubles which are offensive to the sight. Do not try to discover what is passing in the moon, and think a little more of what is happening at home, where we see everything going topsy-turvy. It is not right, and that too for many reasons, that a woman should study and know so much. To form the minds of her children to good manners, to make her household go well, to look after the servants, and regulate all expenses with economy, ought to be her principal study, and all her philosophy. Our fathers were much more sensible on this point: with them, a wife always knew enough when the extent of her genius enabled her to distinguish a doublet from a pair of breeches. She did not read, but she lived honestly; her family was the subject of all her learned conversation, and for hooks she had needles, thread, and a thimble, with which she worked at her daughter's trousseau. Women, in our days, are far from behaving thus: they must write and become authors. No science is too deep for them. It is worse in my house than anywhere else; the deepest secrets are understood, and everything is known except what should be known. Everyone knows how go the moon and the polar star, Venus, Saturn, and Mars, with which I have nothing to do. And in this vain knowledge, which they go so far to fetch, they know nothing of the soup of which I stand in need. My servants all wish to be learned, in order to please you; and all alike occupy themselves with anything but the work they have to do. Reasoning is the occupation of the whole house, and reasoning banishes all reason. One burns my roast while reading some story; another dreams of verses when I call for drink. In short, they all follow your example, and although I have servants, I am not served. One poor girl alone was left me, untouched by this villainous fashion; and now, behold, she

---

[37] Many of the words condemned by the purists of the time have died out; *solicitude* still remains.

[38] To keep them flat.

is sent away with a huge clatter because she fails to speak Vaugelas. I tell you, sister, all this offends me, for as I have already said, it is to you I am speaking. I dislike to see all those Latin-mongers in my house, and particularly Mr. Trissotin. It is he who has turned your heads with his verses. All his talk is mere rubbish, and one is forever trying to find out what he has said after he has done speaking. For my part I believe that he is rather cracked.

PHILAMINTE. What coarseness, O heavens! both in thought and language.

BÉLISE. Can there be a more gross assemblage of corpuscles,[39] a mind composed of more vulgar atoms? Is it possible that I can come from the same blood? I hate myself for being of your race, and out of pure shame I abandon the spot.

SCENE VIII.

[PHILAMINTE, CHRYSALE.]

PHILAMINTE. Have you any other shaft ready?

CHRYSALE. I? No. Don't let us dispute any longer. I've done. Let's speak of something else. Your eldest daughter shows a dislike to marriage; in short, she is a philosopher, and I've nothing to say. She is under good management, and you do well by her. But her younger sister is of a different disposition, and I think it would be right to give Henriette a proper husband, who. . . .

PHILAMINTE. It is what I have been thinking about, and I wish to speak to you of what I intend to do. This Mr. Trissotin on whose account we are blamed, and who has not the honor of being esteemed by you; is the man whom I have chosen to be her husband; and I can judge of his merit better than you can. All discussion is superfluous here, for I have duly resolved that it should be so. I will ask you also not to say a word of it to your daughter before I have spoken to her on the subject. I can justify my conduct, and I shall be sure to know if you have spoken to her.

SCENE IX.

[ARISTE, CHRYSALE.]

ARISTE. Well! your wife has just left, and I see that you must have had a talk together.

CHRYSALE. Yes.

---

[39] A reference to the corpuscular philosophy.

ARISTE. And how did you succeed? Shall we have Henriette? Has she given her consent? Is the affair settled?

CHRYSALE. Not quite as yet.

ARISTE. Does she refuse?

CHRYSALE. No.

ARISTE. Then she hesitates?

CHRYSALE. Not in the least.

ARISTE. What then?

CHRYSALE. Well! she offers me another man for a son-in-law.

ARISTE. Another man for a son-in-law?

CHRYSALE. Yes.

ARISTE. What is his name?

CHRYSALE. Mr. Trissotin.

ARISTE. What! that Mr. Trissotin. . . .

CHRYSALE. Yes, he who always speaks of verse and Latin.

ARISTE. And you have accepted him?

CHRYSALE. I? Heaven forbid!

ARISTE. What did you say to it?

CHRYSALE. Nothing. I am glad that I did not speak, and commit myself.

ARISTE. Your reason is excellent, and it is a great step towards the end we have in view. Did you not propose Clitandre to her?

CHRYSALE. No; for as she talked of another son-in-law, I thought it was better for me to say nothing.

ARISTE. Your prudence is to the last degree wonderful! Are you not ashamed of your weakness? How can a man be so poor-spirited as to let his wife have absolute power over him, and never dare to oppose anything she has resolved upon?

CHRYSALE. Ah! it is easy, brother, for you to speak; you don't know what a dislike I have to a row, and how I love rest and peace. My wife has a terrible disposition. She makes a great show of the name of philosopher, but she is not the less passionate on that account; and her philosophy, which makes her despise all riches, has no power over the bitterness of her anger. However little I oppose what she has taken into her head, I raise a terrible storm which lasts at least a week. She makes me tremble when she begins her outcries; I don't know where to hide myself. She is a perfect virago; and yet, in spite of her diabolical temper, I must call her my darling and my love.

ARISTE. You are talking nonsense. Between ourselves, your wife has absolute power over you only because of your own cowardice. Her authority is founded upon your own weakness; it is from you she takes the name of mistress. You give way to her haughty manners, and suffer yourself to be led by the nose like a fool. What! you call yourself a man, and cannot for once make your wife obey you, and have courage enough to say, "I will have it so?" You will, without shame, see your daughter sacrificed to the mad visions with which the family is possessed? You will confer your wealth on a man because of half-a-dozen Latin words with which the ass talks big before them—a pedant whom your wife compliments at every turn with the names of wit and great philosopher whose verses were never equaled, whereas everybody knows that he is anything but all that. Once more I tell you, it is a shame, and you deserve that people should laugh at your cowardice.

CHRYSALE. Yes, you are right, and I see that I am wrong. I must pluck up a little more courage, brother.

ARISTE. That's right.

CHRYSALE. It is shameful to be so submissive under the tyranny of a woman.

ARISTE. Good.

CHRYSALE. She has abused my gentleness.

ARISTE. It is true.

CHRYSALE. My easy-going ways have lasted too long.

ARISTE. Certainly.

CHRYSALE. And to-day I will let her know that my daughter is my daughter, and that I am the master, to choose a husband for her according to my mind.

ARISTE. You are reasonable now, and as you should be.

CHRYSALE. You are for Clitandre, and you know where he lives; send him to me directly, brother.

ARISTE. I will go at once.

CHRYSALE. I have borne it too long. I will be a man, and set everybody at defiance.

Act III.

Scene I.

[PHILAMINTE, ARMANDE, BÉLISE, TRISSOTIN, LÉPINE.]

PHILAMINTE. Ah! Let us sit down here to listen comfortably to these verses; they should be weighed word by word.

ARMANDE. I am all anxiety to hear them.

BÉLISE. And I am dying for them.

PHILAMINTE. [*to* TRISSOTIN.] Whatever comes from you is a delight to me.

ARMANDE. It is to me an unparalleled pleasure.

BÉLISE. It is a delicious repast offered to my ears.

PHILAMINTE. Do not let us languish under such pressing desires.

ARMANDE. Lose no time.

BÉLISE. Begin quickly and hasten our pleasure.

PHILAMINTE. Offer your epigram to our impatience.

TRISSOTIN. [*to* PHILAMINTE.] Alas! it is but a new-born child, Madam, but its fate ought truly to touch your heart, for it was in your court-yard that I brought it forth, but a moment since.

PHILAMINTE. To make it dear to me, it is sufficient for me to know its father.

TRISSOTIN. Your approbation may serve it as a mother.

BÉLISE. What wit he has!

SCENE II.

[HENRIETTE, PHILAMINTE, ARMANDE, BÉLISE, TRISSOTIN, LÉPINE.]

PHILAMINTE. [*to* HENRIETTE, *who is going away.*] Stop! why do you run away?

HENRIETTE. I fear to disturb such sweet intercourse.

PHILAMINTE. Come nearer, and with both ears share in the delight of hearing wonders.

HENRIETTE. I have little understanding for the beauties of authorship, and witty things are not in my line.

PHILAMINTE. No matter. Besides, I wish afterwards to tell you of a secret which you must learn.

TRISSOTIN. [*to* HENRIETTE.] Knowledge has nothing that can touch you, and your only care is to charm everybody.

HENRIETTE. One as little as the other, and I have no wish. . . .

BÉLISE. Ah! let us think of the new-born babe, I beg of you.

PHILAMINTE. [*to* LÉPINE.] Now, little page, bring some seats for us to sit down. [LÉPINE *slips down.*] You senseless boy, how can you fall down after having learnt the laws of equilibrium?

BÉLISE. Do you not perceive, ignorant fellow, the causes of your fall, and that it proceeds from your having deviated from the fixed point which we call the centre of gravity?

LÉPINE. I perceived it, Madam, when I was on the ground.

PHILAMINTE. [*to* LÉPINE, *who goes out.*] The awkward clown!

TRISSOTIN. It is fortunate for him that he is not made of glass.

ARMANDE. Ah! wit is everything!

BÉLISE. It never ceases. [*they sit down.*]

PHILAMINTE. Serve us quickly your admirable feast.

TRISSOTIN. To satisfy, the great hunger which is here shown to me, a dish of eight verses seems but little; and I think that I should do well to join to the epigram, or rather to the madrigal, the ragout of a sonnet which, in the eyes of a princess, was thought to have a certain delicacy in it. It is throughout seasoned with Attic salt, and

I think you will find the taste of it tolerably good.
ARMANDE. Ah! I have no doubt of it.
PHILAMINTE. Let us quickly give audience.
BÉLISE. [*interrupting* TRISSOTIN *each time he is about to read.*] I feel, beforehand, my heart beating for joy. I love poetry to distraction, particularly when the verses are gallantly turned.
PHILAMINTE. If we go on speaking he will never be able to read.
TRISSOTIN. SONN. . . .
BÉLISE. [*to* HENRIETTE.] Be silent, my niece.
ARMANDE. Ah! let him read, I beg.

TRISSOTIN. SONNET TO THE PRINCESS
URANIA ON HER FEVER.[40]

Your prudence fast in sleep's repose
Is plunged; if thus superbly kind,
A lodging gorgeously you can find
For the most cruel of your foes—

BÉLISE. Ah! what a pretty beginning!
ARMANDE. What a charming turn it has!
PHILAMINTE. He alone possesses the talent of making easy verses.
ARMANDE. We must yield to *prudence fast in sleep's repose is*

---

[40] The sonnet is not of Molière's invention, but is to be found in *Les Oeuvres galantes en prose et en vers de M. Cotin*, Paris, 1663. It is called, *Sonnet à Mademoiselle de Longueville, à présent Duchesse de Nemours, sur sa fièvre quarte*. As, of necessity, the translation given above is not very literal, I append the original.

"Votre prudence est endormie,
De traiter magnifiquement,
Et de loger superbement,
Votre plus cruelle ennemie;

Faites-la sortir quoi qu'on die,
De votre riche appartement,
Où cette ingrate insolemment
Attaque votre belle vie!

Quoi! sans respecter votre rang,
Elle se prend à votre sang,
Et nuit et jour vous fait outrage!

Si vous la conduisez aux bains,
Sans la marchander davantage,
Noyez-la de vos propres mains."

The *die* of *quoi qu'on die* was the regular form in Molière's time, and had nothing archaic about it. This is sufficiently true of "Will she, nill she" [compare Shakespeare's "And, will you, nill you, I will marry you".] to excuse its use here.

plunged.

BÉLISE. A *lodging for the most cruel of your foes* is full of charms for me.

PHILAMINTE. I like *superbly* and *gorgeously*; these two adverbs joined together sound admirably.

BÉLISE. Let us hear the rest.

TRISSOTIN. *Your prudence fast in sleep's repose*
Is plunged; if thus superbly kind,
A lodging gorgeously you can find
For the most cruel of your foes

ARMANDE. *Prudence asleep*!

BÉLISE. *Lodge one's enemy*!

PHILAMINTE. *Superbly and gorgeously*!

TRISSOTIN. *Will she, nill she, quick, out she goes*!
From your apartment richly lined,
Where that ingrate's outrageous mind
At your fair life her javelin throws.

BÉLISE. Ah! gently. Allow me to breathe, I beseech you.

ARMANDE. Give us time to admire, I beg.

PHILAMINTE. One feels, at hearing these verses, an indescribable something which goes through one's inmost soul, and makes one feel quite faint.

ARMANDE.*Will she, nill she, quick, out she goes*
From your apartment richly lined.

How prettily *rich apartment* is said here, and with what wit the metaphor is introduced!

PHILAMINTE. *Will she, nill she, quick, out she goes*! Ah! in what admirable taste that will *she, nill she*, is! To my mind the passage is invaluable.

ARMANDE. My heart is also in love with *will she, nill she.*

BÉLISE. I am of your opinion; *will she, nill she*, is a happy expression.

ARMANDE. I wish I had written it.

BÉLISE. It is worth a whole poem!

PHILAMINTE. But do you, like me, understand thoroughly the wit of it?

ARMANDE. *and* BÉLISE. Oh! oh

PHILAMINTE. *Will she, nill she, quick, out she goes*! Although another should take the fever's part, pay no attention; laugh at the gossips; *will she, nill she, quick, out she goes. Will she, nill she, will she, nill she.* This *will she, nill she*, says a great deal more than it seems. I do not know if everyone is like me, but I discover in it a hundred meanings.

BÉLISE. It is true that it says more than its size seems to imply.

PHILAMINTE. [*to* TRISSOTIN.] But when you wrote this charming

Will she, nill she, did you yourself understand all its energy? Did you realise all that it tells us, and did you then think that you were writing something so witty?

TRISSOTIN. Ah! ah!

ARMANDE. I have likewise the *ingrate* in my head; this ungrateful, unjust, uncivil fever that ill-treats people who entertain her.

PHILAMINTE. In short, both the stanzas are admirable. Let us come quickly to the triplets, I pray.

ARMANDE. Ah! once more, *will she, nill she*, I beg.

TRISSOTIN. *Will she, nill she, quick, out she goes*!

PHILAMINTE., ARMANDE. *and* BÉLISE. *Will she, nill she*!

TRISSOTIN. From your apartment richly lined.

PHILAMINTE., ARMANDE. *and* BÉLISE. *Rich apartment*!

TRISSOTIN. *Where that ingrate's outrageous mind.*

PHILAMINTE., ARMANDE. *and* BÉLISE. That ungrateful fever!

TRISSOTIN. *At your fair life her javelin throws.*

PHILAMINTE. *Fair life*!

ARMANDE. *and* BÉLISE. Ah!

TRISSOTIN. *What*! *without heed for your high line, She saps your blood with care malign. . .*

PHILAMINTE., ARMANDE. *and* BÉLISE. Ah!

TRISSOTIN. *Redoubling outrage night and day*! *If to the bath you take her down, Without a moment's haggling, pray, With your own hands the miscreant drown.*

PHILAMINTE. Ah! it is quite overpowering.

BÉLISE. I faint.

ARMANDE. I die from pleasure.

PHILAMINTE. A thousand sweet thrills seize one.

ARMANDE. *If to the bath you take her down,*

BÉLISE. *Without a moment's haggling, pray,*

PHILAMINTE. *With your own hands the miscreant drown.* With your own hands, there, drown her there in the bath.

ARMANDE. In your verses we meet at each step with charming beauty.

BÉLISE. One promenades through them with rapture.

PHILAMINTE. One treads on fine things only.

ARMANDE. They are little lanes all strewn with roses.

TRISSOTIN. Then the sonnet seems to you. . . .

PHILAMINTE. Admirable, new; and never did anyone make anything more beautiful.

BÉLISE. [*to* HENRIETTE.] What! my niece, you listen to what has been read without emotion! You play there but a sorry part!

HENRIETTE. We each of us play the best part we can, my aunt, and to be a wit does not depend on our will.

TRISSOTIN. My verses, perhaps, are tedious to you.

HENRIETTE. No. I do not listen.

PHILAMINTE. Ah! let us hear the epigram.

TRISSOTIN. ON A CARRIAGE OF THE Color OF AMARANTH GIVEN TO ONE OF HIS LADY FRIENDS.[41]

PHILAMINTE. His titles have always something rare in them.

ARMANDE. They prepare one for a hundred flashes of wit.

TRISSOTIN. *Love for his bonds so dear a price demands,*
E'en now it costs me more than half my lands,
And when this chariot meets your eyes,
Where so much gold emboss'd doth rise
That people all astonished stand,
And Laïs rides in triumph through the land. . .

PHILAMINTE. Ah! Laïs! what erudition!

BÉLISE. The cover is pretty, and worth a million.

TRISSOTIN. *And when this chariot meets your eyes,*
Where so much gold emboss'd doth rise
That people all astonished stand,
And Laïs rides in triumph through the land,
Say no more it is amaranth,
Say rather it is o' my rent.

ARMANDE. Oh, oh, oh! this is beyond everything; who would have expected that?

PHILAMINTE. He is the only one to write in such taste.

BÉLISE. Say no more it is *amaranth, say rather it is o' my rent*! It can be declined; *my rent*; *of my rent*; *to my rent*; *from my rent.*

PHILAMINTE. I do not know whether I was prepossessed from the first moment I saw you, but I admire all your prose and verse whenever I see it.

TRISSOTIN. [*to* PHILAMINTE.] If you would only show us something of your composition, we could admire in our turn.

PHILAMINTE. I have done nothing in verse; but I have reason to hope that I shall, shortly, be able, as a friend, to show you eight chapters of the plan of our Academy. Plato only touched on the subject when he wrote the treatise of his Republic; but I will complete the idea as I have arranged it on paper in prose. For, in short, I am

---

[41] This epigram is also by Cotin. It is called, '*Madrigal sur un carosse de couleur amarante, acheté pour une dame.*'

"L'amour si chèrement m'a vendu son lien
Qu'il me coûte déjà la moitié de mon bien,
Et quand tu vois ce beau carrosse,
Où tant d'or se relève en bosse,
Qu'il étonne tout le pays,
Et fait pompeusement triompher ma Laïs,
Ne dis plus qu'il est amarante,
Dis plutôt qu'il est de ma rente."

truly angry at the wrong which is done us in regard to intelligence; and I will avenge the whole sex for the unworthy place which men assign us by confining our talents to trifles, and by shutting the door of sublime knowledge against us.

ARMANDE. It is insulting our sex too grossly to limit our intelligence to the power of judging of a skirt, of the make of a garment, of the beauties of lace, or of a new brocade.

BÉLISE. We must rise above this shameful condition, and bravely proclaim our emancipation.

TRISSOTIN. Everyone knows my respect for the fairer sex, and that if I render homage to the brightness of their eyes, I also honor the splendour of their intellect.

PHILAMINTE. And our sex does you justice in this respect: but we will show to certain minds who treat us with proud contempt that women also have knowledge; that, like men, they can hold learned meetings—regulated, too, by better rules; that they wish to unite what elsewhere is kept apart, join noble language to deep learning, reveal nature's laws by a thousand experiments; and on all questions proposed, admit every party, and ally themselves to none.

TRISSOTIN. For order, I prefer peripateticism.

PHILAMINTE. For abstractions I love Platonism.

ARMANDE. Epicurus pleases me, for his tenets are solid.

BÉLISE. I agree with the doctrine of atoms: but I find it difficult to understand a vacuum, and I much prefer subtile matter.

TRISSOTIN. I quite agree with Descartes about magnetism.

ARMANDE. I like his vortices.

PHILAMINTE. And I his falling worlds.[42]

ARMANDE. I long to see our assembly opened, and to distinguish ourselves by some great discovery.

TRISSOTIN. Much is expected from your enlightened knowledge, for nature has hidden few things from you.

PHILAMINTE. For my part, I have, without boasting, already made one discovery; I have plainly seen men in the moon.

BÉLISE. I have not, I believe, as yet quite distinguished men, but I have seen steeples as plainly as I see you.[43]

ARMANDE. In addition to natural philosophy, we will dive into grammar, history, verse, ethics, and politics.

PHILAMINTE. I find in ethics charms which delight my heart; it was formerly the admiration of great geniuses; but I give the preference to the Stoics, and I think nothing so grand as their founder.

---

[42] Notes do not seem necessary here; a good English dictionary will give better explanations than could be given except by very long notes.

[43] An astronomer of the day had boasted of having done this.

ARMANDE. Our regulations in respect to language will soon be known, and we mean to create a revolution. Through a just or natural antipathy, we have each of us taken a mortal hatred to certain words, both verbs and nouns, and these we mutually abandon to each other. We are preparing sentences of death against them, we shall open our learned meetings by the proscription of the diverse words of which we mean to purge both prose and verse.

PHILAMINTE. But the greatest project of our assembly—a noble enterprise which transports me with joy, a glorious design which will be approved by all the lofty geniuses of posterity—is the cutting out of all those filthy syllables which, in the finest words, are a source of scandal: those eternal jests of the fools of all times; those nauseous commonplaces of wretched buffoons; those sources of infamous ambiguity, with which the purity of women is insulted.

TRISSOTIN. These are indeed admirable projects.

BÉLISE. You shall see our regulations when they are quite ready.

TRISSOTIN. They cannot fail to be wise and beautiful.

ARMANDE. We shall by our laws be the judges of all works; by our laws, prose and verse will both alike be submitted to us. No one will have wit except us or our friends. We shall try to find fault with everything, and esteem no one capable of writing but ourselves.

SCENE III.

[PHILAMINTE, BÉLISE, ARMANDE, HENRIETTE, TRISSOTIN, LÉPINE.]

LÉPINE. [*to* TRISSOTIN.] Sir, there is a gentleman who wants to speak to you; he is dressed all in black, and speaks in a soft tone.

[*they all rise.*]

TRISSOTIN. It is that learned friend who entreated me so much to procure him the honor of your acquaintance.

PHILAMINTE. You have our full leave to present him to us.

[TRISSOTIN *goes out to meet* VADIUS.]

SCENE IV.

[PHILAMINTE, BÉLISE, ARMANDE, HENRIETTE.]

PHILAMINTE. [*to* ARMANDE *and* BÉLISE.] At least, let us do him all the honors of our knowledge. [*to* HENRIETTE, *who is going*.] Stop! I told you very plainly that I wanted to speak to you.
HENRIETTE. But what about?
PHILAMINTE. You will soon be enlightened on the subject.

SCENE V.

[TRISSOTIN, VADIUS, PHILAMINTE, BÉLISE, ARMANDE, HENRIETTE.]

TRISSOTIN. [*introducing* VADIUS.][44] Here is the gentleman who is dying to see you. In presenting him I am not afraid, Madam, of being accused of introducing a profane person to you; he can hold his place among the wits.
PHILAMINTE. The hand which introduces him sufficiently proves his value.
TRISSOTIN. He has a perfect knowledge of the ancient authors, and knows Greek, Madam, as well as any man in France.
PHILAMINTE. [*to* BÉLISE.] Greek! O heaven! Greek! He understands Greek, sister!
BÉLISE. [*to* ARMANDE.] Ah, niece! Greek!
ARMANDE. Greek! ah! how delightful!
PHILAMINTE. What, Sir, you understand Greek? Allow me, I beg, for the love of Greek, to embrace you. [VADIUS *embraces also* BÉLISE *and* ARMANDE.]
HENRIETTE. [*to* VADIUS, *who comes forward to embrace her*.] Excuse me, Sir, I do not understand Greek. [*they sit down*.]
PHILAMINTE. I have a wonderful respect for Greek books.
VADIUS. I fear that the anxiety which calls me to render my homage to you to-day, Madam, may render me importunate. I may have disturbed some learned discourse.
PHILAMINTE. Sir, with Greek in possession, you can spoil nothing.
TRISSOTIN. Moreover, he does wonders in prose as well as in verse, and he could, if he chose, show you something.
VADIUS. The fault of authors is to burden conversation with their productions; to be at the Palais, in the walks, in the drawing-rooms, or at table, the indefatigable readers of their tedious verses. As for

---

[44] It is probably Ménage who is here laughed at.

me, I think nothing more ridiculous than an author who goes about begging for praise, who, preying on the ears of the first comers, often makes them the martyrs of his night watches. I have never been guilty of such foolish conceit, and I am in that respect of the opinion of a Greek, who by an express law forbade all his wise men any unbecoming anxiety to read their works.—Here are some little verses for young lovers upon which I should like to have your opinion.

TRISSOTIN. Your verses have beauties unequalled by any others.

VADIUS. Venus and the Graces reign in all yours.

TRISSOTIN. You have an easy style, and a fine choice of words.

VADIUS. In all your writings one finds *ethos* and *pathos*.

TRISSOTIN. We have seen some eclogues of your composition which surpass in sweetness those of Theocritus and Virgil.

VADIUS. Your odes have a noble, gallant, and tender manner, which leaves Horace far behind.

TRISSOTIN. Is there anything more lovely than your canzonets?

VADIUS. Is there anything equal to the sonnets you write?

TRISSOTIN. Is there anything more charming than your little rondeaus?

VADIUS. Anything so full of wit as your madrigals?

TRISSOTIN. You are particularly admirable in the ballad.

VADIUS. And in *bouts-rimés* I think you adorable.

TRISSOTIN. If France could appreciate your value—

VADIUS. If the age could render justice to a lofty genius—

TRISSOTIN. You would ride in the streets in a gilt coach.

VADIUS. We should see the public erect statues to you. Hem. . . [*to* TRISSOTIN.] It is a ballad; and I wish you frankly to. . . .

TRISSOTIN. [*to* VADIUS.] Have you heard a certain little sonnet upon the Princess Urania's fever?

VADIUS. Yes; I heard it read yesterday.

TRISSOTIN. Do you know the author of it?

VADIUS. No, I do not; but I know very well that, to tell him the truth, his sonnet is good for nothing.

TRISSOTIN. Yet a great many people think it admirable.

VADIUS. It does not prevent it from being wretched; and if you had read it, you would think like me.

TRISSOTIN. I know that I should differ from you altogether, and that few people are able to write such a sonnet.

VADIUS. Heaven forbid that I should ever write one so bad!

TRISSOTIN. I maintain that a better one cannot be made, and my reason is that I am the author of it.

VADIUS. You?

TRISSOTIN. Myself.

VADIUS. I cannot understand how the thing can have happened.

TRISSOTIN. It is unfortunate that I had not the power of pleasing you.

VADIUS. My mind must have wandered during the reading, or else the reader spoilt the sonnet; but let us leave that subject, and come to my ballad.

TRISSOTIN. The ballad is, to my mind, but an insipid thing; it is no longer the fashion, and savours of ancient times.

VADIUS. Yet a ballad has charms for many people.

TRISSOTIN. It does not prevent me from thinking it unpleasant.

VADIUS. That does not make it worse.

TRISSOTIN. It has wonderful attractions for pedants.

VADIUS. Yet we see that it does not please you.

TRISSOTIN. You stupidly give your qualities to others.

[*they all rise.*]

VADIUS. You very impertinently cast yours upon me.

TRISSOTIN. Go, you little dunce! you pitiful quill-driver!

VADIUS. Go, you penny-a-liner! you disgrace to the profession!

TRISSOTIN. Go, you book-maker, you impudent plagiarist!

VADIUS. Go, you pedantic snob!

PHILAMINTE. Ah! gentlemen, what are you about?

TRISSOTIN. [*to* VADIUS.] Go, go, and make restitution to the Greeks and Romans for all your shameful thefts.

VADIUS. Go and do penance on Parnassus for having murdered Horace in your verses.

TRISSOTIN. Remember your book, and the little noise it made.

VADIUS. And you, remember your bookseller, reduced to the workhouse.

TRISSOTIN. My glory is established; in vain would you endeavour to shake it.

VADIUS. Yes, yes; I send you to the author of the 'Satires.'[45]

TRISSOTIN. I, too, send you to him.

VADIUS. I have the satisfaction of having been honorably treated by him; he gives me a passing thrust, and includes me among several authors well known at the Palais; but he never leaves you in peace, and in all his verses you are exposed to his attacks.

TRISSOTIN. By that we see the honorable rank I hold. He leaves you in the crowd, and esteems one blow enough to crush you. He has never done you the honor of repeating his attacks, whereas he assails me separately, as a noble adversary against whom all his efforts are necessary; and his blows, repeated against me on all occasions, show that he never thinks himself victorious.

VADIUS. My pen will teach you what sort of man I am.

---

[45] Boileau.

TRISSOTIN. And mine will make you know your master.
VADIUS. I defy you in verse, prose, Greek and Latin.
TRISSOTIN. Very well, we shall meet each other alone at Barbin's.[46]

SCENE VI.

[TRISSOTIN, PHILAMINTE, ARMANDE, BÉLISE, HENRIETTE.]

TRISSOTIN. Do not blame my anger. It is your judgment I defend, Madam, in the sonnet he dares to attack.

PHILAMINTE. I will do all I can to reconcile you. But let us speak of something else. Come here, Henriette. I have for some time now been tormented at finding in you a want of intellectuality, but I have thought of a means of remedying this defect.

HENRIETTE. You take unnecessary trouble for my sake. I have no love for learned discourses. I like to take life easy, and it is too much trouble to be intellectual. Such ambition does not trouble my head, and I am perfectly satisfied, mother, with being stupid. I prefer to have only a common way of talking, and not to torment myself to produce fine words.

PHILAMINTE. That may be; but this stupidity wounds me, and it is not my intention to suffer such a stain on my family. The beauty of the face is a fragile ornament, a passing flower, a moment's brightness which only belongs to the epidermis; whereas that of the mind is lasting and solid. I have therefore been feeling about for the means of giving you the beauty which time cannot remove—of creating in you the love of knowledge, of insinuating solid learning into you; and the way I have at last determined upon is to unite you to a man full of genius; [*showing* TRISSOTIN.] to this gentleman, in fact. It is he whom I intend you to marry.

HENRIETTE. Me, mother!

PHILAMINTE. Yes, you! just play the fool a little.

BÉLISE. [*to* TRISSOTIN.] I understand you; your eyes ask me for leave to engage elsewhere a heart I possess. Be at peace, I consent. I yield you up to this union; it is a marriage which will establish you in society.

TRISSOTIN. [*to* HENRIETTE.] In my delight, I hardly know what to tell you, Madam, and this marriage with which I am honored puts me. . . .

HENRIETTE. Gently, Sir; it is not concluded yet; do not be in such a hurry.

---

[46] Barbin, a famous bookseller. The arms chosen for the duel would no doubt be books. See "The Lutrin," by Boileau.

PHILAMINTE. What a way of answering! Do you know that if . . . but enough. You understand me. [*to* TRISSOTIN.] She will obey. Let us leave her alone for the present.

SCENE VII.

[HENRIETTE, ARMANDE.]

ARMANDE. You see how our mother's anxiety for your welfare shines forth; she could not have chosen a more illustrious husband. . . .

HENRIETTE. If the choice is so good, why do you not take him for yourself?

ARMANDE. It is upon you, and not upon me, that his hand is bestowed.

HENRIETTE. I yield him up entirely to you as my elder Sister.

ARMANDE. If marriage seemed so pleasant to me as it seems to be to you, I would accept your offer with delight.

HENRIETTE. If I loved pedants as you do, I should think the match an excellent one.

ARMANDE. Although our tastes differ so in this case, you will still have to obey our parents, sister. A mother has full power over us, and in vain do you think by resistance to. . . .

SCENE VIII.

[CHRYSALE, ARISTE, CLITANDRE, HENRIETTE, ARMANDE.]

CHRYSALE. [*to* HENRIETTE, *as he presents* CLITANDRE.] Now, my daughter, you must show your approval of what I do. Take off your glove, shake hands with this gentleman, and from henceforth in your heart consider him as the man I want you to marry.

ARMANDE. Your inclinations on this side are strong enough, sister.

HENRIETTE. We must obey our parents, sister; a father has full power over us.

ARMANDE. A mother should have a share of obedience.

CHRYSALE. What is the meaning of this?

ARMANDE. I say that I greatly fear you and my mother are not likely to agree on this point, and this other husband. . . .

CHRYSALE. Be silent, you saucy baggage: philosophize as much as you please with her, and do not meddle with what I do. Tell her what I have done, and warn her that she is not to come and make me angry. Go at once!

Scene IX.

[CHRYSALE, ARISTE, HENRIETTE, CLITANDRE.]

ARISTE. That's right; you are doing wonders!

CLITANDRE. What transport! what joy! Ah! how kind fortune is to me!

CHRYSALE. [*to* CLITANDRE.] Come, take her hand and pass before us; take her to her room. Ah! what sweet caresses. [*to* ARISTE.] How moved my heart is before this tenderness; it cheers up one's old age, and I can still remember my youthful loving days.

Act IV.

Scene I.

[PHILAMINTE, ARMANDE.]

ARMANDE. Yes, there was no hesitation in her; she made a display of her obedience, and her heart scarcely took time to hear the order. She seemed less to obey the will of her father than affect to set at defiance the will of her mother.

PHILAMINTE. I will soon show her to which of us two the laws of reason subject her wishes, and who ought to govern, mother or father, mind or body, form or matter.

ARMANDE. At least, they owed you the compliment of consulting you; and that little gentleman who resolves to become your son-in-law, in spite of yourself, behaves himself strangely.

PHILAMINTE. He has not yet reached the goal of his desires. I thought him well made, and approved of your love; but his manners were always unpleasant to me. He knows that I write a little, thank heaven, and yet he has never desired me to read anything to him.

SCENE II.

[ARMANDE, PHILAMINTE, CLITANDRE (*entering softly and listening unseen*).]

ARMANDE. If I were you, I would not allow him to become Henriette's husband. It would be wrong to impute to me the least thought of speaking like an interested person in this matter, and false to think that the base trick he is playing me secretly vexes me. By the help of philosophy, my soul is fortified against such trials;

by it we can rise above everything. But to see him treat you so, provokes me beyond all endurance. Honor requires you to resist his wishes, and he is not a man in whom you could find pleasure. In our talks together I never could see that he had in his heart any respect for you.

PHILAMINTE. Poor idiot!

ARMANDE. In spite of all the reports of your glory, he was always cold in praising you.

PHILAMINTE. The churl!

ARMANDE. And twenty times have I read to him some of your new productions, without his ever thinking them fine.

PHILAMINTE. The impertinent fellow!

ARMANDE. We were often at variance about it, and you could hardly believe what foolish things. . . .

CLITANDRE. [*to* ARMANDE.] Ah! gently, pray. A little charity, or at least a little truthfulness. What harm have I done to you? and of what am I guilty that you should thus arm all your eloquence against me to destroy me, and that you should take so much trouble to render me odious to those whose assistance I need? Tell me why this great indignation? [*to* PHILAMINTE.] I am willing to make you, Madam, an impartial judge between us.

ARMANDE. If I felt this great wrath with which you accuse me, I could find enough to authorize it. You deserve it but too well. A first love has such sacred claims over our hearts, that it would be better to lose fortune and renounce life than to love a second time. Nothing can be compared to the crime of changing one's vows, and every faithless heart is a monster of immorality.

CLITANDRE. Do you call that infidelity, Madam, which the haughtiness of your mind has forced upon me? I have done nothing but obey the commands it imposed upon me; and if I offend you, you are the primary cause of the offence. At first your charms took entire possession of my heart. For two years I loved you with devoted love; there was no assiduous care, duty, respect, service, which I did not offer you. But all my attentions, all my cares, had no power over you. I found you opposed to my dearest wishes; and what you refused I offered to another. Consider then, if the fault is mine or yours. Does my heart run after change, or do you force me to it? Do I leave you, or do you not rather turn me away?

ARMANDE. Do you call it being opposed to your love, Sir, if I deprive it of what there is vulgar in it, and if I wish to reduce it to the purity in which the beauty of perfect love consists? You cannot for me keep your thoughts clear and disentangled from the commerce of sense; and you do not enter into the charms of that union of two hearts in which the body is ignored. You can only love with a gross and material passion; and in order to maintain in you the love I have created, you must have marriage, and all that follows. Ah! what strange love! How far great souls are from burning with these terrestrial flames! The senses have no share in all their ardour; their noble passion unites the hearts only, and treats all else as unworthy. Theirs is a flame pure and clear like a celestial fire. With this they breathe only sinless sighs, and never yield to base desires. Nothing impure is mixed in what they propose to themselves. They love for the sake of loving, and for nothing else. It is only to the soul that all their transports are directed, and the body they altogether forget.

CLITANDRE. Unfortunately, Madam, I feel, if you will forgive my saying so, that I have a body as well as a soul; and that I am too much attached to that body for me totally to forget it. I do not understand this separation. Heaven has denied me such philosophy, and my body and soul go together. There is nothing so beautiful, as you well say, as that purified love which is directed only to the heart, those unions of the soul and those tender thoughts so free from the commerce of sense. But such love is too refined for me. I am, as you observe, a little gross and material. I love with all my being; and, in the love that is given to me, I wish to include the whole person. This is not a subject for lofty self-denial; and, without wishing to wrong your noble sentiments, I see that in the world my method has a certain vogue; that marriage is somewhat the fashion, and passes for a tie honorable and tender enough to have made me wish to become your husband, without giving you cause to be offended at such a thought.

ARMANDE. Well, well! Sir, since without being convinced by what I say, your grosser feelings will be satisfied; since to reduce you to a faithful love, you must have carnal ties and material chains, I will, if I have my mother's permission, bring my mind to consent to all you wish.

CLITANDRE. It is too late; another has accepted before you and if I were to return to you, I should basely abuse the place of rest in which I sought refuge, and should wound the goodness of her to whom I fled when you disdained me.

PHILAMINTE. But, Sir, when you thus look forward, do you believe in my consent to this other marriage? In the midst of your dreams, let it enter your mind that I have another husband ready for her.

CLITANDRE. Ah! Madam, reconsider your choice, I beseech you; and do not expose me to such a disgrace. Do not doom me to the unworthy destiny of seeing myself the rival of Mr. Trissotin. The love of *beaux esprits*,[47] which goes against me in your mind, could

[47] No single word has given me so much trouble to translate as this word *esprit*. This time I acknowledge myself beaten.

not have opposed to me a less noble adversary. There are people whom the bad taste of the age has reckoned among men of genius; but Mr. Trissotin deceives nobody, and everyone does justice to the writings he gives us. Everywhere but here he is esteemed at his just value; and what has made me wonder above all things is to see you exalt to the sky, stupid verses which you would have disowned had you yourself written them.

PHILAMINTE. If you judge of him differently from us, it is that we see him with other eyes than you do.

SCENE III.

[TRISSOTIN, PHILAMINTE, ARMANDE, CLITANDRE.]

TRISSOTIN. [*to* PHILAMINTE.] I come to announce you great news. We have had a narrow escape while we slept. A world passed all along us, and fell right across our vortex.[48] If in its way it had met with our earth, it would have dashed us to pieces like so much glass.

PHILAMINTE. Let us put off this subject till another season. This gentleman would understand nothing of it; he professes to cherish ignorance, and above all to hate intellect and knowledge.

CLITANDRE. This is not altogether the fact; allow me, Madam, to explain myself. I only hate that kind of intellect and learning which spoils people. These are good and beautiful in themselves; but I had rather be numbered among the ignorant than to see myself learned like certain people.

TRISSOTIN. For my part I do not believe, whatever opinion may be held to the contrary, that knowledge can ever spoil anything.

CLITANDRE. And I hold that knowledge can make great fools both in words and in deeds.

TRISSOTIN. The paradox is rather strong.

CLITANDRE. It would be easy to find proofs; and I believe without being very clever, that if reasons should fail, notable examples would not be wanting.

TRISSOTIN. You might cite some without proving your point.

CLITANDRE. I should not have far to go to find what I want.

TRISSOTIN. As far as I am concerned, I fail to see those notable examples.

CLITANDRE. I see them so well that they almost blind me.

TRISSOTIN. I believed hitherto that it was ignorance which made fools, and not knowledge.

CLITANDRE. You made a great mistake; and I assure you that a

---

[48] *Tourbillon.* Compare act iii scene ii. Another reference to Cotin.

learned fool is more of a fool than an ignorant one.

TRISSOTIN. Common sense is against your maxims, since an ignorant man and a fool are synonymous.

CLITANDRE. If you cling to the strict uses of words, there is a greater connection between pedant and fool.

TRISSOTIN. Folly in the one shows itself openly.

CLITANDRE. And study adds to nature in the other.

TRISSOTIN. Knowledge has always its intrinsic value.

CLITANDRE. Knowledge in a pedant becomes impertinence.

TRISSOTIN. Ignorance must have great charms for you, since you so eagerly take up arms in its defence.

CLITANDRE. If ignorance has such charms for me, it is since I have met with learned people of a certain kind.

TRISSOTIN. These learned people of a certain kind may, when we know them well, be as good as other people of a certain other kind.

CLITANDRE. Yes, if we believe certain learned men; but that remains a question with certain people.

PHILAMINTE. [*to* CLITANDRE.] It seems to me, Sir. . . .

CLITANDRE. Ah! Madam, I beg of you; this gentleman is surely strong enough without assistance. I have enough to do already with so strong an adversary, and as I fight I retreat.

ARMANDE. But the offensive eagerness with which your answers. . . .

CLITANDRE. Another ally! I quit the field.

PHILAMINTE. Such combats are allowed in conversation, provided you attack no one in particular.

CLITANDRE. Ah! Madam, there is nothing in all this to offend him. He can bear raillery as well as any man in France; and he has supported many other blows without finding his glory tarnished by it.

TRISSOTIN. I am not surprised to see this gentleman take such a part in this contest. He belongs to the court; that is saying everything. The court, as everyone well knows, does not care for learning; it has a certain interest in supporting ignorance. And it is as a courtier he takes up its defence.

CLITANDRE. Your are very angry with this poor court. The misfortune is great indeed to see you men of learning day after day declaiming against it; making it responsible for all your troubles; calling it to account for its bad taste, and seeing in it the scapegoat of your ill-success. Allow me, Mr. Trissotin, to tell you, with all the respect with which your name inspires me, that you would do well, your brethren and you, to speak of the court in a more moderate tone; that, after all, it is not so very stupid as all you gentlemen make it out to be; that it has good sense enough to appreciate everything; that some good taste can be acquired there; and that the common sense found there is, without flattery, well worth all the learning of pedantry.

TRISSOTIN. We See some effects of its good taste, Sir.

CLITANDRE. Where do you see, Sir, that its taste is so bad?

TRISSOTIN. Where, Sir! Do not Rasius and Balbus by their learning do honor to France? and yet their merit, so very patent to all, attracts no notice from the court.

CLITANDRE. I see whence your sorrow comes, and that, through modesty, you forbear, Sir, to rank yourself with these. Not to drag you in, tell me what your able heroes do for their country? What service do their writings render it that they should accuse the court of horrible injustice, and complain everywhere that it fails to pour down favors on their learned names? Their knowledge is of great moment to France! and the court stands in great need of the books they write! These wretched scribblers get it into their little heads that to be printed and bound in calf makes them at once important personages in the state; that with their pens they regulate the destiny of crowns; that at the least mention of their productions, pensions ought to be poured down upon them; that the eyes of the whole universe are fixed upon them, and the glory of their name spread everywhere! They think themselves prodigies of learning because they know what others have said before them; because for thirty years they have had eyes and ears, and have employed nine or ten thousand nights or so in cramming themselves with Greek and Latin, and in filling their heads with the indiscriminate plunder of all the old rubbish which lies scattered in books. They always seem intoxicated with their own knowledge, and for all merit are rich in importunate babble. Unskilful in everything, void of common sense, and full of absurdity and impertinence, they decry everywhere true learning and knowledge.

PHILAMINTE. You speak very warmly on the subject, and this transport shows the working of ill-nature in you. It is the name of rival which excites in your breast. . . .

SCENE IV.

[TRISSOTIN, PHILAMINTE, CLITANDRE, ARMANDE, JULIAN.]

JULIAN. The learned gentleman who paid you a visit just now, Madam, and whose humble servant I have the honor to be, exhorts you to read this letter.

PHILAMINTE. However important this letter may be, learn, friend, that it is a piece of rudeness to come and interrupt a conversation, and that a servant who knows his place should apply first to the people of the household to be introduced.

JULIAN. I will note that down, Madam, in my book.

PHILAMINTE. [*reads.*] "*Trissotin boasts, Madam, that he is to marry your daughter. I give you notice that his philosophy aims only at your wealth, and that you would do well not to conclude this marriage before you have seen the poem which I am composing against him. While you are waiting for this portrait, in which I intend to paint him in all his colors, I send you Horace, Virgil, Terence, and Catullus, where you will find marked in the margin all the passages he has pilfered.*"

We see there merit attacked by many enemies because of the marriage I have decided upon. But this general ill-feeling only prompts me to an action which will confound envy, and make it feel that whatever it does only hastens the end. [*to* JULIAN.] Tell all this to your master; tell him also that in order to let him know how much value I set on his disinterested advice, and how worthy of being followed I esteem it, this very evening I shall marry my daughter to this gentleman [*showing* TRISSOTIN.]

SCENE V.

[PHILAMINTE, ARMANDE, CLITANDRE.]

PHILAMINTE. [*to* CLITANDRE.] You, Sir, as a friend of the family, may assist at the signing of the contract, for I am willing to invite you to it. Armande, be sure you send for the notary, and tell your sister of my decision.

ARMANDE. There is no need of saying anything to my sister; this gentleman will be pretty sure to take the news to her, and try and dispose her heart to rebellion.

PHILAMINTE. We shall see who has most power over her, and whether I can bring her to a sense of her duty.

SCENE VI.

[ARMANDE, CLITANDRE.]

ARMANDE. I am very sorry to see, Sir, that things are not going quite according to your views.

CLITANDRE. I shall go and do all I can not to leave this serious anxiety upon your mind.

ARMANDE. I am afraid that your efforts will not be very successful.

CLITANDRE. You may perhaps see that your fears are without foundation.

ARMANDE. I hope it may be so.

CLITANDRE. I am persuaded that I shall have all your help.
ARMANDE. Yes, I will second you with all my power.
CLITANDRE. And I shall be sure to be most grateful.

SCENE VII.

[CHRYSALE, ARISTE, HENRIETTE, CLITANDRE.]

CLITANDRE. I should be most unfortunate without your assistance, Sir, for your wife has rejected my offer, and, her mind being prepossessed in favor of Trissotin, she insists upon having him for a son-in-law.
CHRYSALE. But what fancy is this that she has got into her head? Why in the world will she have this Mr. Trissotin?
ARISTE. It is because he has the honor of rhyming with Latin that he is carrying it off over the head of his rival.
CLITANDRE. She wants to conclude this marriage to-night.
CHRYSALE. To-night?
CLITANDRE. Yes, to-night.
CHRYSALE. Well! and this very night I will, in order to thwart her, have you both married.
CLITANDRE. She has sent for the notary to draw up the contract.
CHRYSALE. And I will go and fetch him for the one he must draw up.
CLITANDRE. And Henriette is to be told by her sister of the marriage to which she must look forward.
CHRYSALE. And I command her with full authority to prepare herself for this other alliance. Ah! I will show them if there is any other master but myself to give orders in the house. [*to* HENRIETTE.] We will return soon. Now, come along with me, brother; and you also, my son-in-law.
HENRIETTE. [*to* ARISTE.] Alas! try to keep him in this disposition.
ARISTE. I will do everything to serve your love.

SCENE VIII.

[HENRIETTE, CLITANDRE.]

CLITANDRE. However great may be the help that is promised to my love, my greatest hope is in your constancy.
HENRIETTE. You know that you may be sure of my love.
CLITANDRE. I see nothing to fear as long as I have that.
HENRIETTE. You see to what a union they mean to force me.
CLITANDRE. As long as your heart belongs entirely to me, I see nothing to fear.
HENRIETTE. I will try everything for the furtherance of our dearest

wishes, and if after all I cannot be yours, there is a sure retreat I have resolved upon, which will save me from belonging to anyone else.

CLITANDRE. May Heaven spare me from ever receiving from you that proof of your love.

ACT V.

SCENE I.

[HENRIETTE, TRISSOTIN.]

HENRIETTE. It is about the marriage which my mother has set her heart upon that I wish, Sir, to speak privately to you; and I thought that, seeing how our home is disturbed by it, I should be able to make you listen to reason. You are aware that with me you will receive a considerable dowry; but money, which we see so many people esteem, has no charms worthy of a philosopher; and contempt for wealth and earthly grandeur should not show itself in your words only.

TRISSOTIN. Therefore it is not that which charms me in you; but your dazzling beauty, your sweet and piercing eyes, your grace, your noble air—these are the wealth, the riches, which have won for you my vows and love; it is of those treasures only that I am enamoured.

HENRIETTE. I thank you for your generous love; I ought to feel grateful and to respond to it; I regret that I cannot; I esteem you as much as one can esteem another; but in me I find an obstacle to loving you. You know that a heart cannot be given to two people, and I feel that Clitandre has taken entire possession of mine. I know that he has much less merit than you, that I have not fit discrimination for the choice of a husband, and that with your many talents yon ought to please me. I see that I am wrong, but I cannot help it; and all the power that reason has over me is to make me angry with myself for such blindness.

TRISSOTIN. The gift of your hand, to which I am allowed to aspire, will give me the heart possessed by Clitandre; for by a thousand tender cares I have reason to hope that I shall succeed in making myself loved.

HENRIETTE. No; my heart is bound to its first love, and cannot be touched by your cares and attention. I explain myself plainly with you, and my confession ought in no way to hurt your feelings. The love which springs up in the heart is not, as you know, the effect of merit, but is partly decided by caprice; and oftentimes, when someone pleases us, we can barely find the reason. If choice and wisdom guided love, all the tenderness of my heart would be for you; but love is not thus guided. Leave me, I pray, to my blindness; and do not profit by the violence which, for your sake, is imposed on my obedience. A man of honor will owe nothing to the power which parents have over us; he feels a repugnance to exact a self-sacrifice from her he loves, and will not obtain a heart by force. Do not encourage my mother to exercise, for your sake, the absolute power she has over me. Give up your love for me, and carry to another the homage of a heart so precious as yours.

TRISSOTIN. For this heart to satisfy you, you must impose upon it laws it can obey. Could it cease to love you, Madam, unless you ceased to be loveable, and could cease to display those celestial charms. . .

HENRIETTE. Ah! Sir, leave aside all this trash; you are encumbered with so many Irises, Phyllises, Amaranthas, which everywhere in your verses you paint as charming, and to whom you swear such love, that. . . .

TRISSOTIN. It is the mind that speaks, and not the heart. With them it is only the poet that is in love; but it is in earnest that I love the adorable Henriette.

HENRIETTE. Ah, Sir, I beg of you. . . .

TRISSOTIN. If I offend you, my offence is not likely to cease. This love, ignored by you to this day, will be of eternal duration. Nothing can put a stop to its delightful transports; and although your beauty condemns my endeavours, I cannot refuse the help of a mother who wishes to crown such a precious flame. Provided I succeed in obtaining such great happiness, provided I obtain your hand, it matters little to me how it comes to pass.

HENRIETTE. But are you aware, Sir, that you risk more than you think by using violence; and to be plain with you, that it is not safe to marry a girl against her wish, for she might well have recourse to a certain revenge that a husband should fear.

TRISSOTIN. Such a speech has nothing that can make me alter my purpose. A philosopher is prepared against every event. Cured by reason of all vulgar weaknesses, he rises above these things, and is far from minding what does not depend on him.[49]

HENRIETTE. Truly, Sir, I am delighted to hear you; and I had no idea that philosophy was so capable of teaching men to bear such accidents with constancy. This wonderful strength of mind deserves to have a fit subject to illustrate it, and to find one who may take pleasure in giving it an occasion for its full display. As, however, to say the truth, I do not feel equal to the task, I will leave it to another; and, between ourselves, I assure you that I

---

[49] Compare 'The School for Wives,' act iv. scene vi.

renounce altogether the happiness of seeing you my husband.

TRISSOTIN. [*going.*] We shall see by-and-by how the affair will end. In the next room, close at hand, is the notary waiting.

Scene II.

[CHRYSALE, CLITANDRE, HENRIETTE.]

CHRYSALE. I am glad, my daughter, to see you; come here and fulfil your duty, by showing obedience to the will of your father. I will teach your mother how to behave, and, to defy her more fully, here is Martine, whom I have brought back to take her old place in the house again.

HENRIETTE. Your resolution deserves praise. I beg of you, father, never to change the disposition you are in. Be firm in what you have resolved, and do not suffer yourself to be the dupe of your own good-nature. Do not yield; and I pray you to act so as to hinder my mother from having her own way.

CHRYSALE. How! Do you take me for a booby?

HENRIETTE. Heaven forbid!

CHRYSALE. Am I a fool, pray?

HENRIETTE. I do not say that.

CHRYSALE. Am I thought unfit to have the decision of a man of sense?

HENRIETTE. No, father.

CHRYSALE. Ought I not at my age to know how to be master at home?

HENRIETTE. Of course.

CHRYSALE. Do you think me weak enough to allow my wife to lead me by the nose?

HENRIETTE. Oh dear, no, father.

CHRYSALE. Well, then, what do you mean? You are a nice girl to speak to me as you do!

HENRIETTE. If I have displeased you, father, I have done so unintentionally.

CHRYSALE. My will is law in this place.

HENRIETTE. Certainly, father.

CHRYSALE. No one but myself has in this house a right to command.

HENRIETTE. Yes, you are right, father.

CHRYSALE. It is I who hold the place of chief of the family.

HENRIETTE. Agreed.

CHRYSALE. It is I who ought to dispose of my daughter's hand.

HENRIETTE. Yes, indeed, father.

CHRYSALE. Heaven has given me full power over you.

HENRIETTE. No one, father, says anything to the contrary.

CHRYSALE. And as to choosing a husband, I will show you that it is your father, and not your mother, whom you have to obey.

HENRIETTE. Alas! in that you respond to my dearest wish. Exact obedience to you is my earnest wish.

CHRYSALE. We shall see if my wife will prove rebellious to my will.

CLITANDRE. Here she is, and she brings the notary with her.

CHRYSALE. Back me up, all of you.

MARTINE. Leave that to me; I will take care to encourage you, if need be.

SCENE III.

[PHILAMINTE, BÉLISE, ARMANDE, TRISSOTIN, A NOTARY, CHRYSALE, CLITANDRE, HENRIETTE, MARTINE.]

PHILAMINTE. [*to the* NOTARY.] Can you not alter your barbarous style, and give us a contract couched in noble language?

NOTARY. Our style is very good, and I should be a blockhead, Madam, to try and change a single word.

BÉLISE. Ah! what barbarism in the very midst of France! But yet, Sir, for learning's sake, allow us, instead of crowns, livres, and francs, to have the dowry expressed in minae and talents, and to express the date in Ides and Kalends.

NOTARY. I, Madam? If I were to do such a thing, all my colleagues would hiss me.

PHILAMINTE. It is useless to complain of all this barbarism. Come, Sir, sit down and write. [*seeing* MARTINE.] Ah! this impudent hussy dares to show herself here again! Why was she brought back, I should like to know?

CHRYSALE. We will tell you by-and-by; we have now something else to do.

NOTARY. Let us proceed with the contract. Where is the future bride?

PHILAMINTE. It is the younger daughter I give in marriage.

NOTARY. Good.

CHRYSALE. [*showing* HENRIETTE.] Yes, Sir, here she is; her name is Henriette.

NOTARY. Very well; and the future bridegroom?

PHILAMINTE. [*showing* TRISSOTIN.] This gentleman is the husband I give her.

CHRYSALE. [*showing* CLITANDRE.] And the husband I wish her to marry is this gentleman.

NOTARY. Two husbands! Custom does not allow of more than one.

PHILAMINTE. [*to the* NOTARY.] What is it that is stopping you? Put down Mr. Trissotin as my son-in-law.

CHRYSALE. For my son-in-law put down Mr. Clitandre.

NOTARY. Try and agree together, and come to a quiet decision as to who is to be the future husband.

PHILAMINTE. Abide, Sir, abide by my own choice.

CHRYSALE. Do, Sir, do according to my will.

NOTARY. Tell me which of the two I must obey.

PHILAMINTE. [*to* CHRYSALE.] What! you will go against my wishes.

CHRYSALE. I cannot allow my daughter to be sought after only because of the wealth which is in my family.

PHILAMINTE. Really! as if anyone here thought of your wealth, and as if it were a subject worthy the anxiety of a wise man.

CHRYSALE. In short, I have fixed on Clitandre.

PHILAMINTE. [*showing* TRISSOTIN.] And I am decided that for a husband she shall have this gentleman. My choice shall be followed; the thing is settled.

CHRYSALE. Heyday! you assume here a very high tone.

MARTINE. 'Tisn't for the wife to lay down the law, and I be one to give up the lead to the men in everything.

CHRYSALE. That is well said.

MARTINE. If my discharge was as sure as a gun, what I says is, that the hen hadn't ought to be heard when the cock's there.

CHRYSALE. Just so.

MARTINE. And we all know that a man is always chaffed, when at home his wife wears the breeches.

CHRYSALE. It is perfectly true.

MARTINE. I says that, if I had a husband, I would have him be the master of the house. I should not care a bit for him if he played the henpecked husband; and if I resisted him out of caprice, or if I spoke too loud, I should think it quite right if, with a couple of boxes on the ear, he made me pitch it lower.

CHRYSALE. You speak as you ought.

MARTINE. Master is quite right to want a proper husband for his daughter.

CHRYSALE. Certainly.

MARTINE. Why should he refuse her Clitandre, who is young and handsome, in order to give her a scholar, who is always splitting hairs about something? She wants a husband and not a pedagogue, and as she cares neither for Greek nor Latin, she has no need of Mr. Trissotin.

CHRYSALE. Excellent.

PHILAMINTE. We must suffer her to chatter on at her ease.

MARTINE. Learned people are only good to preach in a pulpit, and I have said a thousand times that I wouldn't have a learned man for my husband. Learning is not at all what is wanted in a household.

Books agree badly with marriage, and if ever I consent to engage myself to anybody, it will be to a husband who has no other book but me, who doesn't know *a* from *b*—no offence to you, Madam—and, in short, who would be clever only for his wife.[50]

PHILAMINTE. [*to* CHRYSALE.] Is it finished? and have I listened patiently enough to your worthy interpreter?

CHRYSALE. She has only said the truth.

PHILAMINTE. And I, to put an end to this dispute, will have my wish obeyed. [*showing* TRISSOTIN.] Henriette *and* this gentleman shall be united at once. I have said it, and I will have it so. Make no reply; and if you have given your word to Clitandre, offer him her elder sister.

CHRYSALE. Ah! this is a way out of the difficulty. [*to* HENRIETTE and CLITANDRE.] Come, do you consent?

HENRIETTE. How! father. . . !

CLITANDRE. [*to* CHRYSALE.] What! Sir. . . !

BÉLISE. Propositions more to his taste might be made. But we are establishing a kind of love which must be as pure as the morning-star; the thinking substance is admitted, but not the material substance.

SCENE IV.

[ARISTE, CHRYSALE, PHILAMINTE, BÉLISE, HENRIETTE, ARMANDE, TRISSOTIN, A NOTARY, CLITANDRE, MARTINE.]

ARISTE. I am sorry to have to trouble this happy ceremony by the sad tidings of which I am obliged to be bearer. These two letters make me bring news which have made me feel grievously for you. [*to* PHILAMINTE.] One letter is for you, and comes from your attorney. [*to* CHRYSALE.] The other comes from Lyons.

PHILAMINTE. What misfortune can be sent us worthy of troubling us?

ARISTE. You can read it in this letter.

PHILAMINTE. "*Madam, I have asked your brother to give you this letter; it will tell you news which I did not dare to come and tell you myself. The great negligence you have shown in your affairs has been the cause that the clerk of your attorney has not forewarned me, and you have altogether lost the lawsuit which you ought to have gained.*"

CHRYSALE. [*to* PHILAMINTE.] Your lawsuit lost!

PHILAMINTE. [*to* CHRYSALE.] You seem very much upset; my

---

[50] In this scene, as in act ii. scenes v. and vi., Martine speaks very correctly at times.

heart is in no way troubled by such a blow. Show, show like me, a less vulgar mind wherewith to brave the ills of fortune. "Your want of care will cost you forty thousand crowns, and you are condemned to pay this sum with all costs." Condemned? Ah! this is a shocking word, and only fit for criminals.

ARISTE. It is the wrong word, no doubt, and you, with reason, protest against it. It should have been, "You are desired by an order of the court to pay immediately forty thousand crowns and costs."

PHILAMINTE. Let us see the other.

CHRYSALE. "*Sir, the friendship which binds me to your brother prompts me to take a lively interest in all that concerns you. I know that you had placed your fortune entirely in the hands of Argante and Damon, and I acquaint you with the news that they have both failed.*" O Heaven! to lose everything thus in a moment!

PHILAMINTE. [*to* CHRYSALE.] Ah! what a shameful outburst Fie! For the truly wise there is no fatal change of fortune, and, losing all, he still remains himself. Let us finish the business we have in hand; and please cast aside your sorrow. [*showing* TRISSOTIN.] His wealth will be sufficient for us and for him.

TRISSOTIN. No, Madam; cease, I pray you, from pressing this affair further. I see that everybody is opposed to this marriage, and I have no intention of forcing the wills of others.

PHILAMINTE. This reflection, Sir, comes very quickly after our reverse of fortune.

TRISSOTIN. I am tired at last of so much resistance, and prefer to relinquish all attempts at removing these obstacles. I do not wish for a heart that will not surrender itself.

PHILAMINTE. I see in you, and that not to your honor, what I have hitherto refused to believe.

TRISSOTIN. You may see whatever you please, and it matters little to me how you take what you see. I am not a man to put up with the disgrace of the refusals with which I have been insulted here. I am well worthy of more consideration, and whoever thinks otherwise, I am her humble servant. [*exit.*]

Scene V.

[ARISTE, CHRYSALE, PHILAMINTE, BÉLISE, ARMANDE, HENRIETTE, CLITANDRE, A NOTARY, MARTINE.]

PHILAMINTE. How plainly he has disclosed his mercenary soul, and how little like a philosopher he has acted.

CLITANDRE. I have no pretension to being one; but, Madam, I will link my destiny to yours, and I offer you, with myself, all that I possess.

PHILAMINTE. Yon delight me, Sir, by this generous action, and I will reward your love. Yes, I grant Henriette to the eager affection. . . .

HENRIETTE. No, mother. I have altered my mind; forgive me if now I resist your will.

CLITANDRE. What! do you refuse me happiness, and now that I see everybody for me. . . .

HENRIETTE. I know how little you possess, Clitandre; and I always desired you for a husband when, by satisfying my most ardent wishes, I saw that our marriage would improve your fortune. But in the face of such reverses, I love you enough not to burden you with our adversity.

CLITANDRE. With you any destiny would be happiness, without you misery.

HENRIETTE. Love in its ardour generally speaks thus. Let us avoid the torture of vexatious recriminations. Nothing irritates such a tie more than the wretched wants of life. After a time we accuse each other of all the sorrows that follow such an engagement.

ARISTE. [*to* HENRIETTE.] Is what you have just said the only reason which makes you refuse to marry Clitandre?

HENRIETTE. Yes; otherwise you would see me ready to fly to this union with all my heart.

ARISTE. Suffer yourself, then, to be bound by such gentle ties. The news I brought you was false. It was a stratagem, a happy thought I had to serve your love by deceiving my sister, and by showing her what her philosopher would prove when put to the test.

CHRYSALE. Heaven be praised!

PHILAMINTE. I am delighted at heart for the vexation which this cowardly deserter will feel. The punishment of his sordid avarice will be to see in what a splendid manner this match will be concluded.

CHRYSALE. [*to* CLITANDRE.] I told you that you would marry her.

ARMANDE. [*to* PHILAMINTE.] So, then, you sacrifice me to their love?

PHILAMINTE. It will not be to sacrifice you; you have the support of your philosophy, and you can with a contented mind see their love crowned.

BÉLISE. Let him take care, for I still retain my place in his heart. Despair often leads people to conclude a hasty marriage, of which they repent ever after.

CHRYSALE. [*to the* NOTARY.] Now, Sir, execute my orders, and draw up the contract in accordance with what I said.

[*curtain.*]

www.ingramcontent.com/pod-product-compliance
Lightning Source LLC
LaVergne TN
LVHW011151080426
835508LV00007B/347
9781420955330